Effective Methods of Teaching Linguistics

Effective Methods of Teaching Linguistics

R.N. Sharma

ABD PUBLISHERS
Jaipur ■ New Delhi

ABD PUBLISHERS

Regd. Off. "Bony Residency", Gate No. 2
Opp. Tilak Public School, Vishweswariya Nagar,
Gopalpura Road, Jaipur - 302018, India
Ph: 0141 - 2761280, Telefax: 2761381
Email: abdpublishersjpr@gmail.com

Delhi Office: 102, 1st Floor, Satyam House,
4327/3, Ansari Road, Darya Ganj,
New Delhi - 110002, India
Ph: 011-45652440

visit us: www.oxfordbookcompany.com

Distributed By
KEYA INTERNATIONAL PRESS LLP
E-mail: keyainternationalpressllp@gmail.com

Published in India, 2025

ISBN : 978-81-19343-40-9

Typeset by Shivangi Computer, Jaipur

Printed and bound in India by Thomson Press Ltd.,
New Delhi

Preface

Linguistics in language studies is scientific comprehension and explanation of sounds, the forms, the functions of words and their parts and the constructions of sentences. Becoming an linguistic expert needs a thorough understanding of all basic concepts, techniques and methods like concepts of change in sound, morphology, syntax, semantics, lexicon and culture; transformations; phonetics; syntactic devices; communicative grammar, etc.

Methodology of teaching a subject has a great bearing and ability of learners to grasp the subject depends to a great extent on it. The effective, innovative and latest methods of teaching linguistics are explained in the book. Each and every aspect has been elaborately discussed both in traditional and modern context to bring before the reader the concept of evolution in linguistics.

The editor gratefully acknowledges the assistance taken from the Central Institute of Foreign Languages, Hyderabad for the preparation of this book.

R.N. Sharma

Contents

1

Sound Change—Change in Phonological Systems

Modification and Change

What do we mean by sound change? When languages are compared at various periods, we find correspondences between their elements. In comparing Middle English with Modern or New English, for example, we observe obvious correspondences between ME *set,* NE *set,* somewhat less obvious correspondences between ME *wīf;* NE *wife*; ME *hūs*, NE *house*. We conclude that NE *set, wife, house* are the contemporary forms of ME *set, wīf, hūs,* and we label these New English forms **replacements** for the Middle English. The replacements [wayf] for ME [wi:f] and [haws] for ME [hu:s] have resulted from modifications in the language. Modifications that lead to the introduction of new phonological elements in a language, to loss or to realignments of old elements, we refer to as a **sound change**. This term is used only for events that result in disruption of the phonological system.

The investigation of sound change is one of the chief concerns of historical linguistics. Through knowledge derived from observation of the sound changes that have been documented in many languages we are able to explain modifications that take place in any further language. For the processes are much the same, though they must be scrutinised within the structure of the language being investigated.

Moreover, that knowledge assists us in reconstructing languages of the past. Again, we have observed that change in past periods has taken place in ways that have been documented in well-known languages, such as the Romance. In view of the importance of understanding change within a given structure, our examples of change will be taken from English as much as possible, since its stages have been well described.

In the next four chapters we will examine change at various levels, the phonological, morphological, syntactic and semantic. In each chapter we examine correspondences between elements at two or more stages of a language, and then we discuss the processes, patterns and spread of such change within given systems. Finally, we examine proposed explanations for modifications and change.

Between the English of Chaucer (d.1400) and that spoken today, probably all elements in the phonological system have been modified. Some of the modifications were very minor; Chaucer's pronunciation of Me *set* would probably be understood by us today, though in details it might seem peculiar. Other pronunciations of his, we might not understand at all, such as his ME *see*/se:/ versus our NE *see*/siy/, ME *tōth* /to:θ/ versus our *tooth*/tuwθ/. Historical grammars concern themselves largely with such striking changes. Yet to understand the process of change in language, we will first examine briefly replacements that do not disrupt the system and that therefore seem minor or not worth notice in general historical surveys of a language, but that may eventually lead to changes.

One feature of Chaucer's pronunciation of *set* that may have differed only slightly from ours is his articulation of /t/; it would probably remind us of the *t* used by a Spanish speaker. Since we have no descriptions of Chaucer's pronunciation, we cannot be sure of this conclusion, but we can assume that at one time English /t d n/ were dentals. Over the past centuries their articulation has been progressively retracted, so that they are now alveolars. As this retraction took place, it did not bring about changes in the morphological, syntactic or semantic systems of the language. Nor was the system of phonemic contrasts affected; NE/t/ contrasts with NE/p k/etc., just as did ME /t/ with ME /p k/ etc. This modification of /t/ has accordingly not led to a sound change.

Another modification that must have been introduced in the

course of the history of English is the aspiration of voiceless stops before stressed vowels when not preceded by /s/, as in *pool* [pʰuwl] versus *spool* [sp⁼uwl], *tool* [tʰuwl] and *cool* [kʰuwl]. We assume that Germanic /p t k/ in such words were unaspirated because they developed from /b d g/, or from glottalics in accordance with glottalic theory. At some time between the changes described in Grimm's law and the present, aspiration must have been added in words like *pool, tool, cool*. But like the alveolar pronunciation of NE /t d n/, this modification has had no effect on the phonological system of English. For the aspirates are automatic variants, or allophones of /p t k/ in specific environments.

In time, such modification may lead to disruptions of the phonological system, that is, to sound change. Most linguists assume, for example, that PIE /p t k/ first became aspirates [p^h t^h k^h] before they were changed to fricatives in the Proto-Germanic etyma of words like NE *five, three, hundred.* But since the phonological system of contemporary English has not been changed by the introduction of [ph th kh], the altered pronunciations are simply modifications, not sound changes.

While such modifications are apparently going on constantly in language, we have little information about them in languages of the past. Speakers, including scribes, take account only of changes in phonological systems, not of modifications. Scribes may introduce new spellings after sound changes take place, or they may betray changes by inconsistencies or errors in spelling. With a long series of texts, we can therefore document changes that have taken place in individual languages.

Historical English linguists are fortunate in having many texts by means of which they can study change. As illustration we will examine the beginning of Chaucer's Prologue to the *Canterbury Tales.* The lines are given first in conventional Middle English spelling, accompanied by a literal translation, then in phonemic transcription, accompanied by a Modern English phonemic transcription. Middle English patterns of morphology and syntax have been maintained so that phonological changes would be better illustrated.

Middle English

1. Whan that Aprille with his schoures swoote
2. the drought of March hath perced to the roote

3. and bathed evry veyn in swich licour,
4. of which vertu engendred is the flour;
5. whan Zephirus eek with his swete breeth
6. inspired hath in evry holt and heeth
7. the tendre croppes, and the younge sonne
8. hath in the Ram his halve cours yronne,
9. and smale fowles maken melodye,
10. that slepen al the nyght with open ye –
11. so priketh hem nature in her corages –
12. than longen folk to goon on pilgrimages.

Translation

1. When (that) April with its sweet showers,
2. has pierced the drought of March to the root,
3. and bathed every vein in such moisture (liquor),
4. from whose effects (virtue) flowers are produced;
5. When Zephirus also with his sweet breath,
6. has inspired in every wood and heath,
7. the tender crops, and (when) the young sun
8. has run half of his course through Aries,
9. and (when) the small birds (fowls) make (their) melodies,
10. which sleep all the night with open eyes –
11. thus nature inspires them in their spirits –
12. at that time people want to go on pilgrimages.

Middle English phonemic representation

1. hwan θat a:pril wiθ his šu:res swo:te
2. θe druχt of marč haθ pe:rsed to: θe ro:te
3. and ba:ðed evri vein in swič liku:r
4. of hwič verteu enǰendred is θe flu:r
5. hwan zefirus e:k wiθ his swe:te bre:θ
6. inspi:red haθ in evri holt and hɛ:θ
7. θe tender kroppes and θe yunge sunne
8. haθ in θe ram his halve ku:rs irunne
9. and smales fu:les ma:ken melodi:e
10. θat sle:pen al θe niχt wiθ ɔ:pen i:e
11. sɔ: prikeθ hem nateur in her kura:ǰes
12. θan longen folk tō gɔ:n on pilgrima:ǰes

New English phonemic representation

1. hwen (ðæt) eypril wið hiz šawərz swiyt
2. ðə drawt əv marč hæz pirst tuw ðə ruwt
3. ænd beyðd evriy veyn in səč likər
4. əv hwič vərčuw enjendərd iz ðə flawr
5. hwen zeførəs iyk wið his swiyt breθ
6. inspayrd hæz in evriy holt ænd hiyθ
7. ðə tendər kraps ænd ðə yəŋ sən
8. hæz in ðə ræm hiz hæf kɔrs rən
9. ænd smol fawlz meyk melədiy
10. ðæt sliyp ɔl ðə nayt wið owpən ay
11. sow priks ðem neyčər in ðer kərəǰəz
12. ðen lɔŋ fowk tə gow ɔn pilgriməǰəz

Comparing the Middle English and the New English texts, we note that the vowels have changed considerably, notably the long vowels. Further, many unstressed syllables have been lost, leading to consonant clusters in New English, as in /pirst beyðd kraps/, and to syllables ending in consonants rather than vowels, as in /swiyt ruwt sən/. Furthermore, the accent of the words that were borrowed from French has generally been moved towards the beginning of words in keeping with the Germanic accent position, as in /likər mélədiy kə́reǰ/. In accordance with such accent placement, the vowels of formerly stressed syllables have been shortened, as in the second syllable of *liquor.* These changes brought about great differences between Middle English and New English.

The most notable changes affected the Middle English long vowels, all of which underwent change, as we see from the following examples. ME /i:/, as in inspi:red/, line 6, and /i:e/, line 10, has changed to NE /ay/. ME /u:/, as in /šu:res/, line 1, and flu:r/, line 4, has changed to NE /aw/. ME /e:/, as in /e:k/, line 5, has changed to NE /iy/, as has ME /ɛ:/, as in /hɛ:θ/, line 6. Moreover, ME /a:/, as in /a:pril/, line 1, has changed to NE /ey/. Further, ME /o:/, as in /ro:te/, line 2, has changed to NE /uw/, and ME /ɔ:/, as in /ɔ:pen/, line 10, has changed to NE /ow/. We will examine these changes again below. They are cited here as examples of the kind of sound change with which historical treatments of phonology are especially concerned.

By means of other words in these twelve lines we also note that not every Middle English long vowel is replaced by one of the New English elements given above. For example, *breath,* the modern form of ME /brɛ:θ/, line 5, no longer rhymes with *heath.* Its vowel was shortened, as were the vowels of other words ending in dental consonants, such as *dead, red, bread* and *thread*; thus, they did not undergo the change of ME /ɛ:/ to NE /iy/. A different type of disruption is found for /swo:te/; like *root* from /ro:te/, its modern form should have the element /uw/. Instead, the form found in line 5, /swe:te/ /swiyt/ has been generalised, ousting a potential */swuwt/. As this discussion may indicate, when we write the history of a language, we first determine the regular correspondences of its phonemes, including its major sound changes; and then we account for exception. The illustrate this procedure, we will examine the principal correspondences between the sound systems of Middle English and New English.

The Middle English and The New English Phonological Systems as Examples of Phonological Change

In dealing with sound change, we require not only that grammars discuss individual changes but also that they present them within the systems of two successive stages of a language. For, as we have noted above, sound change always involves alterations in a system. Unless we know the systems concerned, we cannot interpret the changes. In studying the changes of Middle English, then, we examine the consonant and vowel systems of New English as well as of Middle English.

Comparing the Middle and the New English consonant systems, we find little difference between them in number of phonemes.

Middle English

```
p  t  č  k
b  d  ǰ  g
 f θ  s  š x  h
 v ð  z
m  n
w    l r y
```

New English

```
p  t  č  k
b  d  ǰ  g
 f θ  s  š
 v ð  z  ž
m  n       ŋ
w    l r y  h
```

One Middle English consonant phoneme /x/ has been lost, as in *light;* compare NHG *Licht* [lixt]. If, however, ME *x* is interpreted as an allophone of *h*, this is merely an allophonic change.

Two new consonant phonemes have been added: /ž/, which developed from the cluster /zy/ as in *vision,* and was carried over in French loanwords such as *rouge;* /ŋ/, which was an allophone of ME /n/ before velars. Italian still has such variation for the phoneme /n/, with the allophone /ŋ/, occurring only before [k] and [g]. Middle English [ŋ] became a separate phoneme when voiced stops after nasals were lost in late Middle English, as in *climb, lawn* (cf. OFr. *launde*) and *long,* cf. *longer.* Through the loss of –g, the [ŋ] allophone was split from the phoneme /n/, becoming a separate phoneme as in NE /lɔŋ/ vs. /lɔn/. Apart from the loss of /x/ and the addition of two phonemes, the consonant systems of the two successive stages are similar in structure and number of members.

While the consonant systems differ little, the vowel systems are strikingly different. We give first the Middle English system, using a notation similar to Middle English orthography.

Short vowels	*Long vowels*	*Diphthongs*
i u	i: u:	
e o	e: o:	ei eu oi ou
a	ɛ: a: ɔ:	ai au

Apart from rearrangements, the principal allophones of vowels of the Middle English short-vowel system underwent few modifications, as we may illustrate:

ME ship NE ship ME bush NE bush
ME set NE set ME lock NE (Brit.) lock
ME bak (OE bæk) NE back

In the environments given here, the pronunciation of the Middle English short vowels and that of New English short vowels agree, though ME /a/ was probably articulated further back than is NE /æ/. Simply listing these correspondences, however, gives an inadequate view of the relationships between the two systems. For between Middle English and New English, the characterisation of vowels and consonants by quantity was abandoned. Moreover, ME [ə] has become a New English phoneme, with additions from ME /u/, which became

NE /ə/. as in *cut, tusk, hull,* except after labials, as in *put, bush, full, wolf.*

To illustrate the quantity distinction between long and short consonants in Middle English, we may cite *sunne* 'sun' and *sune* 'son'. Because of the difference in length of *n,* these words did not rhyme in Middle English. With the loss of long ccnsonants, however, they became homophones in New English, Similarly, Middle English vowels that were distinguished by length (somewhat like the vowels in NHG *Stadt* [štat] 'city' and *Staat* [šta:t] 'state') lost the distinction. ME *shamle* 'shamble' had short *a* before two consonants, but ME *sādel* 'saddle' had a long *ā* before consonant plus vowel. When the final syllables of both words came to be pronounced alike, the stem vowels became [æ] as in their New English forms. On the·other hand, long vowels maintained until the time of the Great English Vowel Shift, as in *crādel* 'cradle,' underwent the shift described in the following paragraph. In Middle English the vowels were distinguished by quantity as well as by quality, whereas in New English the primary distinction is by quality. The loss of the quantity distinction has resulted in a totally different vowel system.

The change of long vowels between Middle English and the present is known as the Great English Vowel Shift, often abbreviated GVS in historical grammars of English. This change is remarkable. All the Middle English vowels are modified similarly, by raising; /i:u:/, however, were already high vowels and could be raised no further. Their counterparts in Modern English are the diphthongs /ay/and /aw/. ME /e:/ and /ɛ:/ have fallen together to yield NE /iy/; ME /a:/ was fronted and raised to NE /ey/; ME /o:/ was raised to NE /uw/; ME /ɔ:/ was raised to NE /ow/. Examples are:

ME	NE	ME	NE	ME	NE
wif [wi:f]	wife /wáyf/			hous /hu:s/	house /háws/
seen [se:n]	seen [síyn]			spon /spo:n/	spoon /spúwn/
see [sæ:]	sea /síy/			ham /hɔ:m/	home /hówm/
		name/ na:me/	name / néym/		

These changes alone would have resulted in a totally different vowel system, but the Middle English symmetrical system of diphthongs (the three low short vowels followed by the two high) was also changed.

Middle English /ei ai/, which had probably fallen together by the time of Chaucer, merged with the reflex of ME /a:/, for example ME *vein*, NE *vein* /véyn/, ME *day, dai*/dai/, NE *day*/déy/. ME /oi/ remained unchanged, for example ME *boi, boy* /boi/, NE *boy* /bɔ́y/.

ME /eu/ merged with /uw/ from ME /o:/, for example ME *fruit* /freut/, NE *fruit* /frúwt., ME /*virteul*, NE *virtue* /vərtʃuw/ (also in New English forms with /yuw/, e.g. *pure*). ME /ou/ merged with /ow/ from ME /a:/, for example ME *boue* /boue/, NE *bow*/bów/. ME /au/ became a low, back vowel, for example ME *cause* /kauze/, NE *cause* /kɔ́z/.

It is clear from these examples that the Middle English vowel system was modified so greatly that it is difficult to plot the Modern English system beside it, as we have done for the consonants. In accordance with the diphthongal analysis proposed by Sweet, Wyld, Bloomfield, Bloch, Trager and others, the Modern English vowel system characteristic of Midland American English speakers may be presented as follows:

i ship		u bush	iy see		uw spoon
e set	ə some		ey say		ow bow
æ back	a lock	ɔ cause	ay wife	ɔy boy	aw house

In the vowel system proposed for education British English, these words are arranged as follows:

Simple	*Complex*	
i ship	i^i see	
e set	e^i say	
a back	a^i wife	a^u house
ə some	ɔy boy	$ə^u$ bow
ɔ not		
u bush		u^u spon

In addition, the six simple vowels of British English, and the vowels of *tie* and *town*, may be followed by [ə], as in *tear, tire, tower*; in the Midland dialect of American English, the corresponding sound is [r]. Except for these combinations with [ə], the British and American systems differ primarily in the low short vowels. In both of these systems, however, the set of Middle English vowels has been completely changed. The conservatism of the consonants, side by side with the innovations in the vowel system and in syllabic structure, may illustrate how languages change in some of their segments while undergoing little change in others.

The Processes Involved in Sound Change

From the changes between the Middle English and the New English phonological systems, we may illustrate the essentials necessary for a general understanding of sound change. As may be observed from English, sound changes take place by modification of sounds to similarly articulated sounds. For example, ME [e:] became NE [iy] rather than the totally different [uw] or [s]. Moreover, allophones of phonemes often differ in accordance with their environment; when sound changes take place, the direction may be a result of the phonetic surroundings of the sounds concerned. For example, we might expect a rounded vowel like [u] to be maintained in the neighbourhood of labial consonants, as was ME [u] in words like *put, bull, full,* when in other environments it became a central vowel, as in *tuck, duck, cut.* A thorough knowledge of articulatory phonetics is thus essential for understanding the processes of change.

Understanding the processes of sound change also involves a knowledge of the kinds of changes that sound systems can undergo. In setting up correspondences between Middle and New English, grammars often list only the most frequent correspondences, as if all Middle English phonemes had merely one reflex in New English, for example, as if all ME /u/ had become NE /u/. Furthermore, accounts of the Great Vowel Shift suggest that all ME /i:/ became NE /ay/. Yet, as we see in the few lines cited from Chaucer above, ME /i:/ also underwent other changes, as in *melodīe,* where it was shortened when the accent was placed on the first syllable. Simple treatments of sound systems are accordingly unrealistic, justifiable only for pedagogical reasons. Sound change of the type we have been considering takes place by subclasses of phonemes, labelled allophones. ME /u/, for example, became NE /u/ only after labials, as noted in the preceding paragraph; elsewhere it became /ə/. The Middle English long vowels underwent the Great Vowel Shift only when they had primary accent. As with the addition of NE /ŋ/, the differing developments correlate with differing allophones in Middle English. The changes we have been discussing, we therefore label change by allophones.

Conditioned versus Unconditioned Change

Allophones are restricted to certain environments in which they are conditioned by their surroundings. For example, ME /n/ was conditioned to velar articulation [ŋ] by a following velar consonant. When such allophones undergo a change, we speak of a **conditioned**, or a **combinatory, change**. Other examples are PGmc /f θ s χ/ to PGmc /b ð z g/ when not preceded by the primary accent, as in the words accounted for by Verner's law.

Much more rarely, all members of a phoneme change, and we speak of **an unconditioned change**. Examples are: PIE /o/ to PGmc /a/, as in Goth. *asts* "branch" from PIE /ósdos/ [ózdos] (with loss in Germanic of the second vowel); PGmc /z/ to OE /r/, as in OE wǣron "were." It should be noted, however, that when handbooks speak of unconditioned change, they do not take into account losses of certain members of the earlier phoneme. Thus the change of PIE /o/ to PGmc /a/ is called unconditioned, even though the *o* of unstressed syllables was lost, as in the second syllable of PIE /ósdos/. Moreover, some PGmc /z/ were lost, as in OE *mēd* "meed." Accordingly, it may be true that no change affects all occurrences of a phoneme. Completely unconditioned changes may, then, be impossible to document in languages.

Phonetic Processes Involved in Change

When changes take place, they usually involve modification of one or more distinctive features of a phoneme. NE /t/, for example, is a stop produced by alveolar closure while the velum is raised and the glottis is open. Some of its allophones are also characterised by aspiration, such as its allophone before stressed vowel, as in *top*; that after /s/, as in *stop,* is unaspirated. The allophone of /t/ after stressed vowels and before unstressed, as in *butting, butter, bottom* etc., came to be unaspirated and very short for many speakers of American English; articulated in this way, it became voiced between voiced sounds, so that *butting* and *budding, latter* and *ladder* and so on became homophones. For such speakers the short *t* between vowels became voiced, that is, instead of the distinctive feature [–voice], the distinctive feature [+voice] was introduced. In accounts of changes, we accordingly identify the distinctive features of phonemes and allophones, for through their modification sound changes take place.

From the time of Jacob Grimm, historical linguists have indicated sound changes by means of rules. Handbooks of the past state rules of sound change by means of classes of sounds or phonemes, specifying when necessary the environments concerned. Many current analyses state them by means of distinctive features. In the examples given below, rules of both types will be illustrated; the distinctive-feature rules will be provided for only the first few rules, for in general their formulation requires thorough control of the language in question, and these illustrations provide the format that can be followed for any analysed language.

A change may occur in **place of articulation**: labials may become labiodentals, dentals may become alveolars, velars may become palatals and so on. A change from dental to alveolar occurred when PGmc /t/ became OHG /s/; cf. Eng. hate = Germ. hassen. A change of velar to palatal occurred when PIE /k/ under certain conditions became [ʃ] in some of the dialects; cf. Lat. *centum* = Skt *śatam* "hundred."

This last change is stated as follows in terms of phonemes:

Rule 1a PIE k g gh > PIndic ʃ ž

In terms of distinctive features, it is stated:

Rule 1b [+cns] [–back]
[+high] → [+std]
[–ant]

The distinctive-feature rule indicates that Proto-Indo-European consonants which had the further distinctive features of height and—anterior (that is, no obstruction in the front of the mouth, i.e. back articulation) became strident and palatal.

The rule in both forms indicates that the change is unconditional, that is, that all Proto-Indo-European /k g gh/ became Proto-Indic [ʃ ž]. Yet this change is not found in all words with Proto-Indo-European /k g gh/. For a precise statement of the changes, to the extent they can be determined, one would have to consult a specialised handbook or article; yet even these have been inadequately precise. Complete and accurate descriptions of phonological changes remains to be provided for all languages.

A change may occur in **manner of articulation**: stops may

become fricatives or affricates, obstruents may become semivowels or vice versa and so on. A change from stop to fricative occurred when Proto-Indo-European /p/ became PGmc /f/; cf. Lat. *Pater* = Goth. *fadar*. A change from stop to affricate occurred when PGmc /p/ became HG /pf/; cf. Eng. *Pool* = Germ. *Pfuhl*. A change from semivowel to stop occurred when PGmc *ww* became North and East Gmc *ggw*, as in Goth. *triggws*, ON *tryggr* = OHG *triuwi* "true, faithful"; the two g's indicate that the sound in question was a stop, not a fricative.

The last change is stated as follows in terms of phonemes:

Rule 2a PGmc *ww* > NEGmc *gw* (spelled *ggw*)

In terms of distinctive features, it is stated:

Rule 2b $\begin{bmatrix} +\text{cns} \\ +\text{back} \\ -\text{vd} \end{bmatrix} \rightarrow -\text{rd} \,/\, \_\_ \begin{bmatrix} -\text{cns} \\ +\text{back} \\ +\text{rd} \end{bmatrix}$

This rule indicates a conditioned change. The conditioning feature is indicated after the slant line; by the condition PGmc *w* became North and East Germanic [g] only in the environment preceding *w*. For the interpretation of this rule, the omission of the feature [tense] is significant; the change did not take place before PGmc g^w, which was distinguished from PGmc *w* by tenseness. As the rule may indicate, while indication by means of features provides precision, the result may have a somewhat formidable mathematical flavour.

A change may occur in the **position of the velum**: nasal sounds may become denasalised, non-nasals may become nasals. OIcel. *ellefo* "eleven" corresponds to Goth. *ainlif*; OIcel. *annar* "other," on the other hand, corresponds to Goth, *anpar*. Nasal consonants were lost in Old English with lengthening of the preceding vowel, when they occurred before voiceless fricatives; cf. Eng. *five* = Germ. *fünf*, Eng. *goose* = Germ. *Gans*. Nasal articulation may not be completely lost, but may affect a neighbouring vowel, as in Fr. *vin* [vɛ̃] < Lat. *vinum* "wine."

The change of short vowels to long vowels in pre-Old English, with loss of following nasal, is stated as follows in terms of phonemes:

Rule 3 Pre-OE $\breve{V}$ + m/n + f/θ/s > OE $\bar{V}$ + f/θ/s

A change may take place in **glottal articulation**: voiced sounds may be devoiced, voiceless sounds may be voiced. An example of voiced sounds becoming devoiced is PIE /b d g/ becoming PGmc /p t k/; cf. Lat. *duo* = Eng. *Two.* An example of voiceless sounds becoming voiced is PGmc /f θ s χ/, without chief accent on the preceding syllable becoming PGmc /b ŏ z g/, as in PGmc **tugún*> PGmc *tugun* > OE *tugon* "pulled."

The last change is stated as follows in terms of phonemes:

Rule 4 PGmc f θ s χ χ^w > b ŏ z g g^w when not preceded by the chief accent.

A change may involve loss: OE /h/ before /l n r/ was lost, as in *loud* < OE *hlūd, nut* < OE *hnutu, ring* < OE *hring.* ME /g/ was lost after [ŋ] as in *long.* Final, weakly stressed vowels were lost in early New English, as in /persed/ > /pirst/*pierced, roote* > *root,* and so on. As in these examples, losses may be complete, though they may also have an effect on a neighbouring element. When, for example, [x] was lost in *light, thought, fight* (cf. Germ. *Licht, dachte, fechten*) and so on, in early Modern English, the preceding vowel was lengthened. This phenomenon is known as **compensatory lengthening**. Other examples are OE *gōs* < Pre-OE **gans,* cf. Germ. *Gans* 'goose,' OE *ūs* < Pre-OE **uns,* "us," in which nasals were lost before voiceless fricatives, with compensatory lengthening of the preceding vowel, as indicated in Rule 3 above. The same change occurred earlier in OE *brōhte* < PGmc /branχta/ "brought" and OE *pōhte* < PGmc /þanχta/ "thought."

Changes may also take place in the characteristic features of vowels, as in the degree of vowel opening. Open vowels may become more closed; closed vowels, more open. In Middle English /δ:/, as in *sea,* became more closed, so that we now rhyme its vowel with that of *see.* The closed vowels /i:/ and /u:/ of *wife* and *house,* on the other hand, came to be more open. The change of ME /e:/ to NE /iy/ is stated as follows in terms of phonemes:

Rule 5 ME ε: > NE iy

Changes may take place in the degree of fronting. Back vowels may become front vowels, and vice versa. When umlaut was carried through in Pre-Old English, when for example /u:/ became /y:/, as in /my:s/, the plural of /mu:s/ "mouse," back vowels were fronted.

The change of Pre-Old English long and short *o* and *u* to front rounded vowels is stated as follows in terms of phonemes:

Rule 6 Pre-OE ŏ̄ ŭ̄ > early ø̆̄ y̆̄ OE before i i: j

Changes may take place in labial articulation. The /y:/ of /my:s/, which was fronted in Pre-Old English times, later lost its lip rounding and coalesced with /i:/, so that in Middle English the vowel in *mice* fell together with that of *wife*. This change is stated as follows:

Rule 7 early OE ø̆̄ y̆̄ > late OE ĕ̄ ĭ̄

The examples given here illustrate changes that have taken place in the Indo-European languages. Examples of the processes illustrated here can also be cited from other languages that have been thoroughly investigated.

Assimilation and other Processes

The discussion of processes involved in sound change has examined the effects of change involving one or more distinctive features. Processes also follow general kinds of change. One of the most widely observed of these is **assimilation**, a change in the articulation of a sound to one more like that of neighbouring sounds. To illustrate it, we may note changes in the consonant of Lat. *ad* "to" when it was prefixed to morphs beginning with consonants. Lat. *apparātus* "apparatus," from *ad* + *pārāre* "make ready," illustrates assimilation in place of articulation; the dental *d* was changed to a labial. Lat. *assimulatiō* "assimilation," from *ad* + *simulāre* "resemble," illustrates assimilation in manner of articulation; the stop *d* was changed to a fricative. Lat. *annexus* "annex," from *ad* + *nectere* "bind," illustrates assimilationin position of the velum; the oral *d* was changed to a nasal. Lat. *attempto* "attempt," from *ad* + *temptāre* "try", illustrates assimilation in attitude of the glottis; the voiced *d* has become unvoiced.

As in these four examples, the preceding element is commonly assimilated, and the articulation of the second element is anticipated. This type of assimilation is referred to as **regressive**.

The articulation of the prior element may also be maintained, as in the pronunciation [sévm̩] for *seven;* in this pronunciation the labial articulation is maintained for the nasal from the preceding fricative. This type of articulation is referred to as **progressive**.

The articulation of both elements may be modified, by reciprocal assimilation, as in [sébm̩]; in this pronunciation the closure of the second element is anticipated in the *b*, and the position of the *b* is maintained for the nasal.

The assimilated sound may not always be contiguous with the sound to which it is changed. An example is Eng. *Orangutang,* which was taken over from Malay *orang* "man" + *ūtan* "forest; wild." The nasal of *ūtan* was modified to the velar position of the nasal in *orang* by **assimilation at a distance**, or **distant assimilation**. Skt *n* is changed to retroflex ṇ if preceded in the same word by a retroflex semivowel or sibilant, as in *rudreṇa* "by Rudra." Umlaut is an example of assimilation at a distance; as in OE *fõēt* < **fōti*, the back vowel *ō* was assimilated to the place of articulation of the following front vowel.

Assimilation may be complete, resulting in two identical sounds, as in *annexus,* or partial, as in [sévm̩].

Assimilation varies greatly from language to language. The Slavic languages have undergone repeated palatalization, that is assimilation of sounds to palatal articulation. English, too, has examples from several periods, as given later. But German exhibits little palatalization. We might expect that speakers would find it easier to articulate neighbouring sounds alike, and that they would accordingly introduce assimilation. But the structure of individual languages varies so greatly that we cannot propose such a generalisation. Before we assume that any one process may have led to specific changes or may be expected to, we must noted the characteristic articulation in a given language, as for the following processes.

Changes in word-ending position may lead to development of an additional consonant, as in the pronunciation [sinst] for *since.* In this pronunciation the tongue makes a closure against the alveolar ridge before articulation of the word is completed. The hearer may interpret this hold as a stop [t], and may then imitate the pronunciation, adding the stop, release and all. Such additional consonants are referred to as **excrescent**. Further examples may be taken from English, for example *varmint* < *vermin,* or from German; compare Germ. *Axt,* Eng. *ax*; Germ. *Sekt* "champagne," Eng. *sack* "dry sherry"; Germ. *Habicht,* Eng. *hawk.*

Moreover, final vowels may be lost, a process known as **apocope**. In Old English the first person singular present ended in *-e*, for example *helpe*; in the late Middle English period such final vowels were lost. Apocope, and **syncope**, the loss of medial vowels, are prominent in languages with a strong stress accent on initial syllables. In the Germanic languages many medial and final vowels have been lost, until in present-day English many native words have become monosyllabic. The Old English first singular preterite of *temman* "tame" was *tēmede*; both weakly stressed vowels have been lost, to yield NE *tamed* [teymd].

Vowels may also be introduced, a process called **epenthesis**. We find epenthetic vowels, for example, in OE *æcer,* cf. OIcel. *akr* "acre," OE *ofen,* cf. OIcel. *ofn* "oven," and in many other words before *r l m n*; we find epenthetic consonants in OE *bræmbel* beside *brēmel* "bramble," OE *gandra beside ganra* "gander" and so on. If initial, such elements are called **prothetic**. Prothetic vowels were introduced in French before *s* plus consonant, as in Fr. *école* < OFr. *escole* from Lat. *schola, scola* "school." Similar developments may be noted in Span. *esuela,* Port. *escola,* though in these languages the development of the prothetic vowel is more narrowly circumscribed.

The Patterns of Sound Change

In discussing examples and processes of sound change, we have observed that sound change only occurs when there is a disruption of the phonological system. Such disruption may occur in one of two ways, either by merger or by split.

Merger occurs when sounds change so completely that they fall together with the sounds of another phoneme, for example NE *t* as in *bitter* merging with the /d/ as in *bidder*. It was the pattern by which ME /o:/, as in *roote,* became established as NE /uw/; for reflexes of ME *ō* merged with those of ME *eu,* as in *fruit* and *virtue*. Other examples are given below.

By means of split, one or more allophones of a phoneme may move away from the other allophones of that phoneme: for example, ME [ŋ] split off from the ME /n/ phoneme upon loss of a following /g/, as in *young.* By means of split, new phonemes may be introduced, as was NE /ŋ/, or the diverging allophones may merge with another phoneme as did the reflexes of PGmc /z/ with Pre-OE /r/, as in *were.*

Merger is the more important of these patterns; for often when a sound change results from split, the rearrangement has taken place in such a way that one of the split allophones has merged with allophones from another source. The [e] which split off from Pre-OE /a/ before *i ī j,* for example, merged with /e/, as in *men*. Moreover, allophones may become phonemes when their conditioning entities merge with others; Pre-OE short and long [ø] and [y] became phonemes when following *i ī j* merged with reflexes of other weakly stressed vowels or were lost. Merger may therefore be considered the central mechanism of sound change.

Merger may be conditioned or unconditioned. Unconditioned merger, when a phoneme merges completely with another phoneme, is relatively infrequent. An example is PGmc /z/, which merged in Pre-Old English and other Germanic dialects with PGmc /r/. When such mergers take place, we cannot determine the earlier forms solely from one language, unless we have enough linguistic material to use the method of internal reconstruction. By comparing *was* with *were,* for example, we can distinguish the source of the *r* in *were* (PIE *s*) from that of the *r* in *four* (PIE *r*). Examples of other unconditioned mergers are: that of PIE /o/ with PIE /a/ to PGmc /a/; PIE /bh dh gh/ with /b d g/ in Iranian, Baltic, Slavic and Celtic.

Much more frequent is conditioned merger, as when NE [t] merged with /d/ after stressed vowels preceding other vowels plus consonants, but not /n/; *bitten* did not become a homophone of *bidden*. Numerous instances of such merger can be cited: NE /u:/ in closed syllables merged with earlier ME /u/, as in *blood,* ME *blōd,* cf. Germ. *Blut* [blu:t], and *nut*, ME *nute,* cf. Germ. *Nuss* [nus]. As another example, NE /ž/ from /zy/ merged with /ž/ in borrowings from French, like *rouge.*

Often after such mergers we find alternations that reflect the earlier situation, such as the /ž/ in *vision,* which alternates with the /z/ in *visible*. These alternating entities are used in applying the method of internal reconstruction.

Since split may be brought about in two different ways, we distinguish two kinds of split. **Primary split** results from a change of some of the members of a phoneme, which then merge with a different phoneme. In this way the fricative reflex of OHG /t/ merged with OHG /s/ from PGmc /s/, as in NHG *hassen,* cf. Eng. *hate*; the phoneme

/t/ was maintained as in MHG *treu*, cf. NE *true*. As another example, allophones of ME /u:/ merged with short ME /u/ before consonants, as in late-ME *blud* "blood," but ME /u:/ was maintained, as in *cū* "cow." As these examples indicate, primary split leads to an increase in the number of occurrences of one phoneme; after the merger of late ME /u/ from /u:/ with ME /u/, /u/ occurred more frequently. But primary split does not generally introduce new phonemes.

Secondary split results from a change in the conditioning features of allophones. Such a change may lead to the introduction of new phonemes in a system. In this way the Pre-Old English front rounded allophones [ø: y y:] of /o o: u u:/ became phonemes when the conditioning /i i: j/ were modified. Pre-OE /o o: u u:/ were continued into Old English, but from some of their allophones four new phonemes /ø ø: y y:/ were added to the system. Secondary split, however, does not necessarily lead to the introduction of new phonemes. For example, no new phonemes were produced from the fronted allophones of Pre-OE /a a:/ when the conditioning /i i: j/ were modified; for these allophones fell together with earlier /e e:/.

In sum, disruption of phonological systems, that is sound change, is brought about in accordance with two patterns: merger and split. In each of these patterns, the processes that lead to the change may vary, in accordance with the processes described earlier. Moreover, in languages with large numbers of speakers, the results of sound change may only be adopted over a long period of time, as we will note in the following section.

The Spread of Sound Change

After a sound change has taken place, it may be restricted to a given geographical area or it may be extended to other areas in which a language is spoken. In this way the spread of sound change is comparable to the spread of any linguistic innovation. Words may be adopted throughout the area influenced by a centre of prestige; the French word *lagniappe* was adopted in eastern Taxas through influence from Louisiana, while the Spanish word *pilon* was adopted in southern Texas through influence from Mexico. Phonological innovations may be extended similarly, as demonstrated in Kloeke's classical study concerning the change of MDu. *ū* specifically in the words for "house" and "mouse."

MDu. *ū* changed to *ȳ*, apparently in the area around Antwerp. The results of this change were spread to speakers who were influenced by this focal area; in time the change was extended virtually throughout the entire area in which Dutch was spoken. Near Low German territory, however, *ū* was maintained, probably because of the unchanged *ū* in Low German cognates; *ū* was also maintained more widely in *mūs* than in *hūs*, probably because the word for "mouse" is less widely used in communication with members of other communities than is the word for "house, building." The results of the change accordingly reflect both social and geographical influence. A second change of *ȳ* to [øy] took place in the sixteenth and seventeenth centuries in the Antwerp area and was spread over much of the Dutch-speaking area; it became the standard pronunciation of MDu. *huis* and *muis*. These Dutch phenomena provide an excellent illustration of the spread of sound change, of variation from word to word in adoption of new patterns and of the social forces at work in such spread.

Dialect geographers have carried out many studies which demonstrate that the results of sound changes are extended in accordance with communication patterns among geographical and social dialects.

Among the documented examples of sound change and its spread, the High German consonant shift may be the one most thoroughly investigated. Affecting first the High German area proper, the results of the change have been adopted through more and more of the German-speaking area. With the greater centralisation of government in the nineteenth and twentieth centuries, a form of German was adopted that incorporated most of these changes. Today the dialects of north Germany, that is, the dialects of Low German with unchanged obstruents as in English, are being modified or ousted by High German. The results of the changes introduced by the High German consonant shift are accordingly still being spread, though the changes themselves took place approximately 1,500 years ago.

Gradual Extension of the Great English Vowel Shift

Our observations based on the spread of the Old High German consonant shift and of the Dutch change of *ū*, may help us to understand other such phenomena in language, such as the spread of the results of the Great Vowel Shift.

When we investigate the adoption of the changes of the shift, we find that they were introduced gradually and over a long period of time. Instances of ME [ɛ:], which now rhymes with [e:], were, for example, treated differently in the sixteenth and seventeenth centuries. Dryden rhymed *dream* with *shame, sea* with *obey.* Pope rhymed *weak* with *take, eat* with *state*; Swift rhymed *sea't* with *weight, meat* with *say't,* and so on. Much earlier, the pronunciation [i:] for [ɛ:] is reported by grammarians, but not favoured by them. We assume it was used by Queen Elizabeth I, for she wrote "biquived" for *bequeathed.* Although this pronunciation is known from the sixteenth century, still in 1747 Johnson was troubled about rhyming *great,* whether with *seat* [i:] or with *state* [e:].

We may ascribe Johnson's perplexity in part to the variation of usage among the dialects of Britain, in part to the gradual and slow extension of the shift. A sound change may take place in a focal area and be carried to other areas under its cultural influence through many centuries. The change of ME [ɛ:] and other long vowels must have been similar to the change of intervocalic *t* in contemporary American English, in which some speakers pronounce *butter* [bə́dər], others [bə́tər], still others [bə́tər]. As sounds are modified, the new articulation is extended gradually until words containing them reach a stabilised position in the phonological system of the standard language, as have *dream* and *great* today. Yet even today we find variation in English dialects, some of which preserve the pronunciation [diyf] rather than the shortened [def] of standard English. We also find considerable variation in the pronunciation of words like *root, hoof, roof.* This variation illustrates that even after six centuries the effects of the Great Vowel Shift have not become stabilised in English.

Generalisation of the Results of Sound Change in Small Societies

Just how and when sound changes are adopted in any individual speech community is a complicated problem that requires detailed study. Our information about speech communities of the past is less detailed than is our information on contemporary languages and their use. For this reason our interpretations of the spread of sound changes in the past rely largely on studies of interrelationships between geographical dialects; Kloeke's observations of the difference in extent between the spread of the changed pronunciations in *hūs* and *mūs*, however, also involved consideration of social dialects. In this century, important investigations have been made of linguistic communities in which sound changes have been documented; these investigations provide details about the spread of change among various age groups of speakers and various social as well as geographical configurations.

The most comprehensive survey made of a speech community for historical purposes has provided important information on the gradual spread of the results of sound change. In his investigation of the French-speaking village of Charmey, Switzerland, published in 1905, L. Gauchat found differences in the speech of various age groups of the village. For example, where speakers 69-90 years of age used the back vowel *å,* speakers 30-60 years of age used both *å* and *ao* and younger speakers used only *ao*. Moreover, palatalised *l* was in part replaced by *y* among speakers 30-60 years of age, and totally replaced among speakers under 30.

In 1929 E. Hermann published a follow-up study of Charmey, in which he examined the situation regarding some of Gauchat's conclusions at that time. Hermann found that the change of *ō* to *ao* and other diphthongisation had become even more general. Other sound changes noted by Gauchat, however, had not been generally adopted, apparently because of contrary influence from standard French. The studies by Gauchat and Hermann show that sound changes, when adopted, are spread gradually among a community of speakers, as we have noted for the changes of the Great Vowel Shift.

Alf Sommerfelt found similar results concerning differences among speakers of varying age groups in Welsh- and Irish-speaking communities. Besides supporting the evidence for gradual spread of the results of sound changes, Sommerfelt provided data that illustrate how such gradual shifting takes place. He found that the change was completely carried out in some words, but not yet in others. Sommerfelt's findings remind us of the situation in English after the Great Vowel Shift. A change may not affect all words immediately; but in time it is carried out in all words of similar phonological structure unless social conditions direct the adoption of other patterns.

We may accordingly conclude from the situations in English, in Charmey, and in Wales and Ireland, how sound change takes place and is generalised in relatively small communities. After a sound change has been carried out, it is generalised so that eventually all occurrences of a linguistic element undergo the change, if its environment is the same and if the prestige of the focal area is adequate. If the linguistic community is small and homogeneous, the change may be carried out with complete consistency. This was the situation for the Proto-Germanic consonant shift; we know of no exceptions. If a change were carried out in a small homogeneous community today, we would expect the same results. At the time of the High German consonant shift, however, the linguistic community that spoke High German was so large that the results of the shift were adopted only in a part of the area, presumably the focal area, and those neighbouring areas under its influence. A similar situation existed for English in the fifteenth century, so that today "exceptions" to the Great Vowel Shift are found in the language side by side with the reflexes we expect from the shift.

Generalisation of the Results of Sound Changes in the Large Language Communities of Today

None of the communities discussed in the previous section approaches in size and complexity the linguistic community speaking English today, or even such a portion of this community as the New York City area. The population of the New York City area is much larger than that of England in the fifteenth century, and the speakers are also far more unlike. Recent immigration of Blacks into New York, and of Puerto Ricans, Haitians, and many other groups, is also far more extensive than were any immigrations in Britain at any time, including the fifteenth century. It is instructive to examine how phonological systems change in such a large and complex community.

William Labov has carried out such studies, concentrating on linguistic variables, that is, items which are not found consistently among all speakers. One such item is [r].

In his study of the status of [r], as in *guard*, in New York City society, Labov found that it has high prestige. When speakers wish to be accepted in certain social contexts, they use the [r]. They also extend [r] and other patterns of high prestige to words in which they do not belong, producing in this way **hyperforms**. From his observations of the spread of variant forms with high prestige, Labov has proposed that such forms may be adopted more widely by speakers outside the focal area.

This observation has also been made for languages of the past, though only for occasional forms. Bloomfield (1933: 479-80) cites an instance of a hyperform in Rhaeto-Romance. Another example is OSax. *tins* "taxes." This word is ultimately from Lat. *census,* through OHG *zins.* When Old Saxon speakers adopted the word from Old High German, they apparently assumed that it belonged to the patterns they observed for the Old High German consonant shift, which differentiated their own word *tolna.* from OHG *zollan* "tax" and the like. Rather than adopt the initial late Latin consonant [ts], they introduced the normal Old Saxon equivalent of OHG [ts], converting OHG *zins* to OSax. *tins.* In *tolna* such a conversion is etymologically justified, for the Latin word is *telōnēum*; in *tins*, however, it is not justified, for the initial Latin consonant was [ts].

For languages of the past, we find such changes only in sporadic forms. In the complex societies of contemporary culture, in which speakers master many varieties and dialects of their own language, such changes may be introduced more widely, as in the speech of New York City. As Weinreich, Labov and Herzog have concluded, "the interpretation of the data in terms of language change depends on the entire sociolinguistic structure" (1968).

In conclusion, the studies of Kloeke, Gauchat, Sommerfelt and the numerous scholars who have concerned themselves with the High German consonant shift and the Great English Vowel Shift, indicate that after sound changes take place, they are spread in accordance with social forces in a given community. If a community is small and compact, they may be adopted throughout it. An example we have cited is the Germanic consonant shift, which spread to all speakers of Proto-Germanic. Larger communities, on the other hand, may show only partial adoption of sound changes, as we may note from the results of the Great English Vowel Shift or from the extension of the High German consonant shift. On the other hand, sound changes may be rejected in favour of competing patterns, as occurred in Charmey. We have noted that the shift of certain PIE *k* to sibilants did not take place in the Baltic, the farthest west of stem dialects. To understand the phenomena involved in sound change, linguists have introduced increasingly precise techniques, such as rules in which the various forces involved can be specified. But there are also changes that affect only a small number of words, or only individual words in a language, as we shall note ahead.

Sporadic Change, or Change by Phonemes

As we dealt with sound changes that arise from the rearrangements of allophones. Some allophones of one phoneme in the course of time come to resemble allophones of another phoneme and may merge with them. Allophones may also be split from the phoneme to which they formerly belonged, or they may be lost. In sound changes of this type, all allophones that are similar in articulation undergo the change. Moreover, when the change has taken place, the new alignment is maintained, until another shift occurs. NE /n/, for example, has remained distinct from /n/ since the loss of a following /g/. Besides such change we find in language sporadic changes which affect sounds only in some of their occurrences. As an example we may cite the change of ME *napron* to NE *apron;* it occurred because of false division of the sequence a *napron.* We call the loss of initial *n* in *napron* a sporadic change because it occurred only in a few Middle English words.

Sporadic changes differ from allophonic changes in that they cannot be ascribed to any one phonological pattern. For example, initial *n* was not lost in phonological patterns similar to that of *napron*; it was maintained in *napkin, nape* and so on. By contrast, every *n* was lost before voiceless fricatives in Pre-Old English, as in OE *gōs* "goose" from **gans-*.

Since sporadic changes involve a direct change from one phoneme to another, with no gradual modification of allophones like that in AE-*t*-, we refer to the process as **change by phonemes**. They have also been referred to as **spontaneous**, and **saltatory**—in recognition of the immediate shift from one phoneme to another.

As an example we may cite the pronunciations of NE *seven.* One pronunciation, especially in careful speech is [sévn̩]. But *seven* is often pronounced [sévm̩], or even [sébm̩]. When this pronunciation is used, there has been no long gradual development of a final alveolar nasal to a labiodental or bilabial nasal. Speakers use either one of the two phonemes. Moreover, we find many such changes in rapid, informal speech, especially in everyday words. Although a similar change is often observed for NE *eleven* [əlévm] rather than [əlévn], it would be rare, or nonexistent, in *leaven* [lévn], which has the same phonetic environment for *n* but a different status in the social dialects of the language.

Speakers are often conscious of changes by phonemes, though they are unaware of the changes by allophones, as in the gradual voicing of NE *water, bottle* and so on. Changes by allophone are carried through in all morphs in which the allophone occurs, except possibly by self-conscious speakers; the *t* in Modern English forms like *better, bottom,* for example, is consistently modified. On the other hand, a sporadic change like that of [sévn̩] to [sébm̩], or the pronunciation [irévələnt] for [iréləvənt], is often noted and frowned upon. The different attitude of speakers to change by phonemes probably results from an awareness that such phenomena are associated with specific social dialects or styles.

Many of the processes involved in sporadic change are like those involved in more general sound change. In this way many sporadic changes are assimilatory, such as those of *eleven*. Examples may also be found in the frequent palatalization of *ty* to yield *tš*, as in rapid pronunciation of words ending in *-t* before *you*, such as /betšə/ rather than /bet yə/. Moreover, epenthetic vowels may be introduced, as in the pronunciation /éləm/ rather than /élm/. The same process led to the general introduction of epenthetic vowels in Old English, but in Modern English we do not introduce such vowels in all words with /-lm/; for example, *realm*/relm/, *helm* and so on.

One process that is exemplified primarily in sporadic changes is **dissimilation**, the production of sounds so that they will be more unlike one another. With the notable exception of Grassmann's law, dissimilation is generally attested sporadically in languages. We find dissimilation especially among the more complex sounds, which are also those learned last by children; such are *l* and *r*, as in NE *turtle* < Lat. *turtur,* NE *pilgrim* < Lat. *peregrinus,* NE *marble* < Lat. *marmor*. It is less commonly attested for stops, as in Germ. *Kartoffel* "potato," in which the initial *k* was dissimilated from *t* in the seventeenth century; the early form was *Tartuffeln,* which was borrowed from Ital. *tartuffeli.* (When the plant was imported to Italy, from Peru in the sixteenth century, it was named after the truffle.) As in all of these examples, in dissimilation it is usually the sound of the unaccented syllable that is modified.

Dissimilation may also involve the loss of a syllable; this is called **haplology**. As examples we may cite the Modern English adverbs in *-ly* made from adjectives ending in *-le*. In these, one syllable has been lost, as in *gently* rather than **gentlely, simply* rather than **simplely*. Another example is *England* < *Engla lond* "land of the Angles." Haplology is relatively infrequent.

Another type of change that is primarily sporadic is **metathesis,** the interchange of phonemes. Although few examples can be cited from Modern English, metathesis was remarkably frequent in late West Saxon, where we find *āxian* [a:ksian] "ask," *dox* "dusk," *flaxe* "flask," *waxan* "wash." Metathesis of consonant and vowel (to which some scholars restrict the term metathesis) is also attested in Old English, as in *hors* < *hros,* cf. Germ. *Ross* "horse," *ðirda* < *ðridda* "third," cf. Germ. *dritte* and NE *three.* Reflexes of the nonmetathesised forms are also found in Modern English, as in the dialectal *ask* for *ask,* and in *wal-rus* rather than **whalehorse.* In this way the examples cited here from English illustrate the phenomena of sporadic change, which affects relatively few words of the language, and which often leaves variant forms besides them.

Interpretations of Sound Change

In past treatments of phonological change, and in many current treatments, sound change is interpreted as a change of elements in a phonological system, as we have noted in the discussion of the phenomena described under Grimm's law. For example, the first of the changes in the Germanic consonant shift is interpreted as a change of the Proto-Germanic elements $p\ t\ k\ k^w$ to $f\ \theta\ \chi\ \chi^w$. The elements in question are taken to be abstract elements in the phonological system.

As linguistic theory became more explicit, these abstract elements were precisely defined, and labelled phonemes, that is, classes of sounds with specific relationships to other classes of sounds in a given language. Each class was assumed to have one or more allophones, that is, subclasses of **phonemes**. Sound change takes place in such subclasses, except in the rare instances when it is not combinatory; in such instances, the entire phoneme is changed. The process was stated by Grimm in the form of a rule, and has been subsequently stated by the same device, though the shape of rules has been modified.

When interpreting sound changes as changes of abstract elements in a phonological system, linguists also undertook to analyse the components of these elements, as we noted of Trubetzkoy and Jakobson. Such study led to an analysis of phonemes as bundles of distinctive features. When change occurs, one or more of these components is assumed to have been modified. Thus in the Proto-Germanic change of *p t k* k^w to *f* $\theta \chi \chi^w$ the manner of articulation was modified from that of a stop to a fricative. Phonological changes could in this way be interpreted as addition, alteration or loss of a feature. Thus the feature [+front] was added to the articulation of Pre-OE *a* by umlaut. In the umlaut of Pre-OE *o* and *u*, the feature [+back] was altered to [+front]. The resulting OE phonemes subsequently lost the feature [+round] to merge with *e* and *i*.

By interpreting sound change as a change in features, we can specify more precisely the components of phonemes that are involved in change than if we simply use symbols for the phonemes. But whether depicted as change of subclasses of phonemes, like *p t k* k^w, or as change of features, sound change is interpreted as a change of elements in the phonological system of a language.

Change as Interpreted by Change in Rules

As we noted in recalling the contributions of Trubetzkoy, he regarded phonological elements and processes as rules. The view was continued by generative linguistics, so that in their treatment change consists of modifications of rules in the competence of speakers. Specific changes, then, have been labelled by the effect on rules.

When sound change involves innovations, the event is described as **rule addition.** The changes described in Grimm's law, in Pre-Old English umlaut and in the Great Vowel Shift are examples of rule addition.

When, on the other hand, the application of a rule is no longer maintained, the event is referred to as **rule loss.** As an example, Gothic regularised the fricatives in most inflected sets; it shows voiceless fricatives where the other Germanic languages maintain voiced fricatives, as in the cognate of *choose*:

Goth.	kiusan	kaus	kusum	kusans
cf. OE	cēosan	cēas	curon	coren

Because other evidence has led us to assume that the Gothic verbs at one time had such voiced fricatives, the presence of *s* and other voiceless fricatives in the preterite plural and the preterite participle is ascribed to rule loss.

Voiced fricatives as reflexes of Proto-Indo-European voiceless stops are found in Gothic, as in the form *fadar* "father," and in auxiliaries like *aih* : *aigum* "own." Generative grammarians account for such exceptions to rule loss by stating that words like *fadar* and *aigum* have been entered in the lexicon. Lexicalized forms may escape modification when a rule is lost.

A third type of change is ascribed to **rule reordering**. Two languages or dialects may exhibit the same rules, but the rules may differ in order. In this way the area in central Germany that incorporated some changes from the north and others from the south has different surface forms from those of other dialects but is said to incorporate the same rules.

For example, in the twelfth century, *ī* > *ei* in Austria and south Germany, as in NHG *Seite* < MHG *sīte*. The change was extended northward, and reached the Mosel area in the sixteenth century. Middle High German also had an *ie* diphthong, pronounced [iə]. This *ie* changed to *ī* in the eleventh and twelfth centuries in central Germany, as in NHG *ließ* "permitted," and the change was extended southward. In the dialect of Wetterau, the *ī* > *iə* was adopted before the influence of the *ī* > *ei* was transmitted from the south; as a result, the vowel of *ließ* and other words with earlier *iə* also was changed to *ei* when the *ī* > *ei* change reached the Wetterau dialect.

Grammars of the German dialects would therefore have different rule orders. In a grammar of dialects to the south, the *ī* > *ei* rule would be ordered before that of *ie* > *ī*; in a grammar of dialects to the north, the *ie* > *i* rule would have an earlier order. The relationships between these dialects with regard to these characteristics would therefore be indicated in the order of rules that present the results of previous sound changes.

Besides reinterpreting sound change, and the results of sound change in this way, grammarians with a generative point of view have introduced terms for rules that can be related to other rules. For example, if a rule describes changes that expand the scope of subsequent rules, the earlier rule is labelled a **feeding rule**, and the group of rules is said to stand in a **feeding relationship**. In this way the rules that describe the lengthening of short vowels before the Great Vowel Shift are labelled feeding rules. For, with the addition of more instances of *ī*, a larger number of words underwent the change of *ī* to *ay*. But languages also undergo changes that conflict with the pattern of earlier changes. Such changes are referred to as **bleeding rules; bleeding relationship**, then, results in diminution of scope.

In order to understand the publications that deal with sound change as rules change, students must be aware of their basis, and of their difference from earlier descriptions and historical treatments. The use of rules is not new, for, as we noted above, rules have been used since the days of Grimm. Nor is the use of distinctive features in stated sound changes restricted to such treatments, for linguists of the nineteenth century already dealt with changes by means of features. Rather, it is the identification of linguistic phenomena through rules, and the discussion of linguistic changes as rule changes that are characteristic of this approach.

The rules of the past expressed in terms of phonemes and the rules expressed in terms of distinctive features are equivalent, if both types of rules meet the requirements of observational adequacy and descriptive adequacy. Meeting these requirements is still a greater problem in historical linguistics than is the revision of traditional terminology. For example, rules given in distinctive features may be inadequate if they do not observe the forms (rules) that are exceptions.

Other inadequacies in rules result from our lack of information about the distinctive features of phonemes in languages of the past. For example, we do not know the distinctive features of PIE *bh dh gh* $g^w h$. By one interpretation they were tense voiced stops as opposed to the lenis voiced stops labelled *b d g* g^w. In attempts to understand the changes of the early Germanic consonant system, we must face such problems. By simply rewriting proposed rules formulated by earlier linguists, no new insights into the phenomena themselves are acquired.

Proposed Explanations for Sound Change

Besides studying the processes and patterns by which phonological systems are modified, historical linguists have attempted to determine the causes of modification and to predict its directions.

Some linguists have attempted to account for sound change by proposing that it leads to greater simplicity in language. Such attempts fail when we examine other languages; what is "simple" for speakers of some languages and in specific stages of a language may seem difficult in others, as we noted when we compared sound changes in a given language with the phenomena in other languages. We conclude that assumption of change towards ease of articulation in accordance with the principle of least effort is based on an inadequate view of language. For what seems easy in one language is difficult in another.

For example, German still maintains initial [kn], which has been lost in English and accordingly seems to be a very difficult consonant cluster for English speakers; compare NHG *kneten* "knead," NHG *Knie* "knee," NHG *Knoten* "knot" and so on. As another example we may note that in Latin there was relative freedom of occurrence of final consonants, but in Classical Greek the only final consonants to occur are *r n s*. PIE *-m* in the accusative singular, for example Lat. *lupum* "wolf," shows up as Gk *-n*, *lúkon*. Other final consonants were lost, as illustrated by the vocative singular *paî of paîs,* gen. *Paidós* "boy"; Gk *tí* "what" corresponds to Lat. *quid.* Moreover, Klaus Wedekind (1990) has pointed out that glottalics, which seem to be difficult for linguists working in Indo-European languages, are very common in those of Ethiopia. The observation is important for evaluation of the glottalic theory, because one of its supports is based on the absence of roots with initial and final *b d g* g^w; interpreting these as glottalic, glottalicists use the finding as morphological support for the theory. By Wedekind's observation, the support is empty.

It is obvious from differences like these in various languages that only some sound changes tend toward simplicity and that we must look for other explanations (Jespersen 1922).

Three major reasons are to be proposed for change in language, including change in the phonological system: (1) the effect of one language on another; (2) the effects of modifications introduced when children learn their language; (3) effects of components in the system of a language on other components. We will examine briefly each of these proposed explanations as they apply to sound change.

The Proposed Explanation of Sound Change through the Effects of One Language on Another is Based on Observations of Speakers who Learn a Second Language with Traces of Their First Language

This statement is especially true if the speakers have learned the second language after their adolescence. Thus, many speakers of

English keep their aspirated stops when they learn French, pronouncing *peau* "skin" as [p^how] rather than as [po:]. French speakers may do the converse when they learn English. Moreover, many English speakers keep their diphthongised vowels when they learn Spanish, pronouncing the Spanish *si* 'yes' as [siy], *sé* "be" as [sey], *su* "his" as [suw], in accordance with their own pronunciation of *see, say, sue*. By contrast, many Spanish speakers, who have only five vowels, do not distinguish between such English words as *bit* and *beet, let* and *late, pull* and *pool*. On the basis of such observations, it has been proposed that sound changes may be introduced by the carry-over of articulatory habits from the native language to a second language, with permanent effect. If, then, a large number of speakers adopt a second language, possibly as a result of conquest or migration the sound system of the language can be modified.

The underlying language is known as a **substratum**. The proposed explanation for sound change is therefore known as the **substratum theory**. (The terms **adstratum** for an adjacent influencing language, and **superstratum** for a superior influencing language, may also be used.)

Romance historical linguists especially have attempted to account for the separate developments of Spanish, French and other Romance languages by assuming articulatory modifications carried over by speakers who adopted Latin as their second language. The French front rounded vowels are, for example, ascribed to a Celtic substratum. The changes that Latin has undergone in Rumanian are ascribed to a Dacian substratum.

Our primary difficulty with proposing the substratum theory to account for sound change is the lack of evidence. We do not know what the relationships between the Celtic speakers of Gaul and the Latin-speaking settlers were. We know very little about the varieties of Celtic spoken in Gaul. The problems are similar for Spanish, Rumanian and other languages. Until the substratum theory can be supportd by large-scale observation of sound changes in contemporary languages, we must be cautious about suggesting it as an explanation for sound changes. On the other hand, speakers in societies that use several languages often have similar syntactic constructions in each. The influences of languages on one another may, then, be more weighty in syntax than in phonology.

The effects of language interaction are determined largely by social conditions. When in some areas non-native spekers acquire a new language, the second generation masters it with general adequacy, if the linguistic tradition is well established. In the United States, grandchildren of Italians, Germans, Spaniards, Africans, Asiatics, Irish, and Danes speak the English used by their associates without notable differences in phonological structure. In other societies, however, different conditions may lead to different results.

When substrata have led to modifications in the pronunciation of a language, as of English in India, the linguistic tradition has been less powerful; native speakers have been outnumbered. In India relatively few native speakers from Britain were available to teach English to speakers who constantly used the indigenous languages.

There is now considerable investigation of multilingual communities such as those in India, Africa and other areas of the world that are predominantly multilingual. The effects of one language on another may become clear after further study and may permit generalisations about sound changes resulting from the interplay of languages. Such study has indicated the effects of other languages in the syntax and in the lexicon, as we note later. From our observations, however, we must conclude that sound change has as its major causes other linguistic phenomena.

The Hypothesis that Sound Change is to be Attributed to Children Learning their Language is also Poorly Supported

Under this hypothesis it is assumed that each new generation of speakers must master anew the grammar of their language and that, in the process, phonological change can readily be introduced. It is apparent to anyone observing children learning their language that some of them have difficulty pronouncing certain sounds. An occasional child learning English, for example, may pronounce the *r* as in *rat* with initial rounding, so that the word sounds like *wat*. Although such observations are readily supported, it is also true that these children eventually overcome the difficulties.

Further, even if some young children make idiosyncratic errors in pronunciation, there is no consistency of errors among children. Nor can we determine distinct generations of either young or old speakers who might generalise such mispronunciations. It is difficult, therefore, to conclude that modifications, such as those observed by Gauchat between the speech of different age groups at Charmey, were caused by inadequate learning of the phonemes in question, or of the phonological rules, by children.

Linguists who have studied sound change have observed, however, that when a change has been introduced, it is extended further by young speakers. For example, in 1943 the change of intervocalic AE *t* to *d* was carried through consistently by a group of young speakers (Lehmann 1953). And Sommerfelt observed a sound change in Wales first in a few words, and subsequently in greater numbers, until eventually all sounds in the phonological environment in question were affected. Apparently, when a sound change is adopted, it is observed by more and more speakers in more and more words, until finally it is carried out in all the pertinent environments among a community of speakers.

We assume that if a sound change is carried out "without exceptions," as was the Proto-Germanic consonant shift, the community of speakers was homogeneous and probably small. When a sound change is carried out only partially throughout a relatively large territory, like the High German consonant shift, the community of speakers is exposed to various influences. As the effects of the High German consonant shift were spread towards Low German territory, influences from the important cultural centres of Low-German-speaking northern Germany interfered with the influences leading to modifications. Similarly, the Great English Vowel Shift was not carried out in Scotland. We may conclude, therefore, that the spread of phonological changes is affected by the learning of language among children. But the initial cause of phonological changes cannot be ascribed to language learning.

Ascribing Sound Change to Attempts to Achieve Regularity or Symmetry in Phonological Systems Seems at First Blush Most Attractive

Examples like NE /ŋ/ can be cited that filled out the set of English nasals corresponding to the stops: /p b m t d n k g –/. While this explanation may apply for English, Italian and other languages with similar gaps in the system have not regularised in this way. Clearly, this explanation, too, has its limits.

Even if we may assume a tendency towards symmetry in phonological systems, we cannot predict sound changes: for example, in Middle High German, which had a long-vowel system similar to that of Middle English, the high vowels were also changed to diphthongs, as in MHG *ís* "ice": NHG *Eis,* MHG *hūs* "house": NHG *Haus*. But unlike English, the lower long vowels were not raised. The vowel of NHG *See* "sea" is still pronounced like its Middle High German counterpart, as are the vowels of *Mond* "moon" and *Staat* "state." Thus the Middle High German and Middle English vowel systems are similar in some developments, different in others. If, on the basis of these changes, we should be tempted to speculate that in long-vowel systems like those of the Germanic languages, the high vowels tend to become diphthongised, we would be dismayed by Icelandic, in which the high vowels have remained unchanged but the low vowel has become diphthonised; the *ā* has become [au]. Similarly in Scots English, the *ā*, as in ME *hām*, was modified to *ē,* but the high vowels have not undergone the Great Vowel Shift.

Although we cannot flatly state that changes are caused by the system of a given language, we observe that when changes occur, they are directed by the system. The Germanic reflexes of the Proto-Indo-European stops provide an excellent example of changes that seem to lead to others; after *p t k* k^w became *f* θ χ χ^w, *bh dh gh* g^wh became *ƀ ð ǥ* $ǥ^w$, and finally *b d g* g^w became *p t k* k^w. Accordingly, the elements of the system underwent changes, but in the course of these changes the system was largely maintained. Similarly, in Classical Greek the obstruent system was preserved, except for the labiovelars, though PIE *bh dh gh* became the voiceless aspirated stops *ph th kh.* In Latin, however, the symmetry of the Proto-Indo-European system was disrupted when *bh* and *dh* coalesced with *d,* and *gh* became *g* or *h.* Further, in Celtic, Baltic, Slavic and Iranian, the system was reduced by the merger of *bh dh gh* with *b d g*. As these examples may illustrate, the developments in each of these languages were directed in part by the system, although from the earlier system we could not have predicted the changes in question.

After such changes take place, subsequent changes are also directed in part by the later system. Thus we find parallel series of stops and fricatives developing in English, as we have noted earlier. In Sanskrit, on the other hand, we find parallel series of voiceless and voiced stops, unaspirated and aspirated: *p t ṭ c k* ph th *ṭh ch kh b d ḍ j g bh dh ḍh jh gh.* Just as the development of voiced fricatives seems natural in English, so that of voiceless aspirates seems natural in Sanskrit. Such developments in a specific direction were labelled by Sapir **drift.** Bopp ascribed them to an **inner principle** in a language.

Since the language of one family may undergo a variety of changes, it is not meaningful to speak of a development towards simplicity. It is much more appropriate to observe the general articulatory patterns of the speakers of any given language, for these seem to have an effect on its changes.

This conclusion may be supported by phenomena of assimilation and other combinatory changes. For they seem to be determined by the articulatory habits of the speakers of a language and by the possibilities allowed by the structure of that language. In the history of English, we may observe many instances of assimilation of dentals and alveolars, some of which are sporadic; others are allophonic changes leading to modifications of the system. The following assimilatory changes occur sporadically in Modern English:

won't you	did you	miss you	raise you
[wównčə]	[díǰə]	[míšə]	[réžə]

These forms may be used in rapid speech, are considered informal by some speakers, substandard by others, and have by no means replaced the more careful [wównt yùw] and so on.

Similar changes took place in early Modern English, and many of the changed forms have remained in the language. From the eighteenth century [ty] is attested with the pronunciation [š], as in *nation;* similarly [sy], as in *issue,* and especially before [yŭ], as in *sugar, sure, assure.* (This change also took place in such words as *assume, consume, suet,* but subsequently [s] was reintroduced in these words as a **spelling pronunciation.**) Similarly [zy] became [ž], as in *measure, pleasure, treasure;* [dy] became [ǰ], as in *soldier, grandeur, Indian, educate, hideous;* here, too, all words but *soldier* and *grandeur* were remodelled by spelling pronunciation. *Injun* has survived only as a pejorative term, though the British pronunciation of the country also maintains the [ǰ]. Similarly, many educators consider the regular pronunciation of the word /éǰəkèyt/ undignified and insist on the spelling pronunciation.

In early Old English, allophones of "k" and "g" were palatalised even more generally in the neighbourhood of front vowels, so that modifications arose as follows:

cīdan "chide"	*cū* "cow"	*geard* "yard"	*gold* "gold"
[k'i:dan]	[ku:]	[g'ɛard]	[gold]
pic "pitch"	*bōc* "book"	*dæg* "day"	*longra* "longer"
[pik']	[bo:k]	[dæg']	[longra]

Gradually the palatalised allophones, as in *chide, pitch, yard, day,* came to be further differentiated from the velar allophones, as in *cow, book, gold, longer.* Eventually the palatalised allophone of /k/ fell together with [tj], as in *feccan* [fetjan] "fetch," and the new phoneme /č/ arose; the palatalised allophone of /g/ fell together with the earlier phoneme /j/ as in OE *gear* "year" and split from the /g/ phoneme.

Palatalisation has occurred repeatedly in the Slavic languages. Some phonemes of Slavic can be ascribed to the palatalisation that took place in the Indo-European speech community and gave rise to the isogloss separating the satem languages from the remainder of the Indo-European family. The following are examples:

OCS *pīsati* "write"	cf.	Gk. *poikílos* "variegated"
OCS *zrŭno* "grain"		Goth. *kaurn* "grain"
OCS *zemlja* "earth"		Gk. *khamaí* "on the earth"

At a later time velars were again palatalised in Slavic, for example:

OCS *četyre* "four"	cf.	Lat. *quattuor* "four"
OCS *žena* "woman"		Gk. *guné* "woman"
OCS *četi* "strike"		Hitt. *kuenzi* "strikes"

Later, still in Russian virtually all consonants were palatalised before front vowels, so that today consonants are found in two series: palatalised and nonpalatalised. The two branches of Indo-European, Germanic and Slavic, accordingly provide examples of the assimilatory change known as palatalisation, as do other Indo-European languages.

In the Germanic languages, assimilation also took place in the articulation of vowels. PIE /e/ before [y] became raised in Germanic, so that PIE /ey/ > PGmc /i:/, as in OE *stīgan* "climb," compare Gk *steíkhō* "come"; Modern English cognates are *sty* and *stile.* PGmc /e/ was also assimilated to an *ī* in the following syllable, as in Goth. *midjis,* OE *midd* "mid" = Lat. *medius.*

The most far-reaching of these assimilations in the Germanic languages took place in the early period of the individual dialects, and is generally known by the term **umlaut**, or **mutation**. As we have noted in the first section of this chapter, Pre-Old English short and long *a o u* standing before *y* or short or long *i* of the following syllable became fronted; *a* > *e; o* > *ø*, later *e*; *u* > *y*, later *i*.

Goth. *satjan* = OE *settan* "set"
PGmc *dōmjan* "judge" > *døman* > *dēman* > NE *deem*
PGmc *mūsiz* > OE *mȳs* > ME *mīs* > ME *mice*

Back assimilation occurred in Old Norse. Pre-ON *a* before *u* became *o* [ɔ], for example ON *lǫnd* "lands" from **landu*. Before *w* Pre-ON *a* > *ɔ, e* > *ø,* and *i* > *y,* as in ON *søkkua* "sink" < **sekkwa*, ON *lyng* "heather" < **lingwa*. Since the vowels are also rounded, the assimilation in these old Norse forms involves **labialisation**.

The assimilation in the Germanic languages may be related to a prominent accent on words, which made them into a unit so that one pattern of articulation affected the phonemes of an entire word. Besides assimilation, we also find losses of unstressed vowels, as illustrated below.

By contrast, in Japanese each syllable is pronounced independently. There is no stress accent; all syllables end in a vowel or *ñ*. For as long as Japanese is attested, we find maintenance of vowels; words like *Kojiki,* the name of a literary work completed in AD 712, are pronounced much the same way as they were over a millennium ago. (Syllable-initial consonants were assimilated to following vowels.) But in Proto-Germanic, which had a syllable structure not unlike that of Japanese before effects of the initial stress accent were brought about, words came to be greatly modified. We may illustrate some of the modifications by means of the Gallehus inscription, dated about AD 325, and subsequent developments of the words it contains:

Ek HlewagastiR HoltijaR   horna tawido

Its syllabic structure, consisting primarily of open syllables, was inherited from Proto-Indo-European, which like Japanese had a pitch accent. But as we know from the effects of Verner's law, Proto-Germanic introduced a strong stress accent on the first syllable of words. This strong stress led to the loss of vowels in weakly stressed syllables. By Old English times the inscription would have read:

*Ic Hleogiest Hylte horn tēode

Subsequently, other weakly stressed vowels were lost, leading to the monosyllabic structure of native English words. *I, guest, Holt,* and *horn* may be related directly to the Proto-Germanic words exemplified in the inscription. Moreover, with *hlewa-* "famous" we may compare the adjective *loud;* and *tawido,* the noun *tool.* At these examples illustrate, English has been modified in a specific direction at least in part because of its type of accentuation.

Effects of Phonological Changes at other Levels of a Language

The phonological changes in English that we have pointed out led to loss of morphological markers, and also affected the syntactic patterns of English. The final syllables of Proto-Germanic indicated syntactic relationships; *horna,* for example, could have been interpreted only as an accusative or nominative singular. Since *HlewagastiR* could only be a nominative, the subject of the inscription was identifiable from the morphological markers, as was the object. After the morphological markers were lost, word order came to distinguish syntactic categories, such as subject and predicate. The phonological changes accordingly led to morphological and syntactic changes.

Moreover, numerous function words have been introduced into English, such as articles and prepositions, leading to a considerably different language from Proto-Germanic. For example, on the loss of the dative ending English indicates the indirect object either with a preposition, or by order, as in *She gave the book to the girl, She gave the girl the book.* The differences can be related to phonological changes, many of which in turn we ascribe to one phonological innovation: the introduction of a strong initial stress accent.

While we account for many changes in the Germanic languages by the strong initial stress accent, we do not have adequate information about Germanic in the period before our era to determine the reason for its introduction. That is to say, we cannot account for the sound change by which a stress accent was introduced. Some linguists have proposed that Proto-Germanic adopted the initial stress accent from speakers of adjacent languages whom we cannot identify. In support of this explanation, we can point to a strong stress accent in Celtic as well, which also led to loss of unaccented vowels. Other linguists assume that the accent was developed within the language, without outside influences. We cannot provide an answer to these conflicting views. Possibly a combination of reasons led to the introduction of the change.

In determining the causes of sound change, we will do best to deal with less remote changes than those of Proto-Germanic, such as the change of NE -t- to *-d-*. By documenting fully other such changes, as Gauchat and Hermann did in Switzerland, and as Sommerfelt set out to do in Ireland and Wales, we may come to understand how sound change is introduced as well as how changes are extended. Linguists who have concerned themselves with sound change—for example, Sommerfelt, Weinreich, Labov and Herzog—have pointed out the importance of relating linguistic and social phenomena. With our present knowledge of sound change, based largely on that in Indo-European dialects, we can make assured statements about its processes and patterns; about its direction or causes we can only propose hypotheses. Further study is essential to provide information in these spheres comparable to that gathered over the past century and a half on the processes and patterns of sound change.

2

Morphological Change

Bases for Morphological Change

Because the elements of the morphological system have meaning as well as form, the system is more tightly structured than is the phonological, in which the elements only have form, not meaning. As a result, the elements within the morphological system, especially those in inflectional paradigms, tend to influence one another. That influence, referred to as **analogy**, is one of the two principal bases for morphological change.

To exemplify the close interrelationships in paradigms, we may examine the first three persons singular of the indicative present of verbs in Indo-European languages. These forms of the Proto-Indo-European root **bher-* are as follows in Sanskrit:

bhárāmi "I bear"
bhárasi "thou bearest"
bhárati "he/she/it bears"

Each form consists of three elements: the Sanskrit root *bhar-*; the thematic vowel; the endings *-mi -si -ti*. The forms are highly symmetrical, except for the long middle vowel in the first person. In other respects they exhibit a close fit between meaning and form. The root *bhar-* with the following vowel conveys the lexical meaning "bear"; the three elements *-m-*, *-s-*, *-t-* convey grammatical meaning of person, and the *-i* serves to indicate present tense.

When we compare the forms of the same root in Greek, we find:

phéro "I bear"
phéreis "thou bearest"
phérei "he/she/it bears"

The endings differ remarkably from those of Sanskrit. For the first person we may also note Lat. *ferō*. On the basis of its equivalence to the Greek form, we reconstruct Proto-Indo-European **bherō*. Skt *bhárāmi* then requires explanation. We account for the *-mi* as an addition by spread from the athematic conjugation, which had this ending; it still survives as a residue in Eng. *am*. The change from the Sanskrit ending in *bhárā* (which is found still in some subjunctive forms) to that in *bhárāmi* is readily accounted for by efforts of the speakers to achieve parallelism between the three singular forms, that is, by analogy.

In the second person, phonological change disrupted the parallelism in Greek. While explanations of the ending differ in detail among specialists, a disruption was caused by the loss of intervocalic *-s-* in Greek, yielding **phérei* from PIE **bhéresi*. This form was then influenced by the second singular secondary ending *-s*, as in the imperfect *épheres*. Accordingly, we account for the Greek second singular through the other major basis of morphological change, that is sound change, followed by analogy. As the neogrammarians indicated, sound change operates regularly; all intervocalic *-s-* were lost in Greek. But the resulting form seemed out of keeping with the paradigm. As a result, final *-s* was added by analogy.

The third-person form in Greek is even more problematic. It cannot be derived from PIE **bhéreti*, for that would have given Dor. Gk **phereti*, Att. **bheresi*. The form is explained as based on the second-singular *phéreis* by analogy with the imperfect endings, second-singular *épheres*, third-singular *éphere,* in which *-s* distinguished the second-singular form from the third.

The Greek paradigm, then, shows evidence of both analogical and phonological change.

When we examine the Gothic forms, we find evidence of only phonological change:

baira "I bear"
bairis "thou bearest"
bairip "he/she/it bears"

The Gothic root is pronounced [ber]. Final long *ō* in the first person regularly became *a*; final short vowels were dropped in Germanic, as here in the second- and third-singular; and in Goth. *-e-* shows up as *-i-* except before *r* and *h* (h^w). Of the three sets of forms, only that in Gothic was unmodified analogically. But it is the set that is most affected by sound change. As we noted in chapter 1, vowels of unstressed syllables were weakened or lost in Germanic because of the strong initial stress.

The three sets of forms exemplify the two principal bases for morphological change in their interaction. Means for determining their effects in a given language can best be acquired by examining the bases of morphological change in a number of paradigms that have been accounted for through extensive study. We will review such paradigms in the following sections.

Morphological Changes in Inflectionally Distinct Selection Classes; The Old English Strong Verbs

The history of the strong or irregular verbs in English furnishes us with excellent examples of change in selection classes. The Old English strong verbs are generally divided into seven classes in accordance with internal vocalic variation resulting from Proto-Indo-European ablaut. To summarise the possible forms, principal parts are given: (1) the infinitive, (2) the first and third singular preterite indicative, (3) the preterite indicative plural, (4) the preterite participle. The classes are illustrated with one example for each:

		1	*2*	*3*	*4*
1.	drīfan	"drive"	drāf	drifon	drifen
2.	cēosan	"choose"	cēas	curon	coren
3.	findan	"find"	fand	fundon	funden
4.	beran	"bear"	bær	bǣron	boren
5.	sprecan	"speak"	spræc	sprǣcon	sprecen
6.	standan	"stand"	stōd	stōdon	standen
7.	feallan	"fall"	fēoll	fēollon	feallen

In addition to these strong verbs, there was in Old English a large number of weak or regular verbs, which continued to expand; for almost every new verb was inflected weak. Weak verbs had fewer differing forms than did the strong verbs, as exemplified by three principal parts. Moreover, the only difference between the preterite singular and preterite plural consisted in the endings, as for:

lufian "love" lufode lufodon lufod

In this situation, with the largest number of verbs having relatively few forms while a small number of verbs had many more, there was reduction of the strong-verb set, especially in the preterite.

The source of the preterite vowel in Modern English strong verbs, whether from the singular or plural, varied from verb to verb. In "drive" the vowel of the preterite singular was generalised throughout the preterite, to NE *drive, drove, driven*. In "bite," however, also of class 1, the vowel of the plural was generalised, to NE *bite, bit, bitten;* similarly in "find."

Observing the development of all strong verbs in English, and the basis of selecting either singular or plural vowels in the preterite—or taking over the vowel of the past participle, as in *bear, bore, borne* —would require considerable exposition. Here we are primarily concerned to demonstrate the analogical reduction of forms, on the pattern of weak verbs such as *love, loved, loved*. The general principle of remodelling the strong-verb system is an attempt to distinguish between the stem for the present and that for the preterite, in accordance with the distinction between present and preterite in weak verbs, such as *love*, on the one hand, and *loved, loved,* on the other.

In the process some of the verbs were greatly modified. In *choose,* the vowel of the preterite participle was generalised to the preterite, with [č] and [z], the consonants of the present and preterite singular, generalised throughout, so that the *-r-* was replaced. In *speak* the pattern of class 4 was adopted. In *stand,* the vowel of the preterite was generalised to the preterite participle. In *fall* we find regular developments of the Old English forms, no new remodelled forms.

The history of the principal parts of the English strong verbs then illustrates thoroughgoing remodelling or regularisation. When, as in *drāf, drifon, or cēas, curon,* the differences in a set are regularised, we speak of **levelling**.

Remodelling in the Inflected Forms of Strong Verbs

The inflectional endings of the Old English strong verbs also underwent various modifications as a result of sound change and analogy. We may examine these in two of the major dialects, West Saxon and Northumbrian. The present indicative endings in West Saxon with their older forms are as follows:

Present indicative

1.	sg. *-e*	<	Pre-OE *-a* < *-ū*
2.	sg. -(*e*)*st*	<	Pre-OE *-isi* (with addition of *-t*)
3.	sg. -(*e)ð*	<	Pre-OE *-iÞi*
	pl. *-að*	<	Pre-OE *-anÞi*

Since *-i* following *-e-* of the stem syllable occasioned change of *-e-* to *-i-*, the forms of *beran* in West Saxon were as follows; the Northumbrian forms are also given, to illustrate a paradigm with fewer changes.

		Northumbrian
1.	sg. *bere*	*bero*
2.	sg. *bir*(*e*)*st*	*beres*
3.	sg. *bir*(*e*)*ð*	*bereð, -es*
	pl. *berað*	*beorað*

The Pre-Old English sound change of *e* to *i* before *i* had taken place regularly. After the change the stem *bere, birest,* etc. contained two vowels, in contrast with other verbs that had no such alternation, such as *findan* and *drīfan.* As we know from the forms today, the *e* was extended throughout the present of *bear,* and the difference in vowels was levelled out.

In other ways as well, the verbs in English have become regularised, so that today they have a maximum of five forms. Similar examples of regularisation could be provided from other languages with sets of paradigms.

In the course of levelling, extension may be made from inflected or derived, rather than from base forms. These are known as **back formations**. In Old English the verbs *flēon* "flee" and *flēogan* "fly" were inflected alike in all forms but the infinitive. As in *birest, bireð,* the vowels in the second- and third-singular forms underwent modification, and the present indicative was as follows:

1. sg. *flēo*
2. sg. *fliēhst*
3. sg. *fliēhð*
   pl. *flēoÞ*

The first person singular and the plural, with vowels the same as that of *flēon*, developed into NE *flee.* This should have the following alternation: *I flee, thou fliest, he flies.* Instead, a new infinitive, *fly*, was produced. In *flee,* the base allomorph was extended throughout the present; in *fly*, an inflected allomorph was generalised throughout the present, as a back formation.

We may cite further instances of back formations from nouns. When in Middle English, *-s* came to be the general plural marker, the singular : plural contrast was based on presence and absence of *s*, on the pattern:

ME sg. *fader* "father" *fō* "foe"
pl. *faders* *fōs*

Some nouns that ended in *s* were interpreted as plurals, and a new singular was produced, for example *pes* "pease" from the Lat. sg. *pisum*; the new singular is now commonly used, though the old has survived in the nursery rhyme "Pease porridge hot." Similarly *buriels* < *byrgels* "tomb" was assumed to be plural, and a new singular was produced, which, on the pattern of *funeral,* was spelled with *a, burial.* Other such singulars were made as back formations, such as *riddle* from ME *redels* < *rædels,* compare Germ. *Rätsel,* and *cherry* from ME *cheris* < OFr. *cherise,* later again borrowed as *cerise.* In these nouns the new singular forms rather than inflected forms resulted from analogy.

We may illustrate a further complexity of morphological change with WSax. *eom* "am." Like Goth. *im* "am," this form should have had an *i* in the stem, for it developed from PIE *?és-mi,* cf. Skt *ás-mi.* In Germanic, however, the copula came to be a composite verb, with forms from the root in *be* and that in *was,* as well as that in *is*. From the northern Old English forms such as *bīom, bēom,* we may assume that *eom* is a combination, with the consonant from the root **es-* and the vowel from the root of *be*; such combinations are called **blends** or **contaminations**. Morphological change can in this way lead to forms that have a complex origin, and also to new morphological markers.

Morphological Change as a Source of New Inflectional Markers; Grammaticalisation

The development of blends, as well as back formations, demonstrates that new, unpredictable forms may be produced in a language by the changes that take place in morphological sets. In this way new suffixes and grammatical markers may result. Examples of new suffixes are English *-dom* and *-hood.* In Old English the words from which these arose were used to form compounds, for example *frēo* "free" + *dōm* "quality" > *frēodom* "freedom," *cynedom* "royalty"; similarly, *camp* "battle" + *hād* "state" > *camphad* "warfare," *werhad* "manhood," and so on. The second elements of the compounds then came to be treated as suffixes and distinguished from the free forms, *doom* and *hood.* In German, the cognates of these two elements also came to be suffixes, *-tum* and *-heit;* their distribution is often different from that of the English suffixes, as in *Freiheit* "freedom," but *Königtum* "kingdom."

Established as independent entities, suffixes come to have a development of their own. From forms like OE *æþeling* "nobleman," made from *æþele* "noble" and the suffix *–ing,* an erroneous division was made to produce a new suffix *-ling.* The process has been called **suffix clipping.** The new suffix was used to form further words, such as *darling,* cf. *dēor* "dear." Similarly, *-able* was taken as suffix in such forms as *habitable,* from Lat. *habitabilis,* and was then used in many new forms, such as *bearable, supportable.*

One such element that has enjoyed a wise development is *-burger.* In German, *-er* is commonly used to make adjectives from city names, such as *Berliner* "of Berlin," *Frankfurter* "of Frankfurt," *Wiener* "of Vienna"; these simply meant "of the city," and may have been used as family names, for example *Frankfurter.* Some of them were also used to characterise prepared meats, such as *frankfurter, wiener, hamburger,* a characteristic meat dish of Hamburg. By chance, the first syllable of *hamburger* coincided with the name of the meat "ham"; it was quite irrelevant that ham was never used in hamburgers. One can now buy *fishburgers, chesseburgers* or even burgers labelled for their producer, such as *Mooreburgers.* Other suffixes produced similarly in recent English are *-teria,* from *cafeteria,* cf. *washeteria,* and *-ware,* from (*computer*) *hardware,* to *software,* and so on.

In the same way of improper clipping, inflectional markers have been produced in the process known as **grammaticalisation**. One of the characteristic noun plural markers in German is *-er*, as in *Kind* "child," *Kinder* "children." Historically, it is a derivational suffix, used to form nouns, as in Skt *ján-as,* Lat. *gen-us* "kind, race," from the root PIE **gen-* "beget," In Pre-Old High German, finals of words were lost in such a way that *-er* survived in the plural, in contrast with its loss in the singular, as in *kalb* "calf,": *kelbir.* It was then taken as a plural marker, and widely extended to many neuter nouns in which the suffix had never been added, such as *Haus* "house": *Häuser,* and even to masculines, such as *Mann* "man": *Männer.* We find a similar extension in Middle Dutch, virtually none in English, only *child : children.*

Only by chance do we have material to determine the source of the *-er* suffix. For *kalb* is the only *er*-plural in Old High German that can be connected with the Indo-European nouns in *-es-*. Moreover, the great extension of the *er*-plurals occurred in Old High German and Middle High German times, from which we have a fair number of texts. If inflectional markers were produced in this way at an earlier stage of the language, we can merely hypothesise their origin and extension.

Markers of the preterite and perfect in the early Indo-European dialects may have had their origin in this way, although various hypotheses have been proposed for their source. In Germanic we find a *-d-* marker for the preterite, as in Goth. *lagida,* OE *legde* "laid," and with voiceless dental in Goth. *brāhta,* OE *brohte* "brought." A suffix *-d-* < PIE **-dh-* may have been clipped from stems, and may have come to be used to indicate the preterite tense. Similarly, the *-v-* of the Latin perfect, for example *amāvi* from *amō* "love," the *-k-* of the Greek perfect, for example *pepaideuka* of *paideúō* "educate," and other preterite markers that we find in other dialects may have their origin in this way. In view of the absence of textual evidence at the time of their origin, our support of such a hypothesis on their development lies in general linguistic theory and the structure of the dialects after the splitting of Proto-Indo-European.

Possibly of greater amusement than significance in the development of languages are new formations that represent fanciful modification, such as Eng. *sirloin.* This is from Fr. *sur-loin,* in which the first element derives from Lat. *super* "upper," so that historically the word refers to the upper part of the loin. In English, however, *sur-*, which was not found in other widespread compounds, seemed aberrant and was modified to the apparently sensible *sirloin,* for the upper part of the loin is a noble piece of meat. Somewhat scornfully, this process has been referred to as **folk etymology**. As a further development, such etymologies may be followed by spurious histories. For example, I have been informed that there is a house in Lancashire which has been identified as the place where a ravenous King James I knighted the humble loin of beef. It does not, however, differ essentially from the process by which a contemporary English suffix *-burger* was formed, or an Old English suffix *-ling,* or an Old High German suffix *-er.* Like these, it illustrates how speakers manipulate language for their own purposes.

In folk etymology the sportive manipulation of language by individuals may be more evident than it is in less fanciful remodelling, as well as the approbation or disapprobation of fellow speakers; but what is essentially involved is the remodelling of less frequent and less favoured patterns in the language in accordance with those more highly favoured. When the cognate of Lat. *homo* came to be found in English only in the Old English compound *bryd-guma* "espoused man," cf. Germ. *Bräutigam,* it was modified after the more widespread though illogical *groom* to *bridegroom.* When *pentis,* from Fr. *appentis* < Latin *appendix,* was applied to an outgrowth of a large building, it was remodelled to *penthouse.*

Just as folk etymology shows the inventiveness of some language users in making analogical creations, it may illustrate the conservatism of others. The term *Welsh rabbit* for a cheese dish, like *Cape Cod turkey* for the plainest of piscatorial fare, shows an attempt by the ingenious to make simple food more palatable for the credulous. Their stolid fellow speakers may, however, object to this transparent outrage, and insist on *Walsh rarebit,* in much the same way that we today require inventive children to say *men* not *mans, better* not *gooder, went* not *goes,* and to banish *funner* entirely from their speech.

Reasons for Analogical Change; Internal Influences

In accounting for phonological change, we noted that it takes place in accordance with general modifications for which we have been able to provide no specific reasons. The reasons for changes in morphological markers, however, can often be ascribed to regularisation of the forms in a morphological, syntactic or lexical set, as we may illustrate by means of NE *father.*

When we trace the history of NE *brother,* by successive steps we can take it back to PIE **bhrā́ter.* Between the time of Proto-Indo-European and Modern English, the phonemes of **bhrā́tēr* have undergone various sound changes; by noting these, we can derive all the phonemes of NE *brother* from those of its Proto-Indo-European etymon. NE *father,* however, cannot be directly related to PIE and Pre-Gmc **patḗr* in this way. For the Proto-Indo-European medial *t* became PGmc *þ,* which became *ð,* since the primary accent followed it; this in turn became OE *d,* so that the Old English form was *fæder;* the Middle English, *fader.* Without any further modification, the New English form should also have *-d-*. Yet such a modification did occur. Some time after 1400, [ð] was substituted for *-d-*, giving rise to NF *father.* We assume that the substitution was made partly because the word *father* was associated with the words *brother* and *mother,* and was remodelled after them. The substitution may have also been assisted by the medial, intervocalic position.

Similarly, we would be unable to derive the preterite participle *swelled* from a Proto-Germanic etymon, or even from an Old English form. The earlier preterite participle was *swollen,* which survives primarily as an adjective; *swelled* was made from *swell* on the pattern of such forms as:

fell	=	shell	=	swell
felled	=	shelled	=	x

Swelled, then, replaced the older *swollen.*

Modifications of this type illustrate the chief mode of change introduced in morphological and syntactic systems. By it the members of a morphological, syntactic or lexical set are increased or reduced in number, and the means involved in marking syntactic categories are extended. Since such changes are carried out on the pattern of those already present in the language, they are referred to as **analogical.**

Analogy is a process by which morphs, combinations of morphs, or linguistic patterns are modified, or new ones created, on the pattern of those present in a language.

We can observe analogy most clearly in the learning of language. Most of us have observed children learning forms such as the plural *cups* to *cup* and applying their discovery to other nouns, such as:

cat	=	fork	=	cap
cats	=	forks	=	caps

If then they see a *jet*, and learn the word, they make a plural, *jets*; if they see a specific toy in a toy store, they make a plural, *sputniks*.

We become especially conscious of such extensions if they produce forms that we consider incorrect. Just as children learn to make plurals, they make comparatives, as for:

new	=	old	=	good
newer	=	older	=	gooder

At this point we object, and supply the correct form *better*. If we find a further extension from,

That's new	=	That's find	=	That's fun
That's newer	=	That's finer	=	That's funner

we may even remark on the child's cleverness after providing the correct form. At some time in the past, however, speakers of English were more tolerant of new comparatives, for the form *older* has replaced *elder* (except in restricted usages); *littler, littlest* have generally replaced *lesser* and *least* when adjectives, except in some contexts such as the bird name *least flycatcher*. In this way irregularities may be removed from grammatical sets. But by far the most important use we make of analogy in language learning is in extending forms and patterns that we have mastered.

If we learn a language like German, we do not memorise separately every inflected form. We learn a model such as,

singen	"sing"
ich singe	"I sing"
er singt	"he sings"

and we expect to apply it to *ringen* "wrestle," *bringen* "bring," and so on. We may assume that native speakers learned many forms of their language in much the same way. If on the pattern of the past *ich sang, ich rang,* we make a form *ich brang,* we are corrected. We may even be reminded of the cognate of *ich brachte* "I brought" to reinforce our acquistition of the irregular form. In this way we learn one of the limits of such analogical extension.

We acquire other linguistic patterns similarly. If we master the German syntactic patterns:

Wir gehen heute. "We're going today."
Heute gehen wir. "Today we're going."

we do not need to learn separately every sentence beginning with *heute* or other adverbs to gain control over this type of subject position. If we have under control the normal word order, *Wir reisen heute, Wir lessen morgen,* we have no difficulty saying on the basis of our mastery of the patterns:

Heute reisen wir. "Today we're travelling."
Morgen lesen wir. "Tomorrow we'll read."

In this way analogy is constantly applied when we use a language. As in foreign-language learning, there are limits to its application, some of which we may transgress to the consternation of fellow speakers, others to their mild amusement and still others to their admiring imitation. It is difficult to predict when analogical forms will be accepted, when not. We do, however, know some of the conditions under which analogy operates.

Prerequisites for the Operation of Analogy

For the operation of analogy, some linguistic set is necessary. The set may be inflectional, like the English verbs, in which the *t/d/əd* suffix has been replacing internal change, as it has done in *swelled.* The set may be derivational, such as the English nouns with *-er* suffix, such as *driver;* this suffix, imported from Lat. *-arius,* has come to be used after virtually any verb. The set may also be syntactic. A number of English verbs that formerly took an object in the genitive case were until quite recently followed by *of*-constructions, for example *miss, desire, remember, forget, hope, thirst, wait.* Sir Walter Scott wrote: *I remember of detesting the man.* By contrast, the common transitive pattern in English consists of a verb followed immediately by an object; this pattern accordingly was generalised and extended to the verbs cited.

Sets may also be semantic, such as the relationship terms, *brother, mother, father.* Among such sets are the numerals. In German ordinals, for example, *-te* is used from "two" to "nineteen," for example *der zweite, der neunzehnte*; after that *-ste* is used, for example *der zwanzigste,* until the millionth, where formerly *-te* was used; today *der milligste* is being used widely and promises to replace *millionte.* Numerous examples can be cited from the numerals in the various Indo-European dialects, as we have for English. The spread of Slav. *d-* to "nine," cf. Russ. *d'evyat',* from "ten," cf. Russ. *d'esyat',* is among the clearest.

Such sets are very infrequent at the phonological level. An example of analogy at the phonological level is the extension of *-r* before vowels in New England English. Since retroflection was lost before consonants but not before vowels, two forms of such words as *water* exist side by side: *watə was* . . ., but *water is* . . .; *watə wheels* . . ., but *water always* . . . . Nouns with final ə fell into this pattern, such as *soda, idea,* so that speakers with this variation say: *the idea was* . . ., but the *idea-r is.*

A type of analogy limited to literate cultures is purely graphic. ME *rīm,* for example, came to be written *rhyme* because early Modern English writers thought it was connected with *rhythm.* Me *delite* < OFr. *deliter,* Lat. *dēlectāre* came to be written in Modern English as *delight* because it was considered to be related to *light,* cf. Germ. *Licht.* We are most familiar with this type of analogy from language learners—from errors of students and typesetters, or from our own struggles with English spelling. We may align *proceed* with *precede,* or vice versa; a part of our schooling is spent differentiating among *to, too, two, their, there* and like sets. With our contemporary regard for spelling, a great deal of social prestige is involved in producing the standard spelling; we accordingly resist analogical modifications in our spelling system and maintain the established patterns. Attitudes towards analogical modifications are accordingly of great importance for their acceptance.

Conditions for the Occurrence and Acceptance of Analogical Change

Essential problems of analogy that require further study include the conditions (1) under which it takes place, and (2) by which new patterns get established. We cannot yet provide satisfactory answers. Some linguists have proposed that analogical change leads to simplification, and that such a development is to be expected when children acquire their language. Otto Jespersen reviewed the evidence for this assumption in his book, *Language* (1922), and concluded that the question is complex. His own observations led him to ascribe some linguistic changes to "first learners," whether children or adults. But he did not ascribe a development towards simplicity to children's language, even though he believed that there has been a "tendency . . . [towards] progress, slow and fitful progress, but still progress towards greater and greater clearness regularity, ease and pliancy" in language (*ibid.*). We have mentioned above that children who learn Arabic master the highly complex broken plurals of nouns, and that children who learn Turkish have no difficulty with its intricate rules of vowel harmony.

These and many other examples contradict the view that simplification in language is to be ascribed to children, even though recent scholars have returned to this assumption. By contrast, as Jespersen reported at length, children generally abandon the simplifications they introduced, such as *goed* rather than *went, mans* rather than *men* and so on. Rather than unsubstantiated claims about the role of children in language change, further investigations need to be made. Weinreich, Labov and Herzog have attributed the transmission of new patterns to the "community as a whole," rather than to "the generational gap between parent and child" (1968). The procedures for change they cite are even more intricate than are those considered by Jespersen.

To ascribe simplification to analogical change and to the influence of children as they acquire language is far too simplistic. This is not to deny the findings of Gauchat and others that the younger speakers in a community extend observed changes further than the older. The findings are to be expected, for changes that are not adopted by younger speakers are lost. But claims about the causes of change are far different from observations of their spread.

Kurylowicz (1960) attempted to suggest reasons for the introduction of analogy in morphological sets. He found these reasons in the relationship of forms in a paradigm. Those forms that are basic tend to influence others. For example, in verbal systems with a present tense category and a passive voice, the present active by his view dominates both the present passive and the perfect active; the perfect passive in turn is dominated by both the present passive and the perfect active. Kurylowicz calls the present the **founding** form; a derived form like the present passive he calls **founded.** A founded form might then be modified in accordance with the founding form, on the pattern of the following chart:

Present active → Perfect active
↓ ↓
Present passive → Perfect passive

If then the perfect active has a segment differing from that of the perfect passive, this segment may be introduced into the perfect passive.

Kurylowicz proposed this relationship in inflectional systems as the cause for a phenomenon in early Latin. There, as Karl Lachmann observed more than a century ago, the past participles of stems ending in *-d-* and *-g-* have lengthened vowels, with devoicing of the stop before the participial suffix *-tus*. Thus the past participle of *ăgo* is *āctus,* in contrast with the short vowel in *făctus* from *făciō*; similarly *lēctus* form *legō* "read," *ēsus* from **ēssus* from **ed-t-os,* based on *edō* "eat," and so on. The phenomenon is referred to as Lachmann's law; it had been widely, and ineffectually, discussed before Kurylowicz provided a definitive explanation, explicated further by Calvert Watkins.

The explanation may be illustrated as follows:

Present active *legit* → Perfect active *legit*
↓ ↓
Present passive *legitur* → Perfect passive **lĕctus* > *lēctus*

By this explanation, original *ĕ* in the perfect passive participle was changed to *ē* by analogy. The change differs from the sound changes discussed in Chapter 1 because of its motivation. Kurylowicz has definitely established that some phonological modifications can be brought about by analogy. The reasons for such modifications are the internal patterning in a language.

Kurylowicz finds many more examples of the effects of analogy in the spread of changes in morphological forms rather than in their introduction. For such extension of the results of earlier changes, he has proposed a series of rules. As the counterexamples cited with the rules illustrate, these rules do not permit us to predict when analogy may take place in a given language, nor to determine what its direction has been under poorly known situations in the past. The rules, however, provide explanations for some instances of analogical extension.

Kurylowicz's first rule states that a twofold morphological marker tends to replace one that is single. As example he gives the *-e* plural ending of German nouns, which in some nouns was also associated with umlaut of the stem vowel, for example *Gast* "guest": *Gäste.* This twofold marking has been extended as in *Baum* "tree": *Bäume,* replacing earlier *baume.* Many further instances can be cited in which it does not apply; for example, the German weak verb *trennen, trennte, getrennt* "separate" has maintained a single marker in contrast with *rennen, rannte, gerannt* "run" and similar verbs.

By Kurylowicz's second rule, analogy proceeds from the base form to derived forms. While commonly true, as in *sputnik, sputniks.* changes such as *pease* to *pea* contravene this rule.

By the third rule, any construction consisting of a constant plus a variable is used as a pattern for an isolated entity with the same function. In this way constructions like *wrongly* from *wrong* were used as a pattern for remodelling endingless adverbs such as *slow* to *slowly.*

In the fourth rule, which deals with the results of analogy, Kurylowicz states that a new analogical form takes over the primary function of a contrast, while the replaced form is used for secondary functions. Thus *brothers* is used for the plural of *brother,* while the replaced *brethren* maintains a peripheral function; similarly, *older* versus *elder,* and so on. Yet again, contrary examples can be provided, such as analogical forms in the German article, that is *dessen,* that are used today in the relative pronoun, not in the article itself.

The two other rules proposed by Kurylowicz are of less interest here. A set of such general rules would be highly advantageous if they applied to prehistoric languages, such as Proto-Indo-European or Proto-Afro-Asiatic. Kurylowicz has indeed applied them in this way, especially to problems of Indo-European variation of vowels in ablaut and to accentual problems. Yet if the rules cannot be established in contemporary languages, their application to earlier periods may be unreliable. The problems that we find with the carefully designed rules of Kurylowicz illustrate that modifications of morphological rules are not as consistent as those occurring in sound change.

Interplay of Changes in the Morphological and Phonological Components of Language, and in the Lexicon

As illustrated above, analogy may by viewed as the central process in modifications introduced in morphological systems. The second process, sound change, may also bring about modifications, as through loss of morphological markers. Moreover, it may introduce irregularities in morphological systems that then are restructured in morphological and lexical sets.

As examples of sound changes leading to change in morphological systems we may cite instances from the Germanic languages, such as the Pre-Old English umlaut changes. When Pre-OE *u* and *o* became *y and ø* before *i i*: *y*, a new contrastive marker was possible between many singular and plural forms, for *i i*: *y* were found especially in plural endings. Yet in English this sound change affected the morphological system only to a minor extent, for we have few plurals of the type *man: men, goose: geese, mouse: mice*. In German, on the other hand, this sound change was widely extended to provide one of the prominent plural markers. In this way sound changes may contribute to the possibility of new morphological contrastive devices, which then may be extended by analogy.

Such a contrastive device has recently been made available by the loss of *-t* in some English final clusters. When *-t* is lost in *slept,* a new contrast *sleep : slep* yields new irregular verbs. This phonological change is too recent for its results in the morphological system to be predicted.

As a result of such changes five or more millennia ago, the material was provided for one of the characteristic features of Indo-European languages ablaut. It is generally assumed that the ablaut contrast between root structures of the shapes *Ce*(R)C- (consonant : *e* : possible resonant: consonant) and C(R)C- resulted from a loss of vowel, which in turn was due to varying accentuation. This assumption is based on contrasts found in forms, such as those of PIE *derk-* "see." The Greek present first-singular form, with accent on the root, is *dérkomai* "I see." The Sanskrit past participle, however, with accent on the suffix, is *dṛṣṭás* "seen." The original situation has been obscured by many subsequent changes, so that in most forms it is opaque except to trained Indo-Europeanists. In the participle, the *r* became vocalic on loss of the *e*. The contrast with the Greek present form is, then, in accordance with the shapes given above.

The contrast has been maintained even more clearly in NE *nest* (originally a compound of the adverbial particle **ni-* and the root **sed-* "sit," in which the *e* was lost), as opposed to NE *sit,* a reflex of the Indo-European form with *e* vowel. The contrast has also been maintained between the present stem and the participle of many irregular verbs in English, such as *choose : chosen, bind : band, steal : stolen,* even though subsequent changes have obscured it.

The original Indo-European sound change, which led to a loss of *e,* may have affected few forms originally. But, like the umlaut change in German, it came to be used as an inflectional marker; and the contrast was widely extended, especially in the Germanic system of irregular or strong verbs. The contrast came to be so well established that it was introduced into words borrowed into the Germanic languages three millennia after the sound change took place, as in the Old English verb borrowed from Latin: *scrīfan* "write (shrive)": *scrifen* "written (shriven)."

Another major contrast in Indo-European ablaut, that between *e* and *o,* as reflected in Gk *dérkomai* "I see": *dédorka* "I have seen," has also been explained on the basis of a sound change. While the explanation of this sound change is disputed, the standard reason given is shift of pitch accent from the base, with backing of the *e* vowel to *o*. Russian has a similar change, though with the *o*-vowel under accent, as in the name *Gorbachev* [garbəčɔ́f]. The change to *o* also had a great affect in the morphology of the dialects. It is the basis of the contrast between the present and the past tense in English irregular verbs, for example *sing* : *sang, sit : sat,* and also for the contrast between simple and causative verbs, such as *sit : set, lie : lay*.

In this way many morphological modifications in languages are spread by analogy, though the innovations may be a result of phonological change, or also of some other process, such as borrowing, that has provided a useful characteristic marker for a set.

Analogy in the Lexicon

Similar analogical processes and results are found in the lexicon. In the scientific terminology of today, many entities have been widely spread, with a specific meaning. Thus, *-ide* is used for hundreds of names of chemical compounds, such as *chloride, fluoride;* it was apparently taken from the term *oxide*, which was borrowed from Fr. *oxyde.* The suffix *-ate* is found in many names of salts and esters formed from acids with names ending in *-ic,* for example, *nitrate* from *nitric acid* and so on. The suffix *-eme* has come to be used for entities in linguistics, from *phoneme* to *morpheme* to *grapheme* and others. Analogy in this way is useful in expanding and regularising the derivational system of the greatly expanding vocabularies of contemporary languages as it has served to enlarge and regularise their inflectional and syntactic systems.

The source of the material used in analogy is irrelevant. Any segment of the language may be generalised, whether its origin is in sound change or borrowing, or whether it is simply a segment of the language, like English *-ware* of *hardware,* that has been extended in computer terminology. When new forms are made by analogy in a language, sets of some kind undergo expansion; the process leads to larger sets, and accordingly to greater regularity in the language.

3

Syntactic Change

Long Delayed Recognition of Syntactic Structure

The analysis of sentences discloses only with difficulty the structure of syntax. Unlike morphology, syntax cannot be analysed into regular paradigms. Further, syntactic sequences are more open to pragmatic variation than are those of morphology and phonology. For the purpose of phonological variety, we may select unusual forms and also unusual patterns of sound, as in producing rhymes or alliteration; but typically we choose unmarked patterns in both phonology and morphology for general conversation. Syntax, however, we modify readily, placing objects at the beginning of sentences, like this one, for emphasis of the displaced segment. As a result of the multiple possibilities in syntax, linguists long failed to recognise the basic structures of syntax. Instead, they described phrases, clauses and sentences, identifying their components and the categories to which they belong, as well as their uses. Variant patterns were treated in stylistics.

By contrast with such syntactic treatments, in 1844 Henri Weil published a remarkable monograph on the syntax of Latin. Listing its syntactic patterns, he compared them to the patterns of Turkish. That is to say, he recognised that Latin was verb-final, an OV language. This finding has now been firmly supported by the studies of Charles

Elerick on the syntax of Cicero, Caesar and Livy. For example, the following sentence in the first book of Livy's history of Rome has OV order, and in addition a preposed relative construction *proelio victum*:

Alii proelio victum Latinum pacem cum Aenea, deinde
some battle conquered L. peace with A. then
affinitatem iunxisse tradunt
relationship made they-report

"Some report that Latinus, who was conquered in battle, thereupon made peace with Aeneas and then an alliance of marriage."

In providing support for Weil's conclusions, Elerick not only shows that final position of the verb is statistically most frequent in the three authors whose language he analysed; he also provides rules for the alternative patterns.

Weil's monograph was cited, as by Delbrück, but his insight into the patterning of syntax was not recognised. Delbrück in turn determined the patterns of Vedic syntax, especially in his monograph on the *S'atapathabrāhmana.* He recognised that the verb was final in the sentence, and also that Vedic had postpositions rather than prepositions; further, that adjectives preceded nouns. Moreover, he was greatly interested in intonation. He pointed out that verbs of finite clauses were unaccented when they stood finally, but those of non-finite clauses were accented; and he related this situation to the preposed position of non-finite clauses. Since non-finite clauses precede finite clauses in OV languages, Delbrück provided a great deal of evidence that OV was the "traditional order," as he put it, in the Indo-European languages.

We may illustrate the OV patterning of Vedic by some lines of the *Rigveda.*

Rigveda. 1.12.7
yáḥ sū́riaṃ, yá uṣásaṃ jajā́na,
who sun who dawn created
yó apā́ṃ netā́–sá janāsa, Indraḥ.
who waters' guide he men Indra
"Indra, oh men, is the one who created the sun and the dawn, and who is guide of the waters."

This short Rigvedic passage exemplifies the following OV characteristics. The verb *jajā́na* stands at the end of its clause. The relative clauses introduced by *ya-* precede their antecedent *sa*. The genitive *apā́m* precedes its noun. Moreover, the first line exhibits gapping of the type expected in OV languages; the verb is deleted from the first clause, and is found only in the second. Like early Latin and Hittite, Vedic, then, provides a great deal of evidence for OV structure.

Proto-Indo-European as an OV Language, As Demonstrated by the Comparative Method

If we apply the principles of the comparative method to the syntactic patterns, identified in the early dialects, we conclude that Proto-Indo-European was an OV language. The comparative method is applied to abstract features, not to surface manifestations. In the phonological component it is applied to phonemes and to subclasses of phonemes, not to phones. Similarly, in syntax, the comparative method must be applied to abstract structures like the order of genitives with regard to their head nouns (GN), or the order of relative constructions to their antecedents (RelCl + Ant). Indo-Europeanists in the nineteenth century applied the method only to phonological and morphological patterns, and accordingly they did not reconstruct the syntactic patterns of the proto-language.

The findings of Weil and Delbrück did not lead to recognition of the structure of syntax, nor did the patterning of early texts like the *Rigveda*. When Brugmann wrote his work of 1925 on the simple sentence of Indo-European, he proceeded in his systematic fashion, describing sentences, clauses and phrases and the relationships between their elements. That is to say, his work dealt largely with morphological features that signal syntactic relationship.

Numerous monographs on specific constructions were produced by other historical linguists, but the results were not co-ordinated. George Small, for example, published two monographs on comparative constructions in the early Germanic dialects; in these he showed that the texts included many examples like the following Old English one in *Elene* 565:

Hēo wǣron stearce stāne heardran
"They were immovable, stronger than stone"

In this line the comparative follows the standard *stāne*; an Old Icelandic example shows the same construction with *konu* preceding the comparative:

Hón var hverri konu fríðari
"She was more beautiful than any other woman"

While Small's monographs were and remain important for their data, linguists did not recognise the interrelationships between specific syntactic patterns, and accordingly the findings were received as uncoordinated contributions.

Greenberg's Syntactic Universals

The structure of syntax became clear through an important article published by Joseph Greenberg in 1963. The article made two significant points. As one, it established relationships among syntactic patterns like the relationship between verbs and objects, adpositions and objects, comparatives and standards, labelling them **universals**. These three constructions, and more, some of which will be examined below, are characterised by **government**; if verbs precede objects, as in a VO language, so adpositions (prepositions) will precede nouns, and in comparison adjectives will precede standards when we are dealing with consistent languages. Moreover, if verbs follow the objects that they govern, as in OV languages, the other two constructions will be parallel.

Similarly, elements that modify nouns, like relative clauses, genitives and adjectives stand on the side of objects and other nouns, that is, opposite the verb as exampled early.

As a second significant point, Greenberg proposed **implicational universals**. A consistent language with object-verb order would also have object-adposition order and so on. That is to say, if in texts examined for historical purposes postpositions rather than prepositions were found, the language concerned could be recognised as OV rather than VO.

Both points are significant for historical linguistics. Syntactic pattering is based on abstract rules made up of categories, much like the rules for the formation of cases or the sequence of phonological elements. Such syntactic rules can be treated by the comparative method or by the method of internal reconstruction, and the prior pattern can then be reconstructed. That is to say, a comparative pattern like *stāne heardran* "stone-from harder" = "harder than a stone" in Germanic, Vedic and Latin, provides the data for reconstructing earlier syntactic patterns much as do morphological patterns like the formation of the third-singular indicative active.

Moreover, if we find only characteristic OV patterns, like postpositions or comparatives with standards before adjectives, in a language for which we have few texts, we have grounds enough to conclude that the language is OV.

The universals identified by Greenberg then are highly important for historical linguistic purposes. They enable linguists to interpret the findings of earlier scholars, like Delbrück. They also provide means for reconstruction of syntax comparable to the phonological and morphological reconstruction that had long been carried out.

Re-Examination of Findings by Delbrück and Early Syntacticians

We now deal with syntax through the structures made up of syntactic universals. As in phonology, we propose a framework. The syntactic framework is not as tightly interrelated as is the paradigm of a noun or verb; but we assume that if a characteristic element of the framework, such as use of postpositions, is represented in a given language, that language can be identified as OV.

Yet we must also remember that languages are constantly changing. Changes are slower in syntax than in phonology and morphology. As a result, we commonly find residues of past constructions side by side with the current patterns. We find those residues in literature, and especially in poetry, which tends to follow traditional norms. If, as in Old English, the OV comparative constructions are maintained only in the older language, with gradual replacement by VO constructions, we assume that the language is shifting from OV to VO order. We have more evidence for such a shift in English, as we will see below. Here we may simply note that the other Germanic dialects also contain OV comparative constructions; accordingly, we reconstruct Proto-Germanic as an OV language. We find assurance for our reconstruction in the OV patterning of Vedic Sanskrit and Latin.

We also note the segments of the language that maintain older constructions. As in the lexicon, these are generally the common segments, such as the pronouns; for example, in Latin we find postpositional use of *cum* with pronouns, such as *mēcum* "with me," *sēcum* "with (him)self." Frozen forms like these in syntax are as important for historical reconstruction as are aberrant forms in morphology, for example the English strong verbs, or residues testifying to Verner's law like *was : were, lose : forlorn.*

We must also be aware of the ready modification of some characteristic patterns, such as descriptive adjectives. While literary writers would not modify the comparative pattern, and probably not the order of adpositions, they readily place adjectives after nouns, as in Longfellow's "This is the forest primeval." Because of the ready manipulation of adjectives, and other patterns, we determine basic word order by more fixed patterns, such as comparison, adpositions and the position of the relative clause.

Following such guidelines, we interpret the findings of Weil, Delbrück and others. In one of the many monographs based on a dissertation, Wende (1915) located the postpositions in Old English texts. His findings are in keeping with the statements above. The postpositions occur largely in traditional texts, *ac ðis . . . we willa her æfter areccean* (*Cura Pastoralis*) "but this we will relate hereafter." They become less and less frequent in the course of Old English writings. We interpret such findings as we have those of Small, as residues of OV patterning. Moreover, we find residues in English today in such adverbs as *herein, hereafter,* and the like. It is also useful to note that such residues are more common in archaic style, as in legal language. Even without the Old English texts, we could conclude from the current English forms that English was at one time an OV language.

In the same way, we examine the characteristic constructions in texts of the other dialects, such as the Homeric poems. In them we find comparatives of the OV pattern, as in the first book of the *Iliad*, line 249:

> toû kaï apò glṓssēs mélitos glukíōn hréen audḗ
> his ptc. from tongue honey-than sweeter flowed sound
> "Speech sweeter than honey flowed from his tongue."

While the Homeric poems contain such OV comparative constructions, they also have VO constructions with particles such as "than." In interpreting these constructions, we must note that, like other epic verse, the Homeric poems contain much traditional material. Such passages may be identified by the OV patterns; but we must always be aware that poets may create pseudo-archaic expressions. None the less, the variety of comparative constructions indicates to us that Greek was shifting from OV to VO structure in the early part of the first millennium BC.

Residues of OV patterning in many of the Indo-European languages remain to be interpreted. Similar studies must now be done for other language families. It is clear, for example, that the books of the Old Testament show a progression of change. Unlike the Indo-European languages, however, the progression is from VSO structure to SVO. The change may be illustrated by citing relative constructions. VSO languages may have no relative particle, but may simply place finite verbs after their head. This is the construction in Genesis 1.1:

bəreśith bārāʔ ʔelohim . . .
in (the) beginning created God
"In the beginning when God created . . ."

Only the new translations, as well as the earlier Hebrew grammarians, recognise that the second and third words make up a relative clause modifying the first word. Accordingly, the older translations, like the King James Version, are wrong. The translators were ignorant of VSO patterning, and treated the initial prepositional construction as an adverb with the following principal verb.

Proper interpretation of the type of language, and the types of universals found in it, as well as the other features as illustrated above, are then important for greater understanding of the historical background of individual languages. The constructions have often been described. But since the patterns of syntactic structure were unknown, the interpretation of the constructions is often erroneous, just as the syntactic patterns were unexplained.

Processes in the Shift of the Relative Clause Construction

We may illustrate the change of some characteristic constructions for fuller understanding of the processes involved in syntactic change.

Hittite texts from the eighteenth to the twelfth centuries BC provide materials for understanding the shift from OV relative constructions towards the VO construction. Those materials are supplemented by early Latin texts, which still contain OV relative constructions. Before examining passages, we may note that many relative constructions serve to identify specifically, or to topicalise, the nouns they modify, as in *the girl who left is his sister, or that girl who left is his sister.*

It is also useful to mention that OV languages are more asyndetic than are SVO languages; clauses often seem strung together, without conjunctions. In this way, the earliest Hittite texts contain such parallel clauses, some of which we would treat as relative clauses if we produced them in English.

In Old Hittite, a particle was attached to nouns, topicalising them much as relative clauses do, as in the following example taken from Justus (1975):

kuis	sagais	kisari	ta	LUGALi . . .	tarueni
which	sign	appears	it	to-king	we report

We may translate the sentence: "We report to the king whichever sign appears." But in approximating the meaning of the sentence in English, the translation would be "We report the sign that appears to the king."

In a fuller version of the Old Hittite construction, the relative noun is given in both clauses:

gud-puhugarin	ma	kuedani	Udti	nu-za	UTUSI	apedani	UDti
ox-substitute	ptc	on-which	day	ptc-ptc	my-sungod	on-that	day

warapta
bathed

"The king (< sungod) bathed on the day on which they adorned the substitute-ox."

In both of these examples, the relative noun is topicalised by an element that later came to be used for a relative pronoun.

We may cite a similar example from the Latin Agrarian Laws of about 111 BC:

> Quei ager publicus populi Rom. in terra Italia . . . fuit, de eo agro loco quem agrum locum populus ex publico in privatum commutavit, is ager locus . . . domneis privates ita . . .
>
> "Whatever public land of the Roman people there was in the country of Italy, from that land and place whatever land and place

the people changed from public to private, that land and place shall be private for the owners."

The two initial early clauses beginning with *quei* and *quem* seem, on the one hand, to be preposed relative clauses, on the other hand, to be topicalised statements. The resumption of the relative noun by means of *de eo agro* recalls the Hittite example, indicating that the previous clause is taken as relative in this stage and style of Latin. At a later stage, and in the subsequent language, the sentence would be given as "the land that belonged to the people . . . shall be private for the owners."

As languages become VO in structure, relative clauses generally come to be placed after principal clauses. Moreover, the relative noun is not included in the relative clause, but only in the principal clause, as in the translation of the examples given above. The topicalising pronominal element then becomes a relative marker, generally placed directly after the relative noun, as in "the land that." In this way the relative clause pattern may shift completely from an original OV structure to VO structure such as that we know in English.

We may still note that the relative marker may be omitted at this stage, much as it was in the earliest Hittite. Its omission in English is possible when the relative noun is object of the verb in the relative clause, as in *This is the book she brought.* In medieval German, the relative pronoun could also be omitted when the relative noun was subject of the relative clause, as in the Old High German sentence:

er sār in thō gisagēta thia sālida in thō gaganta
He at-once them then told the fortune them then had-befallen
"He at once told them the fortune that had then befallen them."

The construction is known as *apò koinoū,* common to both clauses. It is found also in Middle High German, where the common element may be object to the verbs of the two clauses, as in:

Gâwân an den zīten
Gawain at the time
sach in der siule rīten
saw in the hall ride
ein rīter und ein frouwen
a knight and a lady
mohy er dâ beidiu schouwen

could he there both see
"Then Gawain saw riding in the hall, a knight and a lady, (whom) he then could see both."

In the long period of shifting from the OV relative construction to the VO there are many further matters of interest. The data may be consulted in handbooks; they are not explained, however, and accordingly many syntactic problems remain to be more fully accounted for. Here we have only provided a few examples to illustrate how relative constructions of OV patterning were shifted to the relative construction we find in English and other Indo-European languages of today.

The Gradual Shift of Other Constructions

If English were an OV language, genitives would be placed before the nouns they modify. This construction is found today only for animate nouns, unless we set out to provide playful examples. We say *Joe's legs were tired after the game,* but we hesitate to say *The table's legs are scratched* rather than *The legs of the table are scratched.* Finding the preposed genitive more frequent in the older period of the language, Fries (1940) investigated the construction as well as others.

In Old English texts of AD 900 52 per cent of genitives stood before nouns, as in the following phrase (*Ben. Rule* 95.14):

on ænium oþerum mynstres þingum
in any other minster's things
"in any other affairs of the minster"

But periphrastic genitives, that is, those made with prepositions, are found in only 0.5 per cent of the uses. By AD 1300 84.5 per cent of all genitives are periphrastic, as in the translation above and in current use. Fries concluded in his article that "in present-day standard English the pressure of position is such that all word groups tend to modify the word immediately preceding." But he did not relate his finding to general conclusions about language, as that the shift in position of the gentitive is expected when a language changes from OV to VO structure. None the less, the essay is of great interest, also for indicating the length of time required for introduction of the VO pattern of the genitive into English.

It is also instructive to examine the development of the comparative pattern in English and the other Germanic languages. As we noted above, in the early period of these languages, the comparative could be simply placed after the dative, as in *stāne heardran.* VO languages, in contrast with OV, require particles between the adjective and its standard, as in our construction: *older than Jack.* As English was moving to VO structure, a number of particles were applied, some of which are still found in dialects. Among these is *as*, which corresponds to the comparative particle *als* of German; another is *nor*; another is *be,* a reflex of an old instrumental *by*. The VO structure required a particle, but allowed a number of possibilities. Only after some time was the particle *than* fixed in standard English; in German, on the other hand, the particle *dann* is dialectal in contrast with *als*.

The Shift in Order of Complements

In OV languages complements, also known as object clauses, are preposed. In Japanese, for example, object clauses precede main clauses. These commonly end in nouns, such as *koto* "fact," which are objects of the principal verb, as in:

fune no deta koto o shiranai
boat ptc. left fact ptc. not-know
"He does not know that the boat has left."

Hittite preserves similar examples, though with participles, as in:

ammuk-war-an akkantan *IQ.BI*
me ptc him dead he stated
"He stated to me that he was dead."

This construction is similar to that in Turkish: for example:

onun gideceğini biliyorum
his coming I know
"I know that he will come."

If a language comes to be VO in structure, such object clauses must stand after the verb. When placed there, they are generally introduced by a marker that indicates complementation.

The various Indo-European languages are highly interesting for the devices that were introduced to mark complements. In Sanskrit, *yád* "what" is a common initial marker; it corresponds to Homeric *hó*. In the course of time other markers were introduced, such as *hóte* in Greek. Moreover, the construction of the accusative with infinitive is also common, in Latin as well as Greek, for example *keleúō se apeltheîn* "I command you to go," Lat. *iter patefierī volēbat* "he wished the road to be opened."

These are the two major patterns for complementation in the Indo-European languages of VO structure. In examining their development in any language, details, like the verbs with which they are used, provide topics for further studies. Grammars of the past list the patterns and the complementisers; but they do not relate them to the structural changes in syntax.

The Germanic languages developed their own constructions, by some views with influence from Latin; yet the independent patterns in each of the languages suggest that the constructions are native. In Old English one of the common patterns is a clause introduced by *þæt*, as in:

> bæd þaet he wære Cristen gedon
> bade that he were Christian made
> "He asked that he be made a Christian."

Like the principal verb here, verbs meaning "request," "make known," "say," "promise," and "intend," are followed by *þæt* complements in Old English. On the other hand, verbs meaning "command," "wish," "begin," and "are" are followed by infinitival complements, as in:

> het hine gan to þam cininge
> commanded him go to the king
> "He commanded him to go to the king."

Only later was the "*-ing*" construction introduced, by some assumptions on the basis of Celtic, as in *she intended driving the children to school, They began going slowly to the door*. Since this third complementation pattern is not found in the other Germanic languages, the proposed origin in Celtic, which has verbal nouns, is highly likely.

Old Icelandic developed a construction introduced by the particle *at,* comparable to OE *þæt,* and also used the infinitive with accusative construction. In Old High German the particle *huueo*, Germ. *wie* "how," was used as well as the *that*-construction and the accusative with infinitive construction. These two constructions are also found in Old Saxon. Except for the English *-ing* construction, the dialects are parallel in complementation types, suggesting that the patterns were being introduced into Proto-Germanic, to be fixed only in the individual dialects.

The dialects and even individual authors of the early period differ in their uses of the possible constructions, indicating that the patterns were still fluid. Moreover, the verbs with which either the *that*-construction or the accusative with infinitive were used often differ from those of Latin. We conclude, then, that complement structures were being devised for each of the Germanic languages, much as were comparative constructions with their particles.

The development is of primary interest here in indicating how complement clauses following verbs arose in one of the Indo-European languages. There were similar needs for the other types of clauses, such as conditional, result, purpose and so on. We find different markers for many such types of clauses, even between English and German, as in Eng. *if* versus Germ. *wenn.* Investigating the origin and development of these provides fascinating syntactic studies, for the Romance languages and the other branches of the Indo-European family as well as for Germanic.

Syntactic Change from Active to Accusative Languages

While the differences between the OV patterning of Hittite or Vedic Sanskrit and the VO patterning of later dialects may seem considerable, the syntactic changes between active and accusative structure are far more comprehensive. Such a shift took place between Pre-Indo-European and Proto-Indo-European. In examining the evidence for the change, we may recall some of the characterstics of active languages.

Active languages differ from accusative and ergative languages in having clauses bound together by agreement rather than by government. Verbs and nouns fall into one of two classes, stative/inanimate or active/animate. Moreover, verbs are the central elements of sentences. In constructing sentences, an active noun is matched with an active verb, and a stative noun with a stative verb. Active languages have other pertinent characteristics; for example, the stative subsystem of the verb has relatively few forms. Nouns have few inflections. Interrelationships in clauses are indicated by a large number of particles.

Before relating these characteristics with those of Proto-Indo-European, we may recall some of the long-standing problems in its verb system. The present system contrasts with the perfect system in tense-aspect. The present system indicates ongoing action; the perfect system indicates a completed action, that is, a state. Moreover, in Sanskrit, Hittite and early Greek, there is a primary contrast in voice between the active and the middle; the middle often indicates a state, and is also used with reflexive meaning. The perfect and the middle have long been aligned with each other by Indo-Europeanists, though the basis for the alignment has been disputed.

Moreover, when we examine the forms in the early dialects, we find that there are few characteristic forms for the perfect and the middle; in building the paradigm, the remaining forms have been built on those of the present. In accounting for this situation, we remember that the stative inflection of active languages has few forms. In view of the correspondence in meaning of the stative with that of the Indo-European perfect and the middle, coupled with the morphological correspondences, we conclude that Pre-Indo-European was an active language.

The conclusion can be supported by additional data. Among these are sets of roots that are inflected only as actives or as middles. Among roots inflected only as actives are those meaning "bite," "blow," "eat," "give," "go"; among those inflected only as middles are "lie (be lying down)," "smile," "fear," "turn," "wish for." These meanings coincide with the meanings of active and stative verbs in active languages. Accordingly, the contrast between such roots may be interpreted as residue from the earlier Pre-Indo-European active structure.

Moreover, we cannot reconstruct a verb "have" for Proto-Indo-European, let alone Pre-Indo-European. The Germanic verb "have" cannot be securely explained; it may be based on the verb found in Latin, *capiō* "seize, take"; if so, the *-p-* should have become *-f-* by Grimm's law. Because of the phonological and semantic difficulties, some Germanic scholars derive "have" from the same root as they do Lat. *Habēō,* with influence from the root in *capiō*. Morover, a totally different root is used for the verb "have" in Gk *ékhein*. Further, a phrase made up of the verb "be" accompanied by a dative is used in Latin to indicate possession, as in *mihi est liber* "to me is book" = "I have a book." Since active languages lack a verb for "have," we account for the diversity of expression in the Indo-European dialects by the assumption that there was no verb for "have" in Pre-Indo-European; the individual dialects developed their own.

The early dialects include other residues of active inflection. We may also recall the lexical evidence provided by the presence of two words for "water" and "fire," as well as for verbs like "lie," "sit"; we have noted that one of these refers to the substance or action as active and animate, that is, the word for "water" attested in Sanskrit as *āp-* and that for "fire" in Latin as *ignis,* while the other refers to the substance or action as inactive or inanimate, that is, the words *water* and *fire* are reflexes of the inactive, inanimate nouns in Pre-Indo-European.

The presentation here may illustrate how, on the one hand, we can account for problems in Proto-Indo-European and the early dialects that have long been unexplained. They may also indicate the great changes that take place when an active language shifts to accusative or ergative structure.

Explanations for Syntactic Changes and Problems in Reconstructing Earlier Syntactic Patterns

In attempting to account for syntactic changes, we take our evidence from modifications that have been attested and from syntactic patterning. There is little question that syntactic change proceeds in accordance with the drift of a language. We have noted that when the Indo-European languages become VO in structure, the various constructions were modified to VO patterning, some like the English genitive construction over a long period of time. As objects were placed after verbs, so were object clauses, in our terminology, complements. Moreover, markers were developed to introduce complements. Some of these were taken from particles, such as forms of Proto-Indo-European **yo-*, or as in the Germanic languages, forms of **to-*.

Similarly, prepositions were introduced, many of them from previous postpositions. And comparative constructions in the VO pattern were developed, with particles selected to function as pivots between the adjective and the standard.

In addition, VO modifier constructions were introduced, as we have seen in reviewing the evidence in Hittite and Latin for relative clauses, and in English for genitive constructions.

In short, the characterstic VO patterns were gradually incorporated in the syntactic structure of the changing languages. Residues survived, as they do in morphology and the lexicon. But the shift is straightforward, so that we may assume similar shifts in other languages that undergo syntactic change. The change may be from other initial types; Hebrew shifted from a VSO language to one of SVO structure. The processes, however, are comparable.

Such observations do not provide us with information on the original cause of the change. Two such causes may be briefly sketched.

The first has to do with adoption of a language by non-native speakers. When large numbers of non-native speakers adopt a language, the language tends to be shifted to SVO structure. Apparently, the basis for the shift is ease in understanding. In both VSO and SOV languages the two frequent nominal constituents of sentences, subject and object, stand side by side. In SVO languages, by contrast, they are clearly separated by the verb. We may note that all widely used languages with more than 100 million speakers today have become SVO. A number of these are Indo-European: English, French, German, Italian, Portuguese, Russian, Spanish. Another example is Chinese, which apparently in an early stage was verb final. The last major language to change towards SVO structure is Arabic, which is increasingly assuming SVO characteristics. An apparent counterexample is Japanese; but it has not been adopted by large numbers of speakers outside Japan. The evidence of widely spoken languages, then, supports the hypothesis that they tend towards SVO structure. If the basic sentence pattern is changed, the remaining constructions gradually change as well, as we have observed above.

A second cause of syntactic change is comparable. Speakers of two or more languages tend to use the same syntax for the language or languages over which they have least control or which they use least. In a personal observation, I found that an individual speaker, a third-generation Fijian of Indian descent, claimed to know Tamil, Fijian and Hindi. When he produced Tamil sentences, however, they were halting and in VO, rather than OV, order. His Fijian was correctly VO. But of the three languages he spoke Hindi most accurately, with consistent OV order. When questioned about Tamil, he replied with some embarrassment that it had been his grandfather's language and that he now used it rarely. Yet it is quite remarkable that he spoke it with the VO order of Fijian rather than the OV order of Hindi, in which he was most at home. Such an example permits no general conclusions, inasmuch as too many variables may be involved; but it does suggest that the basic syntactic patterns of a language may be modified on the basis of patterns in other languages.

Such modifications have been proposed for a number of languages. Akkadian, for example, is OV, in contrast with the basic VO structure of Semitic languages. It was brought into an area occupied by speakers of the OV language Sumerian, and presumably was adopted by many speakers of Sumerian. In time, Sumerian became extinct. The influence it may have exerted on Akkadian, however, is our best explanation of the change in order of Akkadian. Similarly, the Semitic languages of Ethiopia have become OV, presumably also by influence of languages spoken in the area before the Semitic languages were introduced.

Such examples provide further support for the hypothesis that the Indo-European languages became VO in structure when they were introduced into the various regions in which we find them. By the time of Classical Greek, Classical Latin, and the earliest other western dialects, these languages were adopting VO order. The recently found Celtic inscriptions in Spain indicate that early Celtic, like Proto-Indo-European, had OV order; but in Britain the Celtic languages went on to develop VSO order, a change that has been attributed to indigenous speakers of VSO languages. Such explanations find support in the Indo-Aryan languages of today; for like the Dravidian languages, which are spoken by many bi-lingual speakers of Indo-Aryan languages, these are now consistently OV. Yet Classical Sanskrit was ambivalent in structure. The patterns of syntax are apparently less strongly regulated than are those in phonology and morphology, so that they are more likely to be modified under the influence of other languages.

4

Semantics Change and Changes in the Lexicon

Frameworks for Understanding Semantic Change

In the preceding chapter we have seen that an understanding and explanation of linguistic change depends on an adequate framework. Such a framework for sound change was provided in phonological study during the nineteenth century. The well-known rules describing sound change—Grimm's law. Verner's law and many others—were proposed when linguists increased their insights into the sound system of language and worked out a universal treatment of phonology. As information on speech sounds and the principles underlying the sound systems of various languages increased, improved formulations of phonological rules were provided. Subsequently, the formulations for specific changes have been improved and are still being improved. These improvements are based on an increasingly adequate framework for dealing with changes in the phonological component of language, the groundwork for which was provided in the nineteenth century and used subsequently in interpreting sound change.

Treatment of the syntactic component of language has undergone a similar development though more recently. Eduard Sievers and other linguists of the nineteenth and early twentieth centuries dealt with an underlying phonological structure. But only recently have linguists begun to deal with underlying structures in the syntactic component.

The advances have been made possible by the framework of syntax that was initially proposed by Greenberg, as we have noted in the previous chapter.

In order to deal with semantic change, we need a similar framework. As in the study of phonology, morphology and syntax, we need to determine characteristic entities of semantic structures and the characteristic relationships among such entities. In the past many individual changes have been described in semantic study. For example, the Latin word for "maternal uncle" *avunculus* is a form derived from the Latin word for "maternal grandfather" *avus*. The derivation is quite clear, as is the development of Lat. *avunculus* to Fr. *oncle*; NE *uncle* has the same source, through borrowing from French. Although the external development of the Latin terms causes no problems, no explanation could be given for a semantic development that would lead to calling an "uncle" something like "little grandfather." An explanation has recently been provided from study of the systems in language referring to kinship. A variety of distinct systems has been determined. The system in which the mother's brother is associated with the grandfather is known as the Omaha kinship system. In a group of speakers with an Omaha kinship system one can expect to find the same or similar terms for mother's brother and for maternal grandfather. This expectation is parallel to the expectation we have observed in syntactic study of finding postpositions in a language of OV order, or of finding noun-adjective order in VO languages.

The expectation may not be fulfilled, as we have observed for English, with adjective-noun order in a VO language. If it is not, the language is in flux and we look for an explanation. Thus, the system of kinship terms in late Latin was changing to the system of terms we find in the Romance languages today, such as French, Italian, Portuguese and Spanish. Changes in the kinship system led to changes in the kinship terms. French *oncle* is not restricted to "maternal uncle," nor are the further terms Ital. *zio,* Span. *tío,* or Port. *tío*. The kinship system has changed, and with this change the kinship terms have a different meaning from the corresponding term in Latin. But during a period in the development of the Romance languages, the meanings of these terms must have been in flux, just as in late Old English. At that time the distinctive terms for "paternal uncle" OE *fædera,* and "maternal uncle," OE *ēam*, were yielding to a single term *uncle*.

This example of the change in meaning for the term *avunculus* may illustrate the procedures we follow in dealing with semantic change. We determine coherent sets of terms in language corresponding to conceptual sets; we then examine the position of individual items like *avunculus* in such a set. The term **field** was introduced for such sets by the German scholar Jost Trier, who carried out a widely influential semantic study by investigating the terms referring to the intellect in early German. As yet, no sub-classifications of the "intellectual field" comparable to the sub-classifications for kinship terms have been determined. None the less, it is useful in dealing with semantic change to focus one's study on a restricted set of terms, like those for the intellectual field, for colours, for kinship, for numerals and so on.

The observation of semantic changes in kinship systems points to a difference between the study of semantic change, on the one hand, and phonological and syntactic change, on the other. Semantic change may be intimately related to change in other social structures. For example, the shift in meaning of Lat. *penna* "feather" to "writing implement" is related to a change in cultural activities by which feathers came to be used as writing implements. As far as we have been able to determine, there is no such relationship between cultural changes and syntactic, morphological or phonological changes, even though some scholars have proposed such relationships. We may also note that not all semantic changes are related to cultural changes: for example, the restriction in meaning of the word *wife* from "woman," as still in Germ. *Weib*, to "female spouse" is unrelatable to any shift in the cultural status of women in English-speaking areas.

Nevertheless, many semantic features that are prominent in a language, and accordingly many semantic changes, are related to the physical situations of the speakers of a given language. This observation may be supported by semantic changes that are introduced when speakers move to different locations. Edward Sapir provided an excellent example when he demonstrated that the Navaho of the American southwest migrated to their present home from the Athapaskan territory in northern Canada (Sapir 1963). One of these examples in the Navaho verb for "seed lies": *-sàs*, from "underlying *zàs* or *yàs" (ibid.)*. For this word Sapir provided the etymology: Ath **yàxs* "snow lying on the ground." The word maintained its meaning in the Athapaskan languages of the north but changed its meaning remarkably when Athapaskan speakers moved into a region with no snow. In somewhat the same way the words *robin* (*mountain*), *lion,* and so on changed in meaning when English speakers brought these terms to America. The relationship between semantic change and other cultural change adds a complexity to the study of change in meaning that is not found in the study of change in phonological, morphological and syntactic systems.

It is hardly surprising, therefore, that general principles have not been determined for semantic change. Modifications in the means of indicating meaning are associated with modifications in the lexicon, and for these we can propose some general patterns, as will be apparent later in the chapter. But rules have only recently been proposed; they are restricted to small sets like kinship terms. Further such rules may be expected as the study of semantic change is pursued with the rigour applied to phonological, morphological and syntactic change.

To deal with the complexity of semantic change, three terms are used: (1) the **word,** or linguistic **symbol**; (2) the **referent** denoted by a word, whether concrete like "pen" or abstract like "thought"; (3) the **reference,** or notion symbolised. Each of these may change, as examples given below will illustrate. A word like OE *ēam* "uncle" may be lost; a referent like a feather may be replaced by a plastic cylinder with a point; a notion associated with an object, like a bear, may come to convey dread, and changes in the designation may result. In dealing with semantic changes, the meanings of words have come to be expressed increasingly by means of features.

Change in Semantic Features

In proposing a framework for semantic analysis, fields have been analysed for their distinctive features. If we analyse the kinship system for Modern English in this way, we would propose the features: gender, generation, and lineality. The basic set of kinship terms may be presented in a matrix as follows:

	Father	*Mother*	*Brother*	*Sister*	*Son*	*Daughter*	*Uncle*	*Aunt*	*Cousin*	*Nephew*	*Niece*
Sex	0	1	0	1	0	1	0	1	–	0	1
Generation	0	0	1	1	2	2	0	0	1	2	2
Lineality	0	0	0	0	0	0	1	1	1	1	1

Such a matrix permits ready understanding of semantic change. For example, the system of kinship terms in Modern English is not completely symmetrical; it does not have a distinction for gender manifested in the "cousin" relationship. If this feature were extended to the term "cousin," a semantic change would be brought about. As in German, a further kinship term might introduced; a male cousin in German is called *Vetter*, a female cousin *Kusine*. In Classical Greek the term *mḗtrōs* was used for "maternal uncle," *pátrōs* for paternal uncle. Thereupon the feature of consanguinity came to be more important than that for gender, and the word *theíos* "uncle" was introduced for either "father's brother" or "mother's brother." Apparently, cultural changes had led to disregarding distinctions between paternal and maternal relationships. The change in meaning in the new system can be indicated precisely if we analyse the set of kinship terms in Classical Greek into distinctive features.

Moreover, the use of distinctive features in a semantic field may be specified by rules that indicate the relationships among them. For example, in Latin the word *gener* was used for "man's sister's husband" and for "son-in-law." Both designations involve no more meanings than those found in the English set of kinship terms. But English does not have the same rules as Latin. This situation may illustrate the need for proposing rules depicting the use of features in a given language, as well as the need for analysing semantic entities into features. For the Latin word *gener,* Floyd Lounsbury proposed the following rule: "Let any woman's brother, as linking relative, be regarded as equivalent to that woman's son, as linking relative." (1964). Formalised, in symbolism used for kinship terminology, the rule reads ♀B . . . → ♀s. This rule, which Lounsbury labels an asymmetrical skewing rule characteristic of an Omaha kinship system, was replaced by bilaterally symmetrical skewing rules in Italian, French, Spanish and Portuguese. These languages, like English, distinguish between lineal and collateral relatives, containing separate words for "brother-in-law" and "son-in-law."

This example may illustrate that semantic change may be represented much as is phonological, morphological or syntactic change. Features may be added or lost; or rules expressing the relationships between features may be modified or lost.

Other semantic modifications may be understood by means of

feature analysis. For example, NE *mother* is used not only as a kinship term, but also in such expressions as *mother-of-pearl, mother-of-vinegar, mother of battles.* In these expressions the semantic feature < + Human > has been eliminated and the feature < + Relationship > has been aligned in a different way with other features.

Extensions of use for other words may illustrate the discussion of meaning change in this way. The term *clothes' horse* also involves the loss of a feature: < + Animate >. The use of the term *house* for a body of representatives, on the other hand, involves the addition of the features < + Animate > and < + Human >. Few studies have been carried out that exemplify such rules and their role in change of meaning. The examples included in the rest of this chapter may, however, be examined in this way. By analysis of the words into features and by examination of the specific modification involved, the semantic change in question may be more precisely understood.

On Determining Change in Meaning

Change of meaning is readily apparent in any language for which we have a series of texts. As example we may cite *persona,* for which a considerable change of meaning can be substantiated in the several millennia over which it and its reflexes are found in Latin and English texts. When we first encounter *persona,* it means "mask." In Roman drama, masks were used on the stage, and varied in accordance with roles. Soon *persona* came to mean a "character indicated by a mask," thereupon a "character" as such or a "role in a play." From this developed the meaning "representative of a character," then a "representative in general." For us its central meaning is "representative of the human race." A peripheral meaning, "representative of the church," has survived in the form *parson,* which has retained the pronunciation found in such words as *Derby* (British), and is spelled accordingly. The word *persona* has accordingly undergone a considerable change, from referring to an article of stage costume through designation for human roles to a general designation for human being, all of which can be attested in Latin and subsequent English texts.

Even if we lacked these texts, we could make conjectures about its development of meaning by comparing Modern English usages like *ten persons were at the meeting, the three persons of the trinity* and *He is a parson*. Peripheral meanings, as well as the central meaning, may be found in texts produced at one time, and may be used to infer the change of meaning a word has undergone. In the Old English *Beowulf,* for example, the etymon of *thank* is attested in a compound with the meaning "thought," *fore-panc* "forethought." In *Beowulf,* it means "satisfaction, pleasure." On the basis of further examples, we can infer a change of meaning for *thank* from "thought" to "recognition" to "acknowledgement." Numerous examples are available for conjecturing change of meaning from texts for which we have no long succession of predecessors.

As with *thank,* conjectures on meaning change may be supported by a third procedure, comparison with elements similar in form, that is, through etymology. It is scarcely hazardous to assume that *thank* is related to *think.* Internal vowel change is a common device for deriving words in the Germanic languages, as in *drink : drench, wind: wend one's way* and so on. One may therefore suggest for *thank* on the basis of etymology, the earlier meanings we find attested in Old English.

Inferences about meaning from etymology, however, require caution, for forms may be modified in accordance with phonological, morphological and syntactic sets. If, for example, we had only the form Germ. *Sündflut* for the flood that Noah survived, we would relate the first element to *Sünde* "sin" and assume *Sündflut* to be a compound describing the long flood caused by man's sinfulness. Actually, from older forms we find the analysis wrong; the first component was modified by folk etymology from MHG *sin-*, a cognate of Lat. *senex* "old person," so that it originally meant the "long-lasting" flood. Suggesting change of meaning on the basis of etymology or similarity of form may thus be erroneous.

The same caution applies when we attempt to reconstruct change of meaning from forms in related languages. We would have to know considerably more than the fact of their relationship to decide that of the pair Eng. *silly* : Germ. *selig* "blessed," the German form preserves the earlier meaning, while of the pair Eng. *cup* : Germ. *Kopf* "head," the English form does. We can conclude from comparisons of related forms which differ in meaning that change of meaning has indeed taken place. For its exact course we speak with certainty only when we have texts in which the earlier, as well as the later, meanings can be established.

In discussing the changes in semantic systems, for convenience we deal with words. Actually, any morphological element may undergo semantic change. We can observe it in affixes: *super-* in *superman* differs in meaning from *super-* in *superstition* or *superstructure.* In the second chapter we saw how the segment *-burger* has changed considerably in meaning. We must make the same assumption for morphemes consisting of suprasegmental material, such as intonation patterns; but with our ignorance of suprasegmental morphemes of the past, we cannot provide sure examples. In this brief introduction to change of meaning, we will deal only with well-established examples, such as the words used for illustration so far in this chapter. Interpreting such examples, we will discuss semantic change in relation to the processes and to the causes that have been proposed for it.

Processes by Which Semantic Change and Change in the Lexicon are Carried Out

In a celebrated article, Meillet proposes three processes by which semantic change takes place.

The first of these is change in the contexts in which given words are used. An example is the restriction of meaning of Fr. *pas, personne, rien, jamais.* These words were used with *ne* "not" to strengthen the negation: *pas,* for example, originally meant "step." When *ne* was omitted, they came to have a negative meaning.

The second process results from a change in the object referred to, or in the speakers' view of such an object. An example of change in the object referred to is *pen* from Lat. *penna* "feather, quill." Used for a writing implement dispensing some kind of fluid ink, *pen* no longer means "feather." Among such changes Meillet classes those resulting from taboo. One can readily cite circumlocutions for non-favoured objects, such as Gk *aristerós* "better" for "left (hand)," *left,* itself from an Old English word for "weak," Lat. *sinister* "more useful," itself replaced by *gauche* in French, which now also has an unfavourable connotation. The Slavs and Welsh substituted so commonly for "bear" the circumlocution "honey-eater, honey-pig," that the original was lost from their languages. Through enforced disuse of the tetragrammaton JHWH, the Hebrews lost knowledge of its pronunciation. Many tabooed words are restricted in usage only in certain social situations, so that the word is not totally lost from the language. The attempts to bar *Lady Chatterley's Lover* were determined in part by Lawrence's used of a term tabooed in print, even though it is widely used in the spoken language.

Such words under only a partial taboo do not undergo a change in meaning because of the taboo, as can be demonstrated from the long history of the often cited Anglo-Saxon four-letter words, many of which can be traced back to Proto-Indo-European. If, however, a word is under complete taboo, such as the reflex of the Proto-Indo-European word for "bear" in Germanic-speaking areas, it may be lost; the word has reflexes in dialects spoken where the bear was not a present danger, for example Gk *árktos,* Lat. *ursus,* Skt. *ṛ́kṣas.*

The third basis for semantic change, and change in the lexical component of language, Meillet found in the influence of other languages and dialects, including social dialects. The process by which words are imported into a language is known as **borrowing**. It has by far the greatest effect on the lexicon of the three processes discussed by Meillet, as will be illustrated below for English. A large number of words in English have been borrowed from French, though their earlier source is Latin or Greek. An example is priest. Originally a specialised use of the Greek adjective for "older," *presbúteros* became a part of the technical language of the early Christians. The English form *presbyter,* as well as the related *priest,* has retained the specialised meaning, besides leading to a modification of *elder.* Such borrowings and lexical changes result from complex historical, social and linguistic processes. We will discuss some of these, using primarily examples from the history of English.

Semantic Change Resulting from Change in Linguistic Contexts

As we have noted, the omission of a word may lead to a change in meaning of other words. Modifiers may be omitted, as was French *ne* in expressions with *pas,* so that *pas* alone now means "not." An example from English is the word *undertaker,* which once meant "one who undertakes, an energetic promoter." One translation of the Twenty-third Psalm began: "The Lord.is my undertaker." A common context in which the word was used was that of *funeral undertaker; funeral* then was omitted, and until morticians thought they could sweeten their trade with a new name, the chief context for *undertaker* was for people who assist in the obsequies for the dead. The head noun itself may be omitted, as with *main*, which came to be used for "main ocean," as in the *Spanish Main; mainland,* on the other hand, was retained as a compound. As other examples we may cite *fall* "autumn," from "fall of leaves," and *private* "lowest-ranking soldier," from *private soldier.*

Semantic changes brought about by such linguistic modifications are rare. Similarly infrequent are changes resulting from similarities between forms. As examples we may cite NE *demean* and *presently.* NE *demean* "behave" was associated with *mean* "inferior" and today is generally used as a synonym for "debase." NE *presently* "soon" was associated with *present* "now" and has come to be used as an adverb meaning "at present" rather than "in the future." While semantic changes resulting from linguistic influences may be cited, they are far less frequent than changes resulting from modifications in the reference of referent.

Semantic Change Resulting from Change of Reference or Referent

Scientific advances, or social changes, bring about extensions of words to new uses. Examples may be given from almost any field of scientific or social change. As the scale of living has improved, for example, the term *pool* has undergone a change in meaning. Earlier, *garage* came to replace *stable.* In some regions *landing strip* is equally favoured. Other words referring to transportation by air have undergone striking modifications in meaning. The term *plane* was formerly found chiefly in modest scientific contexts, as in the term *plane geometry*. Unless restricted in use by the knowledgeable younger generation, who scorn it in favour of *B-747, DC-10* and the like, it has great frequency. Other items used in its linguistic environment, *pilot, jet,* and so on, have a considerably different meaning from that associated with these words before the age of flight.

We can also cite examples from the past. A *picture* formerly was something painted; now we can have our picture taken with a camera, itself formerly a term for a room. For the Romans a *street, strāta via,* was a "paved way." In the course of time it came to represent any passageway for vehicles.

Other examples may be observed today in the expansion of comfortable living. With the increased shift to suburbia came increased prestige for linguistic items suggesting life in the hills outside the city. Lots on "trails" and "lanes" sell rapidly. While "avenues" were formerly the grand entrances for cities, they may now be the ways along which commercial firms are located, with the former favourable meaning maintained only where some modicum of urban elegance is retained, as in *Fifth Avenue* or *Pennsylvania Avenue.* In many areas the formerly humble *trail* and *lane* have in this way outdistanced *avenue.* What entrepreneurs will do in the future, when all the haves live on trails and the have-mores are in search of elegant housing, will provide students of semantic change with further examples of changes in meaning resulting from non-linguistic influences. It is instructive, as well as amusing, to examine the designations for new developments around a city, with their designations including words like *hill, brook, wood.*

Among the greatest sources of such influences are technical changes, with resultant changes in technical dialects and consequent influences on the language in general. Intellectual historians may look to meteorology, and speak of a *climate of opinion.* The intellectual climate may undergo a *renaissance,* with *nerves* of communication strengthened, especially for those who are *off centre.* The technical dialects of sports have been widely exploited in English. In building a strong group, one tries to avoid *bush leaguers* (baseball) or those with a *bias* (bowling); otherwise one may find oneself *out in left field* as far as the competition is concerned. More recently, the dialect of computer technicians has been extended, as in the words ending in *-ware: hardware, software, courseware* and so on, even *wetware* for the brain. When the former meaning is still the more prominent, we may call such transfers of context metaphors. In the course of time, the new meanings may prevail and cause the **metaphor** to fade. Today we scarcely think of the former meaning of *decide* "cut off" or *detail* "cut in pieces" as we *bat around* a topic.

Often the shift in reference is from a serene to an emotionally active connotation, which corresponds to the hyperbole of literary analysis. *Astonish,* somewhat like *stun,* once meant "strike by thunder." In Shakespeare's *King Henry the Fifth,* Gower points out to Fluellen that he astonished Pistol when he struck him a second time. Such shifts seem to lead to a less vivid meaning, as may be illustrated by words of strong assent, such as *certainly, sure, indeed*—which today have less force than does *yes*; similarly, words that indicate degree, especially of behaviour or appearance, such as *fine,* which now is scarcely more satisfactory than are *superb, grand, perfect, magnificent, great.*

Shifts in reference are readily attested for terms of address, as in Span. *don, donna* from spoken Lat. *domnus, domna* "lord, mistress." In French, *domina* gave rise to *dame, madame.* The similar German *Herr,* like Eng. *Mister,* scarcely carries the connotation of mastery today. Lofty terms, when generalised, come to take on meanings resembling their everyday contexts. Some terms, in shifting from an indication of social to moral inferiority, have undergone even less favourable change. A *villain* was once a worker at a *villa*; other terms for rural work that have developed similarly are *churl* <OE *ceorl* "common man, farmer" and *boor*—compare the stolid Dutch farmers who settled South Africa. A *knave,* as in the *Knave of Hearts,* was a boy; see Germ. *Knabe.* Terms for government officials may also suffer, for example *publican* "a public servant" or *cheater,* earlier *escheater,* an officer whose duty it was to assure the return of property to the state if the owner died without heirs or without leaving a will.

Some shifts result from cultural or geographical changes rather than from modifications introduced by imaginative speakers. When people from Britain settled in America, they gave a red-breasted thrush the name of their robin, a much smaller bird with similar colouring. *Holiday,* which once referred to a sacred festival day, has lost much of its religious connotation.

Other shifts follow attitudes of the speakers. When members of a society consider it essential to use a circumlocution for a tabooed term, it may change entirely to the new meaning. *Bear* is scarcely "the brown one" for any speaker of English today. Various words were changed in meaning as they were introduced for the tabooed names for *hand, left, right* in Indo-European languages, as we may illustrate from the panoply of Indo-European words for hand—OE *folm,* Skt *hastas,* Gk *kheír,* Lat. *manus,* Lith. *rankà,* Goth. *handus.* The tabooed words may then be totally lost, as was the cognate of Gk *árktos* "bear" in Germanic and Slavic.

It should be noted that *taboo,* or avoidance of the unspeakable, varies from culture to culture, and accordingly from language to language. It is applied to clothing in Japanese; to animal names by hunters; and to names of excretory functions, death and divinity for many of us. It also varies with generations; younger speakers today may abandon the taboo on excretory functions. Terms for races, such as *Negro, Black, African-American* or *Mexican, Chicano,* and the like are also candidates for taboo, with considerable variation in attitude and consequent use.

In cultures that absolutely forbid the use of certain words, such as any homophone of the name of a deceased person, taboo may have an effect on the lexical stock of a language. In this way the attitudes towards objects, that is, the **reference** of individual words, may be influential in bringing about semantic change.

Semantic Change Resulting from Borrowing

By far the most important effect on the semantic component of language is brought about by the influence of other languages or dialects, a process referred to by linguists as **borrowing.** Borrowing may be viewed as cultural diffusion. In accounting for it, we set out to determine the conditions under which borrowing takes place.

We also note that there are borrowings of various types. Some borrowings, known as **loanwords,** mirror the phonemes of the foreign language. In Eng. *poet,* for example, the French phonemes were reproduced almost exactly in English. Most recent borrowings in English are of this type; words like *oxygen, hydrogen, telephone* are made up of entities borrowed from Greek, with English sounds substituted for those assumed to be pronounced in the original.

Other borrowings reproduce the morphemes of a foreign language, using native material. Examples are academic terms like *handbook,* a translation of Lat. *manuālis liber,* which itself has survived in the abbreviated form *manual.* Words similarly reproduced by translation are the names for the days of the week: *Monday = diē s Lunae,* "the day of the Moon goddess," *Tuesday = diēs Martis,* "the day of Mars" and so on. These are known as **loan-shifts, loan translations** or **calques**. In German, loan-shifts are especially prominent; instead of taking over the Greek components for "acid" and "material," as did English in *oxygen,* German translated them to form the loan-shift *Sauerstoff*: similarly, *Wasserstoff* for "hydrogen," *Fernsprecher* for "telephone," and so on.

In a further type of borrowing, only the meaning of a linguistic entity may be changed. OE *eorl* "earl" meant "brave warrior"; the present meaning was taken over from Old Norse, where the word indicated a rank of nobility. Similarly, OE *dwellan* meant "lead astray" but was modified in meaning by ON *dvelja* "abide" to present-day "dwell." Changes in meaning under the influence of a foreign language are known as **extensions**.

To understand borrowings of various types, we must know the degree of command that speakers have of the languages in question; for the extent of reproduction is often determined by the extent of control that speakers have acquired of a second language, especially before conventions of borrowing have been established.

We may illustrate possible modifications by noting how English words are treated in Japanese. The English word *violin* is reproduced variously, depending on the speaker's command over English. Sophisticated speakers may use a very similar form when they speak Japanese, that is *vaiorin,* even though their own language does not contain a /v/. Most speakers, however, substitute /b/ for English v, and say *baiorin.* Both sets of speakers reproduce *l* as *r*. But especially among naíve speakers, borrowings show substitution of phonemic, not phonetic, entities, as the examples given below indicate.

The role of phonemic structure in borrowings may be illustrated through the treatment of English *t* in Japanese. The stop [t] occurs in Japanese only before [e a o]; before [u] we find the affricate [ts]; before [i y], the affricate [tš]. If a work like *tank* is borrowed into Japanese, the result is *tanku,* different largely in the mandatory final vowel. For *touring,* the Japanese from is *tsuringu*; for *team* and *tube, tšiimu* and *tšyuubu.* In Japanese, [t ts tš] are in complementary distribution; they are members of the same phoneme. Naive speakers automatically substitute any of the allophones of /t/ in accordance with their distribution before following vowels in Japanese.

To illustrate a different treatment, we may note the forms of *jet* in Japanese. Like [tš], [dž] may occur in Japanese only before [i] and [y]; *jib* is then taken over with the similar pronunciation [džibu]. Before [e a o], on the other hand, [z] is found, in complementary distribution with [dž]. With these limitations of Japanese phonological structure, the word *jet* has been borrowed in two forms: [džietto] and [zetto]. In the first the initial consonant is similar to that of English, with vowel modification; in the second the vowel is unchanged, but the initial consonant has been altered.

For the examples cited, knowledge of the phonological structure of Japanese and English is necessary to explain the Japanese forms. One must know the allophones of the English phonemes and their possible Japanese counterparts. To illustrate the Japanese treatment of English *s,* the following examples may be cited; Jap. *sanmā-sō ruto* corresponds to Eng. *sommersault; setto-pož išon* to Eng. *set position* (of a pitcher); *šinema,* to Eng. *cinema*; *šōradu-rain,* to *shoulder line; supu* to *soup.* As comparison with the statement of correspondences given in the workbook will illustrate, the English words have undergone modifications determined largely by the possibilities in Japanese.

The borrowing language also brings about morphological modifications, for borrowings generally take on the patterns of native elements. When, for example, *bask* was borrowed into Old English from ON *báǒa sik* "bathe oneself" and *busk* from ON *búask* < *búa sik* "ready oneself," they were treated like simple verbs in English. Reflexives were not combined with verbs in English, and accordingly the speakers failed to recognise the final pronouns. To be sure, foreign inflections may occasionally be maintained, especially by sophisticated speakers. Many nouns were imported into English with their Latin or Greek plural inflections, such as *datum : data, colon : cola, skeleton : skeleta, maximum : maxima,* and so on. Except in learned contexts, these now make their plurals in *-s,* with the exception of the first, *data,* which is increasingly treated as a singular, as in *the data is.*

Similarly, in Japanese, borrowings are equipped with the Japanese morphological markers. Words borrowed into Japanese from Chinese, such as *kenkyuu* "study" were treated as verbs with the addition of *suru* "do," *shita* "did," for example *kenkyuu shita* "studied." When English words were borrowed into Japanese, they too followed this pattern. The loanword *taipu,* from Eng. *type,* as well as others, may be accompanied by forms of *suru.* The large number of borrowings into Japanese from Chinese and English could be inflected in this way, though without introducing any new morphological markers.

Further, syntactic expressions borrowed from another language are difficult to maintain. Eng. *marriage of convenience* <Fr. *marriage de convenance* "marriage for advantage" may be misinterpreted today. To be sure, the phrase *it goes without saying* <Fr. *cela va sans dire* has currently become established among many speakers. Yet neither of these expressions has affected the language deeply. A more widespread example of syntactic borrowing may be the German favouring of highly complicated sentence patterns, as a result of the influence of Latin syntax. As with other proposed borrowings of syntactic patterns, such as the introduction of numeral classifiers into Japanese from Chinese, the evidence is not conclusive. For the clearest instances of borrowing are in the lexical and semantic sphere. Below, however, we examine evidence that general syntactic patterns may be affected by borrowing.

Results of Borrowing under Different Social and Linguistic Conditions

Various situations in the history of English provide us with good examples of different results of borrowing. These results may be ascribed to different types of language contact, with differing effects on the language.

Borrowing when a Language of Prestige is Adopted

The first major contact of English speakers was with Celtic speakers. When English was brought to the British Isles in the fifth century AD, presumably there were more Celtic speakers than Germanic invaders. Yet English survived and ousted Celtic. Moreover, it adopted very few words from Celtic, a few common nouns like *bannock* "cake" and *brock* "badger," and numerous place names, such as *London, Thames, Dover.* The resulting linguistic situation is much like that of American English and the American-Indian languages. A few nouns from American-Indian languages were borrowed: *tomahawk, skunk,* and many place names, such as *Chicago, Mississippi, Kentucky*. The two linguistic situations had much in common; from them, with the support of other parallels, we can suggest the typical situation in which few lexical borrowings are made.

When speakers learn a prestige language, they are under social pressure to acquire it without flaws. They speak the acquired language as well as possible and avoid carrying over into it items from their native language. Examples may be taken from America in the nineteenth century. Immigrants who came to this country attempted to learn accurate English. Their own language, however, was grossly modified, often with importations from English, In the German area of Chicago, a mixed German was referred to as *die schönste lengevitsch* "the most beautiful language." It consisted in great part of German structures filled with borrowings from English. On the basis of this situation, and those just cited, we may conclude that speakers modify the language they are certain of much more readily than they do a language that they know imperfectly.

As a further well-documented example, we may cite Germany in the eighteenth century. At the courts French was the language of prestige; German, that of everyday communication. Frederick the Great of Prussia considered German a language fit only for peasants. He often wrote in French; when he did, he avoided German borrowings. His German letters, on the other hand, abound with French loanwords.

From these and other examples, we may view the English-Celtic relationship as a typical situation in the contact of languages. Old English was regarded as the language of cultural prestige. Although they may have been preponderant numerically, native Celtic speakers set out to learn English, gradually abandoning their native language. In the course of time an English resulted with few lexical importations. Apart from place names, only those items were borrowed from the receding into the dominant language for which the dominant language had no readily available terms.

Although we can provide no evidence for this type of language interrelationship in prehistoric situations, from the results we may assume it for many areas. It is especially relevant in the spread of Indo-European languages: of Hittite into Anatolia, of Greek into the Hellenic peninsula, of Italic into Italy, even of Indic into India, although in India there was considerable phonological modification resulting from the borrowing of retroflex consonants. This situation applied also for the spread of Arabic, which was adopted from Iraq to Morocco with little change in grammatical structure. Except for special situations discussed below, it also applied for the spread in recent centuries of three of the most widely spoken languages, today: French, Russian and English.

Borrowing when a Language of Prestige is Used Simultaneously with a Surviving Indigenous Language

A second typical situation, English in the eleventh century, at first glance parallels that of the fifth century. A relatively small group of invaders took over politically control of an established population and continued as the ruling class. Yet the results were quite different. In the centuries after 1066, Norman French was used by a small segment of the population, but eventually it was ousted by English.

We explain the different result by noting that the type of contact was completely different from that in the fifth century. During the eleventh and subsequent centuries, the indigenous speakers adopted words for only those cultural spheres in which they maintained contact with the ruling classes. For everyday communication they used their own language. We may illustrate this restriction of contact by noting the spheres of borrowing.

One notable sphere of borrowing was government and administration. A great number of English words in these areas was borrowed from French, for example *council, country, crown, government, minister, nation, parliament, people, state.* For titles, *prince, duke, marquis, viscount, baron* were borrowed; only the native *earl* was kept, but the earl's wife is a *countess,* and *count* is the equivalent rank for foreign nobles. In the related area of heraldry, many French terms were taken over, including those for colours such as *sable, gules, vert.* Moreover, military words were borrowed: *armor, army, banner, navy, siege, war*; similarly, such legal terms as *court, crime, defendant, judge, jury, justice, plaintiff.* In the sphere of legal terminology, some French idioms were introduced and maintained, presumably because of the extended period of French influence. Although English became the official language in 1362, legal French was not given up in courts of justice until 1731. The phrase *puis né* "later born, lower" was borrowed as an adjective, surviving in *puisne judge,* and more widely as *puny.* Moreover, some syntactic phrases, with adjective following noun, have been maintained: *attorney general, malice aforethought.*

The difference in social status of the two languages may be illustrated in contrasting words: for a small crime, the English *theft* is used; for a serious one, the French *larceny.*

Today still, words for food reflect the social relation between the Norman French and their English subjects. English terms are used for animals in the field: *cow, calf, ox, sheep, boar, swine*; French, for animals on the table: *beef, veal, mutton, bacon, pork.* Moreover, the humble meal *breakfast* has an English name; the more elegant *dinner* and *supper,* at which *jelly* and *pastry* may be served, have French names. The social relationship is further reflected in words for *sport* < *desport*, the *chase*, *falconry, cards*, and *dice*, where even words for numbers were taken over: *ace, deuce, tray.* As with foods, names for artisans in the lower groups are English: *baker, fisherman, miller, shepherd, shoemaker, smith;* those in contact with upper classes are Norman French in origin: *carpenter, mason, painter, tailor.*

The general situation is clear. Upper-class invaders, though in the minority, occupied positions of prestige in Britain for three centuries. They were gradually replaced, however, by bilingual natives of Britain; and descendants of the invaders learned English. The French terms introduced into English reflect a feudal system, with various class distinctions. We conclude that the language of lesser prestige maintained itself because of the numerical, and eventually political, preponderance of its speakers. Yet the language of greater prestige has left a great effect on certain segments of the vocabulary.

We find this situation in other areas as well. The Dravidian languages of India have been maintained, though with numerous borrowings from Indic languages. In early Mesopotamia, Akkadian ousted Sumerian, though it took over many words from the earlier language of prestige. When the Japanese became aware of the higher culture of China in the second half of the first millennium after Christ, they sent emissaries to China, who imported with the higher culture a large number of borrowings; but Japanese was maintained as the national language.

To a certain extent this type of contact exists today wherever western civilisation and science are being imitated or adopted. Words like *electricity, telephone, airplane* are being introduced as loanwords or loan-shifts. We find a variety of parallels to the English-French contact, in which the invading language leaves a marked effect in the native language without replacing it.

Borrowing when the Languages Concerned are on an Equal Plane

A third typical situation is the contact between English and Scandinavian, in the ninth to eleventh centuries. Both languages existed side by side for some time, until eventually Scandinavian was lost; but, unlike Celtic several centuries earlier, it left a considerable imprint on English. This imprint, on the other hand, was not in higher segments of culture, as was the later Norman French influence, but extended through much of the everyday vocabulary. To be sure, there were various martial and legal terms of Scandinavian origin in early English, but few of these have persisted; one that has remained, *bylaw* (*by* = "village"), has merely a vestige of its original sense.

The Scandinavian borrowings show no specific areas of cultural superiority. The term for a possible architectural improvement, window ("wind-eye"), merely replaced an older *eagpyrel* ("eye-hole," cf. ME *nosethirl,* OE *nosþyrl* (nose-hole), *nostril*); it did not accompany a cultural innovation. Little more can be claimed for the borrowed *steak* and *knife*. Unlike French, Scandinavian furnished many elements of the common vocabulary: *gift, husband, root, skill, skin, sky, wing; happy, loose, low, same, wrong; addle, call, die, drown, gape, get, give, hit, screech, take, want*. Still others may have been borrowed, but cannot be identified, for many words were alike in tenth-century Old English and Old Norse.

Most interesting are grammatical elements: *they, them, their* have taken the place of older *hīe, heom, heora.* In these borrowings the central core of the vocabulary was affected. The inflections of English nouns and verbs may even have been simplified by the contact between the two linguistic groups. We can also suggest that the type of contact existing between English and Scandinavian may have been one force in the morphological simplification of English.

This was a contrast between two languages of equal prestige. We are not certain to what extent the two were mutually intelligible; this question may also lack pertinence. For the significant point may be that the two languages were used for communication on an everyday level. The language with the larger number of speakers was maintained, though with simplification of structure.

Still further simplification is evident when speakers communicate only on simple cultural levels. A readily attested example may be found in baby-talk. Speakers, in using it, may avoid lexical items that border on the grammatical, such as pronouns: *Baby like candy?* In even more unabashed utterances, such as *baby go seepee,* we find phonological as well as morphological simplification. Such simplification, used not only to infants when attempting to convey affection, is very similar to that found in the so-called pidgin languages and creolised languages.

Pidgins (apparently a simplification of *business:* Chin. *p* = Eng. *b,* ž = *z,* yielding [pižins] < [biznis] have arisen in areas where people communicated on a very simple level. On the Chinese coast, intercommunication was carried on in English for commerce; in the Pacific islands, it was carried on for the direction of work. In South America, descendants of slaves evolved a simple common language called *Taki-taki*. When such simplified languages are the sole languages of a community, as in Haiti, they are referred to as **creolised languages** or **creoles**. To illustrate the changes that may take place when speakers are in contact on a low cultural level, examples may be cited from Hall (1943).

For a long time Melanesian Pidgin was not learned as a first language by any speaker except possibly by children of parents who could not understand each other's language. It was spoken by speakers with a Melanesian or Papuan background, and by Europeans. Remarkably, when Papua came to have its own government, Pidgin was the only widely used language, and it was adopted as an official language.

When spoken, it is not uniform. Speakers carry over their native speech habits. Melanesians, for example, may pronounce voiced stops with prenasalisation; *nəbawt* "about" may be [nə^{m}bawt]. Germans may use tæsɔl "*but*" like Germ. *aber,* which corresponds to Eng. *but* and *however.*

In Melanesian Pidgin, the sound system of English was considerably simplified. There are no /θ ŏ z ž/; for example, *this* is [dis], *nose* is [nos]. Further, in speaking Melanesian Pidgin English, Melanesians generally substitute the following:

[p] for [f v] :	[pinis]	=	[finis] "already"
	[æp]	=	[hæf] "piece"
[s] for [š č]	[masin]	=	[mašin]

[š] or [tš] for [dž] as in [pičin]

[h] is omitted, as in [bi ayn] "later." Moreover, consonant clusters may be simplified by intercalating vowels, as in [gəris] for [gris] "pig."

In morphology none of the bound forms of English are attested. There are, however, characteristic bound forms. The suffix *-felə* is used as an adjective suffix for monosyllables, and also for numerals, for example:

disfelə havs i-bigfelə	"this house is large"
tufelə pikinini	"two children"
nədəfelə səmtiŋ	"another thing"

It is also added to first- and second-person pronouns to indicate plurals:

mi "I, me"	*mifelə* "we, us"
ju "you"	*jufelə* "you"

Characteristic affixes are also used with verbs; *-im* is used as objective suffix for most verbs when transitive, as in:

ju faytim pig	"you strike the pig"

A predicate marker is used as prefix, unless the subject is *mi, mifelə, ju, jufelə, jumi,* for example:

mašin i-bəgərəp finiš	"the machine is broken"

The syntax too is simple, with sequences of co-ordinated clauses.

In Melanesian and other pidgins, then, we seen an extreme effect of language contact. A language is stripped down for the essentials of communication, with resulting phonological and morphological simplification. How often such processes of simplification took place in the past, we do not know; whether the Assyrian merchants in Asia Minor used simplified forms of communication during the second millennium BC, or the Romans in Gaul, the Hittites in Asia Minor, the Phoenicians in their wanderings. Observing the simplification of structure in contemporary pidgin languages, we may wonder whether a somewhat similar situation may not have led to the form of English that we find spoken after the tenth century, with its progressive loss of inflections, and to other similar reductions of complexity in language structure. This is not to suggest that English is, or ever was, a pidgin.

Borrowing between Dialects

In discussing these three types of contact, we have dealt only with the relations of languages among one another. We must assume, however, similar types of contact between all different forms of speech: geographical dialects, social dialects, technical dialects and even idiolects. Borrowings are made from any such dialect to any other, from all of them into the general language. Illustrations could be given in abundance. For "edible corn on the cob," the northern American *sweet corn* seems to be becoming the standard term rather than the southern *roasting ears*. With the interest in jazz and rock music, many terms have been adopted into the standard language from uneducated speech, such as *the blues*. Technical dialects of the present have introduced so many new terms that we may forget the strong influence of those in the past. We are quite aware of the time of introduction of *x-ray, radium, irradiate, isotope*. Other sources in earlier times were from the technical terms of the ecclesiastical vocabulary. Our *noon* is from OE *nōn,* Lat. *nōna hōra* "ninth hour," the time of the nones, a service held originally at 3 p.m. but later shifted to noon.

The extent to which these have been modified may be illustrated by our use of legal terms. For us, *subpoena,* originally a phrase meaning "under penalty" can be used as a verb. *Affidavit,* on the other hand, a Latin verb form meaning "he has pledged his faith" is a noun today, as is *alibi* "elsewhere," in origin a Latin adverb. Such borrowings then are inflected, as Lat. *caveat* "let him beware" has been, especially by the military with forms like *It was caveated all over the place*.

Although genetics has changed our views on biological inheritance, we still maintain the technical language of medieval science. We may excuse a failing by saying *It's in my blood.* Our disposition we still refer to as our *liquid,* Lat. *humor,* for according to medieval science there were four important liquids in people: blood, phlegm, bile, black bile. Those who were assumed to have too much blood were *sanguine;* too much phlegm, *phlegmatic;* too much bile, *bilious;* too much black bile or melancholy, *melancholic*. Those whose liquids were in balance were *good-humoured.* Their *temperament* was evident in the "weaving together" of the humours, and indicated by their *complection,* now *complexion.*

From words like these in the vocabulary we could reconstruct medieval scientific ideas. As we will see later in Chapter 6, such reconstruction is of great interest for early languages.

Like the borrowings in medieval and Modern English, borrowings adopted in technical dialects are generally based on a learned language. In Arabic-speaking countries, Classical Arabic is used as a source; in India, Sanskrit. In the languages of western Europe, Latin and Greek are the sources for technical terms. Since European technology and science have been spread throughout the world, the influence of Latin and Greek has not been confined to Indo-European languages. Names of chemical elements provide examples. The word for "hydrogen" in Japanese is *suiso* "water-substance"; the word for "nitrogen," *chisso* "suffocating substance" and so on.

Often the translation or adaptation is not literal. In Chinese and Japanese, the morph for "electricity" is extended from the meaning "lightning"; "electricity" in Japanese is *denki* "lightning spirit"; "telephone," *denwa* "lightning speech"; "telegraph," *denpō* "lightning report," and so on.

Moreover, the adaptations may fail to follow forms of the model. In linguistic terminology, for example, the proper Greek suffix for terms ending in *-eme* would be *-ematic; phonematic* would then be the adjective for *phoneme* rather than *phonemic* and so on. Yet the adjectival suffix *-ic* is so common, for example *base, basic,* that it is applied to terms ending in *-eme*, contrary to classical practice. The complexities of such formations and the attitudes of speakers towards these formations are topics that students may find highly interesting to explore.

In contemporary languages we may find results of borrowings made at different times from the same ultimate source. In this way *frail,* ME *freyl,* was borrowed from OFr. *fraile,* which is from Lat. *fragilis,* the source of our *fragile; male* is from Fr. *mâle,* OFr. *mascle,* which is from Lat. *masculus;* a derivative, *masculīnus,* is the source of *masculine* and so on. Such related words are known as doublets.

Borrowings from the Written Language

Another contemporary source for adaptations is the written language. Abbreviations, such as *Prof.* May be used as full words. With the expansion of government agencies, many such terms have been incorporated into everyday speech; /yənéskòw/, *UNESCO*, from *United Nations Economic, Social and Cultural Organisation,* may be as widely used today as /nəbískòw/, *Nabisco,* from *National Biscuit Company.* We also refer to states in this way, for example /yûw ès ès ès ár/, *USSR,* or in the former Soviet Union, /és ès ès ér/. The written language has become such an important source for borrowings of this kind that new names for organisations are generally contrived so that they will provide suitable abbreviations.

Written languages have furnished other modifications for spoken languages. A slight novelty is the odd form of *ye* for the English definite article, as in the name *Ye olde gifte shoppe*; this arose from the use of *y* for *þ* when printing was introduced into England in the fifteenth century. If the form /yíy/ is only jocular and hardly more general than this context, the pronunciations /əšúwm/ or /əšyuwm/ for *assume,* /šuwət/ or /syúwət/ for *suet,* exemplify deeper modifications from the written language. The historically modified /š/ from /sy/ has been maintained only in *sure, assure, sugar,* and among some speakers in *sumac,* while imitation of the written form has brought about change in pronunciation in *assume, consume, ensue, suet,* and others.

Influences from the written language indicate a socially favourable attitude of speakers towards it. Spelling pronunciations, such as /índiyən indyən/ for *Indian* (compare Injun Joe in *Huckleberry Finn* and the British pronunciation of /inǰə/) have completely replaced the former pronunciation.

When such influences are exerted, the effect of individual speakers may be as significant as is that of varying dialects. With the development of widespread education, the idiolects of school teachers, for example, have exerted a considerable effect on languages during the last few centuries. Modifications such as those in *assume* may serve as one illustration. Virtually anyone can supply examples from their schooldays. A favourite target in some American schools was *aunt.* Some teachers considered it undignified to label a close relative with a homonym for an insect. The spelling contributes a possible distinctive pronunciation, /áhnt/, /ɔ́hnt/, or the like. Another is *buoy*; it apparently would not do to suggest that a youth was floating in the water directing traffic. The spelling provided a way out of the difficulty.

Teachers and the bureaucracies supporting them may be responsible for even greater modifications in the language. Since the high front offglide used in parts of New York City instead of retroflection in words like *bird* and *earl* has come to seem substandard, the weight of the New York City school system has been thrown behind an effort to restore retroflection. School teachers are also undoubtedly responsible for depriving American English speakers of a negative in the first person of the auxiliary *be* that is parallel to *isn't, aren't, wasn't, weren't*; for some reason /éynt/ seemed undignified for the graduates of a forward-looking educational system.

Such exertions have given rise to **hyperforms** in contemporary languages. This term is used for attempted corrections that are extended erroneously. Brooklyn children taught to modify /bəyd/ to /bərd/ for *bird* may extend their new learning to /bɔyd/ in *Boyd* or to /ɔyl/ in *oil,* and pronounce these something like *bird* and *earl*. German children speaking dialects without rounded front vowels may round vowels in which rounding is not present in the standard language; taught to change from [filə] to [fýlə] in *Fülle* "abundance," they may also change the vowel in *bilden* "cultivate" and similar words; the use of such hyperforms is referred to as "gebüldetes Deutsch." Such modifications may be introduced without aid from a teacher or a school system, merely in an attempt to speak like the folks in the city; they are therefore also known as **hyperurbanisms**.

Besides illustrating conflicting influences that result from differing dialects, hyperforms are examples of the effects of analogy. If one is taught to substitute *I* for *me* in contexts like *It wasn't me,* one may also be led to say *with Mary and I.* The hypercorrection *I* has been taught as the prestige pattern, and as illustrated, extended in use. Weinreich, Labov and Herzog consider hypercorrection "an important mechanism in the transmission of prestige patterns" (1968). As we have seen in there paragraphs, it is only one of the processes by which borrowings are carried out in language.

The Importance of Borrowing in Language Change

Whether spontaneous or induced, borrowing is one of the important influences on language. In using speech, one of our aims is adequate communication. To achieve the readiest communication, we constantly modify our phonological, morphological and syntactic systems as well as our vocabulary to the speech of our associates. If we wish to impress fellow speakers, we may borrow words they use, or imitate their grammatical patterns. If they prefer a plural verb form with *data,* we may use *the data are.* If they prefer the spelling pronunciations /lítəratyùwr néytyùwr/, we may adopt these. We may also be considered out of date unless we adopt new extensions of meaning.

In their 1968 article Weinreich, Labov and Herzog have re-emphasised the effects on language change of the various subsystems found in any language. They have also attempted to determine precisely how language changes; in this attempt they have assumed a model of language which consists of "discrete layers" that coexist within one speech community and that contain "intrinsic variables." Among the variables they have studied are phonological characteristics, such as the position of *r* in New York City speech, and syntactic characteristics, such as the use of the copula *be* in the speech of young Blacks in northern cities of America.

One of the important processes they identify in linguistic change is the "embedding" of the change, both in the structure of a given language and in the social structure of the society using that language. For example, statements have been made about the lack of the copula *be* in the speech of Black children. Labov has demonstrated that it is not lacking in their grammar (1969). For example, *is,* the most frequently deleted form of the copula, is found in their emphatic sentences, such as *He is an expert.* In order to improve our understanding of language change, precise information such as that presented by Labov is essential. Thereupon the social significance of the variable in question, such as use or absence of *be,* must be determined. After the type of embedding in the language structure and the social structure is understood, the change may be discussed with authority.

Yet such information does not provide the answer to the question on the origin of language change. Weinreich, Labov and Herzog ascribe it to spread of a varying feature. For example, if in a subgroup of speakers a voiced form of intervocalic *-t-* were to spread, and if it were then widely adopted, we would acknowledge a language change. As further groups adopt such a variable, that is, intervocalic [d] rather than [t], it would shift in status to a constant. The change would be considered a completed linguistic change. And the origin of the change would have been in the varying dialects of a contemporary speech community.

Such an explanation for the "actuation" of linguistic changes applies to complex societies of today, which are made up of heterogeneous speakers like those in a large composite community such as New York City. But sound changes or other linguistic changes in the past may not have been actuated in this way. The much smaller communities of the past, like the Proto-Germanic speech community, undoubtedly were far more homogeneous than are today's large urban communities. They may better be compared with the Charmey community, studied by Gauchat and Hermann. Even in these compact communities, we may better understand language by acknowledging a variety of possible causes for linguistic change.

In addition to changes actuated by variation in language, we may assume that changes are brought about by the structure of a given language. Aberrant sound systems or syntactic systems may be modified, as we have noted in chapter 5. Yakov Malkiel ascribed some sound changes to morphological sets (Lehmann and Malkiel 1968).

Another possible cause for change may lie in human imagination. Speakers tire of expressions handed down from generation to generation, as the practice of poets indicates. In everyday speech the desire for change is especially apparent in terms of endearment or evaluation. The inventiveness of individual speakers must, however, be generally accepted, and their new patterns must be adopted to bring about a significant change in a linguistic community.

Van Helmont indeed added the word *gas* to his and other languages, yet his proposed *blas* "emanation from stars" was a failure. George Eastman introduced *Kodak* as a deliberate creation, after he noted the restrictions on the letter *k* in the English writing system; other merchants have followed him in introducing names such as *Kix* for breakfast cereals, *Krax* for crackers, *Klenso* for soaps, yet these have had an effect primarily on external features of the language. Similarly, when Murray Gell-Mann used the word *quark* in Joyce's *Finnegans Wake* for naming elementary particles, the effect was restricted to this one word. For major linguistic changes to be carried out, social factors as well as linguistic factors are involved.

Explanations for changes must draw on both factors. Fortunately, considerable attention is again being given to language change. The resultant study will lead to our understanding of the development of languages in the past, and of language as a phenomenon.

5

Interrelationships among Changes

Interrelationships in the Phonological Component

Changes in the phonological component differ considerably according to the kind of accent. Languages, like Japanese, with pitch rather than stress accent, tend to maintain all the elements of words, including final vowels. Languages, like the Germanic, on the other hand, have undergone many changes, as we have noted above. Some of these changes have resulted from the strong initial stress accent that was introduced into Proto-Germanic before our era. We can determine the Germanic changes by comparing cognates in Sanskrit, Greek and early Latin from the period when they had a pitch accent. Baltic and Slavic languages also maintained a pitch accent for a long period, as Lithuanian does today, and accordingly they maintain many final syllables. By noting forms in these languages we determine losses that the Germanic cognates have undergone. We find support for our conclusions in Finnish borrowings taken from Proto-Germanic or one of the early dialects, such as *kuningas,* cf. ON *konungr* "king." We also have evidence in forms recorded in the runic inscriptions, as in the form *stainaR,* cf. Goth. *stains,* and in forms cited by classical authors.

If we examine nouns, we find that the *-os* ending of the most frequent class of masculine nouns lost its vowel between

Proto-Germanic and the dialects. Goth. *Wolfs,* ON *ulfr,* OE *wulf* "wulf" correspond to Gk *lúkos,* Lat. *lupus,* Lith. *vĩlkas* and so on; PIE *-o-* was lost in the second syllable in Germanic. Moreover, Goth. *gasts* "guest" corresponds to Lat. *hostis;* here PIE *-i-* was lost. We place the loss relatively late in Proto-Germanic because the *-i-* was still written in the Gallehus inscription, *-gastiR;* similarly *-o-* is maintained in the forms we have in Greek and Roman writers, usually in names, like *Marco-manni.* As these examples may indicate, short vowels were lost in final syllables.

Long vowels, on the other hand, were reduced. The dative singular ending of the Indo-European *o*-stems is posited as *-ōi.* In the Germanic dialects this is reflected as *-a* in Gothic, *-e* in the other dialects, as in Goth. *wulfa,* ON *ulfe,* OE *wulfe.* The specific reductions of the various vowels are highly complex; details may be checked in handbooks. Our interest here is simply the observation that segments of the phonological system can bring about changes in other segments of the system. The most evident such process is the one we have exemplified: loss of final or medial syllables as a result of strong stress on the initial syllable.

Losses may vary with the difference in intensity of the stress. When we examine the Romance languages we find that Spanish has preserved final endings while French generally has not, for example Lat. *lupus* "wulf," Fr. *loup,* Spanish *lobo.* We ascribe the difference to difference in strength of the stress in each.

Not only final vowels of final syllables may be affected. In Irish, vowels of alternate syllables, such as the second in trisyllabic words, were lost, as in the borrowing OIr. *apstal,* cf. Lat. *apostolus.*

The results in any language depend on its phonological system. With adequate information on loss in general, we attempt to reconstruct such systems. We can reconstruct the earlier items only if we have related forms in other dialects of the family.

Interrelationships between the Phonological and the Morphological Components

When final syllables are lost, morphological paradigms are disrupted. Thus, the Pre-Germanic *o*-stem inflection was relatively parallel in forms in late Indo-European, with stem vowel varying between *o* and *e,* as in nom. *-os,* acc. *-om,* gen. *-eso.* Upon loss of the vowels of final syllables the three forms in Gothic were nom. *dags,* acc. *dag,* Gen. *dagis,* in OE *dæg, dæg, dæges.* Thus, by Old English times there was no morphological distinction between the nominative and the accusative.

The effects in the verb system were similar, as may be illustrated by comparing the present indicative endings of thematic verbs in Proto-Indo-European and Sanskrit with those in selected Germanic languages. Since the Sanskrit root *bandh-* "bind" is not inflected as is its cognate in Germanic, we give forms of the root *bhū-* here:

	PIE	*Sanskrit*	*Gothic*	*Old Norse*	*Old English*
1.	sg. *-ō	bhavāmi	binda	bind	binde
2.	sg. *-esi	bhávasi	bindis	bindr	bindes
3.	sg. *-eti	bhávati	bindip	bindr	bindeð
1.	pl. *-omos	bhávāmas	bindam	bindom	bindað
2.	pl. *-ete	bhávatha	bindip	bindeð	bindað
3.	pl. *-onti	bhávanti	bindand	binda	bindað

In Gothic the endings are still relatively distinctive, though the third singular and the second plural have fallen together. In Old Norse the second- and third-singular forms have fallen together; in Old English all three persons of the plural have fallen together. The losses of vowels have obscured differences, and forms that were distinctive, like the third plural in Old English, may be taken over in the other persons. Since the strong stress was maintained in the Germanic dialects, the losses also continued. Today all forms of the present are alike in Norwegian; in English a distinction is made only for the third singular.

Losses in the phonological system accordingly have considerable effect on the morphological system. The Sanskrit noun inflection consisted of eight cases. Of these, Lithuanian has maintained the most, lacking only the ablative; on the other hand, by suffxing postpositions it has added three. But most of the dialects have reduced the set of cases greatly. With those reductions other means have been introduced to represent nominal relationships, which is done chiefly through prepositions.

In a similar way, the losses in the verbal system required the use of pronouns to indicate the subject, unless a noun was the subject with third person verb forms. Phonological changes, then, ultimately affect the syntactic system as well as the morphological system.

It should be noted that such changes typically result from modifications in both systems. For example, the shift to SVO structure in the Indo-European languages fostered use of prepositions rather than case endings. Similarly, the requirement of subjects in SVO languages mandates use of first- and second-person pronouns in subject position, reducing the importance of verb endings. When, in addition, the endings were weakly articulated, the tended to be indistinct and were often lost, as in English and French.

Changes Resulting from Interrelationships between Morphological Subsystems

Before examining the effects of morphological losses on the syntactic system we may briefly note changes resulting from lack of symmetry in the morphological system. Indo-European nominal inflection provides examples.

In Proto-Indo-European, declensional endings were added either directly to noun bases or to bases followed by a stem vowel or affix. The so-called root nouns were followed directly by endings, which themselves might be modified, for example Skt *pā́t*, Gk *poús,* Lat. *pēs* "foot," from underlying **pods*. But by far the majority of nouns had affixes added to the root before the inflectional endings, for example PIE *-o-* as in Skt *jánas* "creature," Gk. *Génos* "family," cf. Lat. *genus* "kind"; other nouns added *-i-*, with or without a consonant, as *-ti-*, for example Skt *dā́tis* "gift," Gk *dósis,* Lat. *dōs* "gift"; still others added *-u-*, or *-tu-, -en-* or *-on-* and so on.

When the pitch accent was maintained, the syllables with these vowels were fully pronounced, and the endings as well as the vowels of the root were maintained. When, however, a stress accent was introduced, the vowels of the ending were either reduced, as in Lat. *genus,* cf. Eng. *kin,* or lost, as in Lat. *dōs* and Eng. *kin.* The separate stems then interacted with one another, leading to reduction of inflections through levelling.

The third declension in Latin provides many examples. Root nouns like *pēs*, Gen. *pedis* "foot" belong to it, but also *-ter* stems, like *pater, patris* "father," *-en* stems like *nōmen, nōminis* "name," *–s-* stems, like *flōs, flōris.* Parallelism between such diverse stems led to further reduction and conflation of the various forms.

We find the same conflation in verbs. In Sanskrit there were ten different present classes; in Latin there were only four. Today there is no distinction of present classes in Germanic languages. The different Indo-European classes interacted, and in the course of time the distinctive markers were lost, in part through loss of final syllables but also through loss of different markers by means of analogical levelling.

The loss of such inflectional classes requires the introduction of other devices to convey certain meanings. Thus, Sanskrit had a distinctive method of deriving causatives from simple verbs inherited from Proto-Indo-European **-eyo-*. In Germanic this class was being lost, partly through merger of the distinctive marker with markers indicating other values. In English the class has been reduced to a few forms, for example *set* beside *sit, lay* beside *lie.* Current English conveys causative force with the use of auxiliaries, such as *have,* as in *she had her car repaired, get* in *she got the work done* or *cause* as in *that caused the pump to break.* Similarly, the loss of the subjunctive and the optative required the use of auxiliaries to convey the former meaning. The modal auxiliaries were introduced for this purpose, for example *may, must, might, can, could,* etc.

Internal changes in the morphological system may in this way have a great effect on the syntactic system. It is instructive to compare the situation in Japanese, where morphological elements were not lost by phonological erosion. Roots of verbs end in consonants, for example *yom-u* "read," or in vowels, for example *tabe-ru* "eat." Causatives may be made from these in a long-established inflection based on forms of the verb *suru* "make," for example *yomaseru* "cause to read," *tabesaseru* "cause to eat"; these forms can be found in Japanese of a millennium ago. Other verbal inflections in Japanese are similarly conservative. With a pitch accent and a simple inflectional system, Japanese reduced its conjugation only in details in contrast with the massive reduction in the Indo-European languages. The syntax also has remained constant.

Effects of Morphological Reduction on The Syntactic Component

We have noted above that the loss of morphological markers leads to the introduction of syntactic replacements. Chief among these are function words: adpositions take the place of declensional endings;

auxiliaries take the place of conjugational endings or internal markers. We may illustrate the effects by citing several syntactic patterns.

A pattern common for nouns is that of comparison of inequality. For example, the sequence *She is bigger than you* compares unequals, whereas *She is as big as you* indicates similarity or equality. We have noted above that the comparison of inequality involves, besides the adjective, a standard and a pivot. The standard with pivot was inflected in the ablative case in early Sanskrit, as in the Vedic phrase: *ghṛtā́t svā́dīyaḥ* "ghee-from sweeter" = "sweeter than ghee." As the language was moving towards VO structure, the standard could be placed after the adjective, as in *pāpīyān áśvad gardabháḥ* "poorer horse-from donkey" = "a donkey is less useful than a horse." Even with the shift in location, the standard with its pivot was indicated by inflection.

In Greek the ablative was not maintained, but the genitive replaced it in some uses. As we have noted above, early Greek attests OV comparative constructions like the Vedic above; so does early Germanic, where the dative has replaced the ablative in this use. But as the dative lost its distinctiveness, a particle was introduced, in English of today *than*, in German *als*. Syntactic constructions involving inflections in this way introduce purely syntactic devices when morphological markers are eroded.

In much the same way auxiliaries and other devices, such as derivational constructions, have been introduced as verbal inflections came to be indistinct or not available for extension. The process had already begun in the early Indo-European dialects. Germanic verbs like Goth. *bindan* : *band,* Eng. *bind* : *bound* reflect the basic Indo-European contrast that today indicated tense difference. The phonological distinction, as we noted above, is based on sound changes in Pre-Indo-European and Proto-Indo-European that are referred to as ablaut. These did not fit the structure of derived verbs, such as Goth. *nasjan* "save," *salbon* "anoint," *haban* "have," *fullnan* "fill." Yet pattern congruity required a past-tense form parallel to that of the strong verbs.

A new form was introduced with a *-d-* marker, as illustrated in *nasida* "saved," *salboda* "anointed," *habaida* "had," *fullnoda* "filled." The source of the marker has been strenuously disputed; while its origin is not of primary concern here, in my view it is derivational, like the *-k-* of the Greek perfect, as in *lū́ō* "I loose": *léluka* "I have loosed," and like the -*v*- of the Latin perfect, as in *amō* "I love": *amāvī* "I have loved," as well as other such derivational affixes in the early dialects. This source for morphological categories, however, did not fit the structure of the languages as they became increasingly VO. For VO languages make heavy use of auxiliaries placed before the basic verb to indicate tense, mood and other verbal categories like the causative.

In the historically attested periods of the Indo-European languages such auxiliaries were introduced from a variety of sources. To indicate the perfect forms Germanic made use of the auxiliaries "have" and "be." The auxiliary "have" was used with transitive and many intransitive verbs; the auxiliary "be" was used with intransitive verbs indicating change of place, for example *he is come,* and change of condition, such as *he is become.* In German these rules have been maintained.

In English, on the other hand, *be* is also used to indicate the passive, as in the sentence *Since he is still swimming, the steaks were barbecued by his uncle.* As a result, a form like *he is gone* was ambiguous. Today *have* is the sole auxiliary for the English perfect.

The introduction of auxiliaries, among them *will* for the future, German *werden* for the future and the passive, *esse* "be" for the perfect passive in Latin and others in other languages, has been thoroughly studied. The handbooks, like Jespersen's grammar of English, provide details. These have been reformulated in accordance with the views of individual scholars. The facts are clear; students may wish to examine them in accordance with their own views of language structure.

Greater Fixing of Syntactic Order with Loss of Morphological Markers

When morphological markers or particles are ample in a language, the word order may be relatively free. Latin is notoriously presented as a language with variable word order. Virtually any sentence of Cicero or the classical authors might be cited as an example, for example one of Cicero's orations:

sī hoc optimum factū iūdicārem, ūnīus ūsūram hōrae
if this best for-doing I-had-thought of-one use of-hour
gladiātōrī istī ad vīvendum nōn dedissem

to-gladiator this for living not I-had-given
"If I had thought this the best thing to do, I would not have given this scoundrel the leisure of one hour for living."

Modifiers, like *ūnīus of hōrae* "of one hour" can be separated as here, because their inflections leave no ambiguity about interpretation. If, however, Cicero's sentence were repeated literally in English, it would be difficult to understand.

As inflections were lost in the Romance languages, their word order became relatively fixed. Similarly in the Germanic languages. We cannot place a noun between the modifier of a genitive and the genitive, as in the Latin above *ūnīus ūsōrem hōrae;* nor can we vary the order of sentence components as did Latin writers. English has a relatively fixed word order, with the subject first, followed by the verb, that in turn followed by the object. And if a sentence includes an indirect object, it must precede the direct object unless it is introduced by a preposition, for example *He brought her the lunch/ He brought the lunch to her.*

In general, when languages lose their morphological markers, syntactic patterns are fixed, so that by their position they indicate interrelationships in the sentence that languages with many inflections indicate morphologically.

Syntactic Tedencies and Rules, with Effects on Patterns of Syntax

In the course of syntactic studies various general rules have been determined. These not only regulate syntactic sequences; they may also lead to disruption of syntactic patterning in a given language.

Wackernagel's Law

One of the most commonly discussed rules states that enclitics tend to be placed after the first accented word in sentences. Formulated for Indo-European in an impressive article by the great syntactician, Jacob Wackernagel, the rule places weakly accented words like particles and pronouns in second position; the rule is often referred to as Wackernagel's law. For example, the *Odyssey* begins as follows with the weakly accented pronoun *moi* in second position:

ándra moi énnepe . . .
man me tell
"Tell me of a man . . ."

A number of enclitics may be placed in this position, as in the following clause from Thucydides 4.47:

> eí poú tís tina ídoi ekhthrón . . .
> if anywhere one one may-see enemy
> "If anyone ever saw an enemy anywhere . . . "

Here three clitics are placed after the initial conjunction; in such a sequence each but the last receives an accent, as in this clause.

Since verbs are unaccented in principal clauses in Proto-Indo-European, they are treated as clitics. Consequently, they frequently stand in second place. For example, line 33 of the *Odyssey* begins with the clause:

> eks hēméōn gár phasi kák émmenai
> from us ptc they-say evils are
> "(Humans) say that evil comes from us."

Here the verb *phasi* stands after the initial phrase *eks hēméōn* and a particle; *phasi* shares second position with *gár* rather than standing in final position. The first sentence of Caesar's account of the war in Gaul also has a form of "be" in second position: *Gallia est omnis* . . . "Gaul as a whole is . . ."

Since verbs provide one of the two constituents of the OV/VO nucleus of the clause, any modification of their sequence weakens the standard position. For this reason Wackernagel's law may have been one of the forces that led to the shift from OV order to VO order in the early dialects.

Negative Movement, Strengthening and Attraction

Further syntactic rules have to do with expression of the negative. Patterns of negation received a great deal of attention in the nineteenth century. A short monograph by Otto Jespersen of 1917 summarises the history of negative expression in English, Jespersen, however, did not relate its position to English typology.

In OV languages, negation is expressed by a suffix after the verb, as in Jap. *Tabenai* "does not eat." In VO languages, by contrast, a particle is placed before the verb. This was the situation in Old English, given by Jespersen as the first stage. In that stage negation was expressed by *ne,* as in the example given by Jespersen:

1. *ic ne secge* "I do not say."

The negative marker in this position is weakly stressed. By the process known as **negative strengthening** a noun or particle is added as support later in the sentence, as in more recent examples like *He was not impressed a bit*. In Old English the element *wiht* "thing" was used for this purpose; in this use it is similar to OF. *pas,* and to Lat. *oenum* = *unum* "one thing," which with Lat. *ne* gave rise to the Latin particle *non.*

By the further process known as **negative attraction** the negative marker was prefixed to *wiht,* giving *nawiht, noht, not.* The second stage of negative expression in English, then, may be illustrated by the Middle English sequence:

2. *ic ne seye not.*

The negation is now doubly expressed, producing redundancy that is not favoured in language. Moreover, the weakly stressed *ne* before the verb is open to loss. Accordingly, in a third stage the expression is:

3. *I say not.*

These three stages are paralleled by the development from Lat. *ne dicō* to OFr. *je ne dis pas,* later *je dis pas*. German has remained at this third stage, as in *ich gehe nicht* "I'm not going."

English, on the other hand, came to use auxiliaries extensively in the verb system, among them *do*. Moreover, in a VO language, negation is typically expressed before the principal verb. Accordingly, in a fourth stage the basic pattern is as follows:

4. *I do not say.*

This stage was followed by a fifth, representing current usage.

5 *I don't say.*

English has a large stock of such negative auxiliaries, *aren't, isn't, wasn't, can't, couldn't* etc.; the English linguist John Rupert Firth suggested regarding them as making up a distinct paradigm. However they are treated in grammars, the history of negative expression in English illustrates how syntactic rules bring about changes in the language.

Afterthoughts

A tendency of OV languages places certain elements after the final verb. Delbrück referred to such elements as a *Schleppe* ("train—as of a dress"); a modern term is *afterthought*. In a simple example, the subject is added after the verb, for example Vedic *sá havāca gā́rgyaḥ* "he now said . . . Gargyas" = "Garyas then said."

The afterthough may be prompted by the following sentence, as a discourse effect, as in Delbrück's example: *té 'anyam evá pratiprá jighur áñgirasó' cha* "they another now thither sent . . . to the Angirasas" = "they sent another one . . . to the Angirasas."

If the construction is commonly used, it may lead to a shift from OV structure to VO. Like enclisis of verbs, the use of afterthoughts may have contributed to the shift towards VO order in the early Indo-European dialects.

Influence of Basic Clause Structure on other Syntactic Patterns

Tell now we have observed that languages tend to have characteristic VO or OV patterns, as of adpositions, relative clauses and so on. Few documented instances of changing word order have been carefully investigated, and consequently the evidence for the effects of changing clause order is tentative. Two examples may be cited.

The first example deals with constructions in New High German. At the time of humanism in the fifteenth century and later, writers introduced rules for word order that they viewed as based on that of Latin. The prime targets were dependent clauses; in humanistic style they were to conclude with the finite verb. Such a verbal position was not characteristic of medieval German; but it came to be followed carefully in the written language, and is the rule today.

When we examine the subsequent written language, we find two constructions arising. One is the preposed adjectival or participial modifier of nouns, notorious in scientific German, as in the following sentence of Hermann Hirt:

> die ursprünglich zugrunde liegende Bildung ist nicht mehr
> the originally at-basis lying formation is no longer
> erkennbar
> recognisable

"The formation that originally was underlying is no longer recognisable."

As the translation indicates, the modifier construction is comparable to a relative clause. German, however, as a VO language places relative clauses after their heads. If we analyse the modifier construction rigorously, we find that it is comparable to the relative construction in such OV languages as Turkish. Since its gradual development during the centuries after OV order was introduced in German dependent clauses can be traced in written texts, we may suggest that order led to the introduction of the OV nominal modifier construction in the written language.

The texts document another OV construction, the use of postpositions. These also arose gradually, such as *entgegen* "opposed to," *entlang* "along," *gegenüber* "opposite," *nach* "after," and so on. Used often, though not exclusively, in the written language, these postpositions can be dated in the large German dictionaries; the postposition *entlang,* for example, is first attested as a postposition in 1741. We may suggest that the postposed position was prompted by the OV order of dependent clauses. English cognates, like *along,* have not been moved in this way.

It would be useful if the hypothesis that change in basic verb order can result in change of parallel constructions would be examined in many further languages.

One such shift has been explained in this way for Sinhalese. Like other Indo-Aryan languages of the south of India, Sinhalese has been strongly influenced towards OV word order by the neighbouring Dravidian languages. When we examine Sanskrit, we find that, like the other Indo-European languages, it is shifting from OV to VO word order. We may assume that the modern Indo-Aryan languages would have VO order if they had not been influenced by many speakers of OV languages in the subcontinent. Middle Sinhalese, for example, was strongly VO in order.

The construction of interest in Modern Sinhalese is found in the additive numerals. These, typically "eleven" to "nineteen" are arranged like comparative constructions, with the teen as standard, for example Eng. *seventeen* versus Turkish *onyedi* "ten + seven" = "seventeen." When we examine the Sinhalese teens we find evidence that in Middle Sinhalese they observed VO word order, but then shifted to OV order, as in *daha-hatə* "ten + seven" = "seventeen," presumably due to the strong effect of the OV syntax of Tamil.

These examples may indicate that syntactic patterning and processes may bring about changes within the syntactic component. Syntactic structure is then parallel to phonological and to morphological structure in tending towards pattern congruity, with aberrant constructions modified in accordance with the basic structure.

Syntactic Effects on Derivational Constructions

Syntactic patterning affects derivational constructions, notably compounds. It has also long been noted that OV languages favour suffixes over affixes. We will discuss only compounding rules so affected.

Compounds may be regarded as abbreviated clauses. As such, they might be expected to reflect the order of elements in clauses. Yet, once fixed, they tend to be conservative. In English, for example, the bulk of compounds follow modifier + noun patterning, as in *greenpeace, doghouse* etc. While this is the OV pattern, and might not be expected to be so prominent in a VO language, it may owe some of its predominance to the typical adjective-noun sequence as well as to conservatism in language.

In early Greek and Sanskrit, two different types of compounds were most prominent. Synthetic compounds consist of roots in object-verb order, as in Skt *go-sā́* "acquiring cattle." Possessive compounds consist of a modifier followed by a head, as in Skt *gó-magha* "having an abundance of cattle"; cf. *Bluebeard* "one who possesses a blue beard" beside *bluebird.*

The compounds are exhaustively described by the Sanskrit grammarians, and subsequently by modern grammarians though without explanations for them except for Jacobi's interpetation of synthetics as reduced relative clauses. We explain both synthetics and possessives as abbreviations of clauses. The synthetics are comparable in meaning to relative clauses. Examples with reflexes of PIE *bher-* "bear, bring" are: Skt *vṛṣabhā́rn* "providing virility," Gk *boulēphóros* "providing counsel," Lat. *fructifer* "bearing fruit." As the Sanskrit and Greek forms illustrate, synthetics have the accent on the second component. In this way they correspond to dependent clauses of Proto-Indo-European, which have the verbal element accented.

The possessive compounds are abbreviations of the Pre-Indo-European clause type used for "have"-constructions. That stage of the language expressed possession by means of a dative construction comparable to Lat. *mihi est* . . . . At an earlier stage of the language, the form of "be" would not have been essential. Assuming "have" -clauses of this stage as the pattern for possessive compounds, we propose that in the abbreviated form the pronoun was omitted. Of the numerous possessive compounds in the early dialects we may cite from Sanskrit: *bṛhádratha* "having great chariots," *agnítejas* "having the brightness of fire," *jīvápuťra* "having living sons." It may be noted that these have the accent on the first component as if they were independent clauses, with meanings like "he has great chariots."

In this way we account for the early compounds in the Indo-European dialects. As the languages came to be VO in structure, the basis for the patterning was lost. In English the *Bluebeard* type of compound survives for pejorative use, for example *redneck* "uneducated rustic," etc. When new compounds are created, like *greenpeace,* the modifier + noun sequence is observed.

These examples may illustrate that both in early Indo-European and in Modern English the prevailing types of compounds reflect a predominant syntactic pattern when the compound structure came to be fixed. In this way syntactic structure may affect morphological patterns as well as other syntactic constructions.

Changes that may Result from Discourse Patterning

In recent years linguists have concerned themselves at some length with discourse, that is, complete accounts rather than sentences, whether conversations, paragraphs or longer written texts. Among reasons for the concern is the finding that some languages structure sentences differently in paragraphs. The Fore language of New Guinea has the final verb only at the end of a paragraph, using medial verbs to end sentences within the paragraph (Longacre, 1983). The western languages include no such distinction, but they have various devices like anaphoric constructions, or repeated words like *concerned* and *concern* in the first two sentences above, which bind sentences together within paragraphs. When discourse is studied, it is regarded as a higher level than that of syntax.

Western scholars have long dealt with patterning in larger structures under the label stylistics. The standard grammars of Greek by Schwyzer (1939-53) and of Latin by Leumann, Hofmann and Szantyr (1963-79) include extensive treatments of stylistics. Discourse specialists have not yet correlated their efforts with the massive work in stylistics. Nor have they studied effects of discourse structure on syntactic change. Accordingly, we can only provide examples that may suggest how discourse rules may contribute to change of syntax.

We may use the first paragraph of Caesar's report on the Gallic War as illustration. Caesar is acknowledged to be an excellent stylist; like contemporaries in the period of Classical Latin, he went to great pains to provide an elegant report. It begins:

Gallia est omnis divisa in partes tres, quarum unam incolunt Belgae,
Gaul is entire divided into parts three of which one inhabit Belgae
aliam Aquitani, tertiam qui ipsorum lingua Celtae, nostra Galli
another Aquitani third who of-their tongue Celts in ours Galli
appellantur. Hi omnes lingua, institutis, legibusinter se differunt.
are-called. These all in-tongue institutions laws among self differ
Horum omnium fortissimi sunt Belgae, . . . proximi sunt Germanis . . . .
of-them of-all bravest are Belgae next are Germans

> "Gaul as a whole is divided into three parts, one of which is inhabited by the Belgae, another by the Aquitani, a third by those who in their own language are called Celts, in ours Gauls. All of them differ among themselves in language, institutions, laws. Of all of them the bravest are the Belgae, . . . they are next to the Germans . . . ."

A thorough analysis of the discourse markers would be lengthy, and should be based on the entire passage. Since we are concerned with the effect of discourse on possible syntactic change we may confine ourselves to observing the position of *est* in the first sentence, of *sunt* in the third. As we have noted above, Latin has chiefly OV order in sentences, as in the second here. But these verbs are in second position. That position in the first sentence is all the more remarkable because the form *divisa est* is equivalent to the perfect passive. Apparently, the tendency to place unaccented verbs in second position outweighed any other with reference to its position. Caesar clearly wanted to end the first clause with the phrase *in partes tres* because of the three following qualifiers. As a result, that clause is comparable to the English expression.

With such forces in the language, it is almost inevitable that the OV order would have been modified, as it was in the various areas that adopted Latin. Since we have noted that languages in general change to VO order when they are learned by many non-native speakers, the change from OV order in Latin to VO in late Latin and the dialects may be attributable to that observation. Yet Caesar's rhetorical device of placing the subject *Belgae* after *incolunt* provides support for the proposal that discourse patterning may have been a contributing reason for syntactic change. Interrelationships between the levels of discourse and syntax may in this way lead to changes much as do those between syntax and morphology and still other levels.

6

Linguistic and Cultural Change

Early Attention to Language and Culture

From the beginnings of historical linguistic study scholars concerned themselves with culture as well as with language. Jones's celebrated paragraph (cf. Lehmann, ed., 1967) makes up a very small part of his third anniversary discourse, which is devoted to the culture of the Indians. Schlegel's monograph of 1808 indicates by its title that it deals with culture and the wisdom it may convey as well as with the language. And Bopp's initial work of 1816 gives almost as many pages to his translation of Sanskrit literary works as to the verb system. Many other publications on the two areas appeared in the early part of the century. They include accurate data accompanied errors, so that today they have been superseded. Yet they inform us of the established aim of dealing with the early languages in conjunction with the cultures of their speakers.

To illustrate the early attempts we may recall two of the publications. Friedrich Schlegel's older brother, August, wrote on the names of animals and metals. He recognised accurately that Skt *áyas,* Lat. *aes* and Germ. *Eisen* "iron" are cognates. But he also related Lat. *ursus* "bear" with OHG *ors* "horse." As these examples may illustrate, much remained to be done in determining the actual interrelationships, as well as to avoid error. Celtic was scarcely known at the time, so that the source of *Eisen* as a borrowing from Celtic remained for future scholars to determine. And it soon became clear that the word "horse" is not cognate with the Latin word for "bear."

The publication that raised study of language and culture to a higher level of accuracy is Adalbert Kuhn's essay of 1845 "On the history of the Indo-Germanic peoples in the most ancient times." While cautions in its procedures, the essay proposes the aim of determining the conditions of these peoples at the time before their dispersal, that is, of determining the culture of the Indo-Europeans. From his analysis if kinship terms and words like Skt *rājan,* Lat. *rex* "king," Kuhn concluded that the Indo-Europeans had already progressed beyond a patriarchal society. The terms for domesticated animals led him to propose that the Indo-Europeans already possessed the same animals as those of his day; and words for "to plough," Gk *aróō,* Lat. *arāre* indicated to him that they practised agriculture. They were therefore "a settled people," as terms for habitations substantiate. Kuhn's conclusions, which are remarkably similar to those held today, if not as extensive, indicate that greater control of the early languages, as assembled by Pott and others, brought about improved understanding for the early culture.

In their efforts to determine the culture of the Indo-European peoples, scholars generally maintained the view that Asia was the original home. The phrase *ex oriente lux* was irresistible; it is applied once again by Gamkrelidze and Ivanov (1984), not to the approval of all their critics. Indian literature and philosophy were very impressive. The time of the national archaeologists had not yet come. The general assumptions concerning the Indo-Europeans had them moving from a homeland in India to their later sites in Europe and elsewhere. Whatever the proposals for the Indo-Europeans, procedures were being worked out to determine the origins and the development of early peoples.

Yet similar studies of other language families and their speakers did not appear until later. In 1875 Kremer proposed central Asia as homeland for the Semitic peoples, adding that their oldest centre of civilisation was in Mesopotamia. Using techniques similar to those applied by Pott and Kuhn, he credited the Semites with use of the camel and the donkey in their expansion. Moreover, he assumed that when they were established in their centre, they had goats and sheep, and knew barley, beans, lentils, onions and wheat. In the same year Ahlqvist published his views on the Finnish peoples. He depicted them as making great use of hunting and fishing, though they also possessed horses and cows; but they did not practise agriculture. And unlike the Indo-Europeans, they had no hereditary chiefs and no state organisation.

As in linguistic study, the study of cultural conditions of language families other than the Indo-European did not attract so early nor so wide a group of specialists. Yet when it did, the aims were similar in attempting to determine the culture as well as the language of the early speakers. None the less, the attention to the Indo-Europeans remained much greater than that to speakers of other early languages; as a result the information that has been proposed about their culture is also much fuller. Today Afro-Asiatic specialists would be much more likely to locate the homeland of the family in the Sahara than in central Asia. But they have not provided the extensive handbooks on the early period of the family that we find for the Indo-European family of speakers. As a result, we will deal largely with the procedures taken and methods applied to determine their culture and their homeland.

Words and Things—*Wörter und Sachen*

Interest in the early culture, as well as methods for determining it, were greatly advanced by Jacob Grimm (1848). As in the title of his German grammar, the adjective corresponds to Germanic of today, so that his *History* encompasses the entire subgroup. His methods were announced in a celebrated phrase of the preface, amplified by a metaphor: " I have never been satisfied by words [*Wörter*] without proceeding to things [*Sachen*]. My aim has been not only to build houses, but also to live in them"(1848).

On the basis of his extensive concern with cultural areas, such as law, Grimm presents an account of the Germanic peoples based on their texts, their traditions, and on the evidence in their language. The chapter titles are quite unlike any we would find in a history of language today: 1 "Age (era) and language," 2 "Shepherds and farmers," 3 "Cattle," 4 "Hawking," 5 "Farming," 6 "Feasts and months," 7 "Faith, law, customs." Glancing through the thousand and more pages one is almost surprised to find chapters on linguistic matters like the vowels or the consonants.

Grimm's standing at the close of his career would have brought great attention to any work of his. His *History* was very influential; it is still highly readable and informative on the basis of his extensive control of early texts. The approach attracted numerous scholars. Their journal, *Wörter und Sachen*, was one of the important avenues of publication until its end at the beginning of the Second World War. In its pages languages was not investigated for its own sake but rather for the information it provides on its speakers.

The Beginnings of Specialisation; Concentration on Language

By the middle of the nineteenth century so much information was available and so many problems had to be solved that younger scholars could not deal with as broad a scope as that controlled by Grimm. Moreover, notable advances were being made in solving linguistic problems, so that attention was drawn to the study of the language. While Grim threw up his hands at the prospect of dealing with ablaut in 1822, phonologists were beginning to understand the relationships among the Indo-European vowels. In addition, the first group of exceptions to Grimm's law had been solved, and the second as well by Rudolph von Raumer in 1837, but in brief note that lacked impact. None the less the techniques were being developed that led to Grassmann's important essay of 1862 and Verner's of 1875. (For translations of the cited articles von Raumer, Grassmann and Verner see Lehmann, ed., 1967.) Pure linguistic study accordingly was highly attractive.

On the other hand, archaeology was virtually nonexistent. Grimm despaired about getting information from the "old graves." The secure sources were texts and language. Use of languages of determining culture came to have its own designation: **linguistic palaeontology**. Since the texts were obviously designed for literary rather than for scientific purposes, more information might be determined about the culture of Indo-Europeans from words in the Vedas and the Homeric poems than from their fanciful story, much of it concerned with religion rather than with the Indo-European individual. The use of languages to determine cultural conditions increased the growing concentration on it.

The leading Indo-Europeanist in the middle of the nineteenth century, August Schleicher (1821-68), published a purely linguistic work four years after Grimm's *History* appeared. That work, a morphology of Old Church Slavonic, was followed by a grammar of Lithuanian (1856-7), based chiefly on fieldwork, not literary texts. And in 1861 he published his *Compendium.* The difference between his grammar and Grimm's is apparent from Schleicher's opening sentences (trans. By W.P. Lehmann):

> Grammar forms one part of the science of language; this science is itself a part of the natural history of human beings. Its method is in substance that of natural science generally; it consists in accurate investigation of our object and in conclusions founded upon that investigation .... By grammar we mean the scientific comprehension and explanation of the sounds, the forms, the function of words and their parts, and the constructions of sentences.

There is no mention of culture nor of the speaker. Language is to be treated clinically, in line with procedures that had been developed by the natural sciences. While the languages had been spread by the wanderings of its speakers, those wandering and the peoples were left to the attention of others.

At an early stage, we have sketched a selection of linguistic problems that occupied linguists in the second half of the century. Many more problems might have been cited. The history of each of the languages and each of the subgroups had to be clarified. A glance at the journals of the time provides information on the many attempts at solutions as well as the advances. The increasing publication made it difficult for specialists to deal with the entire family, let alone culture as well as language; instead, individual scholars devoted themselves chiefly to one branch, like Germanic, or to one period, like Classical Latin or to Proto-Indo-European. Brugmann in the manifesto could warn that the speaker was being neglected in favour of the language. Attracted by linguistic problems, linguists disregarded the warning.

Attention to Culture

Much as many of the linguists concentrated on the study of languages, others devoted themselves to study of the early cultures. The most influential of these was Max Müller, whose lectures at Oxford University established him as one of the pre-eminent popularisers of language and culture. Opinions on the culture of the Indo-Europeans were still disputed, for example as to whether they knew iron. Regardless of the uncertainties, Müller presented his views so charmingly that he attracted a large audience. To take one example, he assumed that the word for "daughter" was based on the root **dheugh* "extract, milk." The daughter was therefore the milkmaid in the "poetical and pastoral life of the early Aryans . . . . It discloses a kind of delicacy and humour even in the rudest state of society, if we imagine a father calling his daughter his little milkmaid" (1891). Especially in Germany, novels on early history were very popular.

A comprehensive presentation of the achievements in determining the early culture was given by Otto Schrader (1883, 1890). Using elegant argumentation, Schrader based his conclusions about Indo-European culture on "the three sisters, linguistic research, prehistoric research, and history" (*ibid.*). He indicates the shortcomings of each, and assigns to linguistics the role of taking over when "historical evidence or ambiguous myths and sagas" no longer give "clues." Archaeological palaeontology . . . takes us a step further, and then only where it is possible, with some probability, to assign the monuments recovered by archaeology to a definite people" (*ibid.*). That is to say, Schrader recognised the same problems in dealing with archaeological data that subsequent archaeologists characterise by statements like "stones do not speak" or "pots do not equal people." He also provides a full picture of the early culture, devoting a great deal of space to the use of metals before describing the "primeval period." In view of Schrader's summary of nineteenth-century findings, we may note the twelve topics in his description of the society and culture of the Indo-Europeans. They are: the animal kingdom, cattle, plant-world, agriculture, computation of time, food and drink, clothing, dwellings, traffic and trade, family and state, religion, the original home.

Schrader places the home in the south Russian steppe, about half-way up the Volga. As we note below, this is approximately the site proposed by Gimbutas and also by Childe. Schrader's argumentation is comparable to that we use. The Indo-Europeans were acquainted with the horse, but not with the camel and ass. The proposed location provides the simplest explanation of the early contacts with the Finns. In addition, Schrader makes use of the Finnic Mordwin name for the

Volga, *Rau,* which he relates to the Indo-European root **sreu* " flow," by argumentation that we find less compelling. But, given the restriction to information from the language and texts, it may be clear that his work on Indo-European culture provides a definitive statement on the achievements of nineteenth-century scholars, much like that of Brugmann on the early languages and the proto-language. Brugmann wrote approvingly of Schrader's work.

Its recognised shortcoming consisted in the lack of archaeological support. The last edition of the book appeared at a time when archaeology was beginning to use strict methods. Flinders Petrie introduced the practice of determining strata. Yet for some time the major contributions of archaeology to historical linguistics came from discoveries of materials, the Hittite texts in Turkey, the Tocharian manuscripts in Chinese Turkestan, the Linear B texts in Crete, These contributions have continued. But today the greatest interest comes from precise identification of artifacts and the time of their deposit.

Works on the early culture continued to be published, for example by Hirt. These came to be affected increasingly by nationalism and worse, by racism. Many scholars in Germany now proposed a homeland in northern or in central Europe. A crucial argument for them was provided by the Indo-European etymon of *lox* and the presence of salmon in its rivers. They also relied heavily on the name *beech,* and its habitat only west of a line extending approximately from Danzig to the Crimea. Both arguments ruled out Asia, and also southern Russia, as home. Subsequently, both arguments were nullified; the presence elsewhere of salmon in the third millennium was established, and linguistic evidence for the beech in the eastern dialects was disproved, so that the word may have originated in the western subgroup rather than in the proto-language. But many scholars still place the homeland in areas of Europe.

Articles with racist bias mar an elaborate publication on the state of the art of Indo-European studies that commemorated Hirt's seventieth birthday (Arntz, 1936). The 436 pages of the first volume deal with the results of cultural history and anthropology, the 602 pages of the second with the results of linguistics. Many of the essays are still pertinent, especially in the second volume; but we are taken aback by others with titles like "Origin of the Nordic race and the Indo-European question." The disruption of the Second World War was equally devastating to the study of Indo-European culture. The continuity extending from Kuhn to Hirt was broken. It has taken some time for resumption of concentrated work, and that is to be credited to archaeologists.

Two Further Contributions on Indo-European Culture

While publications on the culture of the Indo-Europeans after the appearance of Schrader's work dealt primarily with details, two further works provided notable advances. One was Franz Specht's book of 1944, reprinted in 1947 to make up for the loss of the first printing. In its major contribution Specht demonstrated the importance of determining chronological strata in the lexicon. That had long been achieved in phonology and grammar. The vowel changes leading to the ablaut relationships clearly took place at various times. And after the discovery of laryngeals, it was also clear that these were being lost in certain environments while the ablaut changes were taking place. Consonant changes also were viewed by strata, though chiefly in the dialects, as by the first Germanic shift and the second, or Old High German, consonant shift.

Specht made use of conclusions that had been reached regarding morphological sets. It was generally held that root noun inflection represented an earlier stage than did the thematic *o* -stems and *ā*-stems. Accepting that finding, Specht pointed out that many of the words for nature and everyday culture were inflected as root nouns. A notable group that is inflected thematically has to do with transportation. The nouns for the wagon and its parts, such as the wheel, Gk *kúklos,* and for the horse, Gk *hípps,* are *o*-stems. On the basis of their formation, Specht proposed that transportation by means of wagons and horses was introduced late in the Indo-European community, shortly before the time of dispersion.

In this way Specht made use of the technique of identifying strata in the proto-language, much as Flinders Petrie had in archaeology. Oddly, archaeologists have failed to use Specht's contributions. Linguists have expanded them, proposing successive strata with data co-ordinated from phonology, morphology and syntax as well as the lexicon.

More recently the eminent Indo-Europeanist, Emile Benveniste, published an impressive work on selected social and cultural topics,

Indo-European Language and Society (1973). Its omissions may be almost as significant as the topics discussed; for, by disregarding the data on everyday life, Benveniste virtually suggests that Schrader's are valid. He concentrates on six topics: economy, the vocabulary of kinship, social status, royalty and its privileges, law, religion, In spite of archaeological advances that provided information on daily life, which was lacking to Schrader, Benveniste confines his study to social practices. As we have noted above, Szemerényi subsequently published a monograph on the Indo-European kinship terms. In directing their attention to specific social practices, Benveniste and Szemerényi have amplified our understanding of Indo-European culture. But the restricted scope of their efforts may also illustrate the expanding body of knowledge about the proto-language and its speakers.

The Kurgan Hypothesis

Marija Gimbutas begins a paper given in 1966 and published in 1970 with the bold statement:

> Post-World War II developments in archaeology in general and the breath-taking pace of excavations in the Soviet Union and the satellite countries have changed many of the old views on "die indogermanische Urheimat." Chronological and geographical gaps gradually are being filled and archaeologists can present some facts with some certainty. The existence of Indo-European homelands advocated by linguists for more than 100 years is no longer an abstraction; results achieved by archaeological research make it possible to visualise the homelands, at a certain time and place, as a historical reality.

Ten years earlier Gimutas had introduced the term **kurgan** ("round mound") as a designation for a culture with various earlier names, among them the Russian Sredniy Stog II and Yamma, as well as Corded, Battle-Axe, Ochre-Grave and so on. Taking the practice of burial under barrows as a significant marker of Indo-European culture, she located their homeland in southern Russia and then identified their extension by numerous barrows found throughout Europe. The practice of burying heroes under mounds is indeed characteristic of Indo-European culture as demonstrated by the final book of the *Iliad* and the conclusion of the *Beowulf*. And archaeological finds, such as the horse bones dated 4400 BC at Dereivka, an archaeological site on the Dnieper, agree well with assumptions about the Indo-Europeans and their culture that had been determined on the basis of linguistic evidence. Further support was given by the "remains of two- and four-wheeled wooden vehicles with solid wheels of oak and their models in clay [that] have been found in the lower Dnieper and Volga region"(*ibid.*). The kurgan culture, as presented by Gimbutas (1970), and by others in numerous subsequent publications, agrees with the conclusions of Schrader and the other scholars who based their conclusions on the texts and inferences from the lexicon. Everything seemed to fall in place.

In her article of 1970 Gimbutas speaks of infiltration by kurgan elements and waves of expansion (*ibid.*). But in subsequent years the kurgan hypothesis came to be associated with spread by migrations similar to those of the Germanic peoples from the first century BC. Moreover, the kurgan peoples came to be regarded as warriors who disrupted the peaceful agricultural peoples living in Europe. The contrast was intensified by the proposal that these agricultural peoples had kindly matrilineal rulers, in contrast with the warlike patriarchal control of the Indo-Europeans.

Whoever proposed these views, they were unrealistic for the period concerned; the sparse population of the time would not have provided large groups comparable to those of the Cimbri and Teutons who invaded southern France around 110 BC. The kurgan hypothesis aroused strong opposition. None the less, it attracted devoted followers, especially in the United States, who published vigorously in its support. Decisive archaeological data in its favour were not assembled. While it remained the hypothesis to disprove, it did not establish itself generally.

Extension of Languages in Conjunction with Economic Advances

While Gimbutas assembled archaeological data that agreed with conclusions determined by linguists, in 1987 the archaeologist Colin Renfrew proposed a solution to " the puzzle of Indo-European origins" purely on archaeological grounds. He associated the spread of the Indo-Europeans and their languages with that of agriculture.

Archaeologists had determind that domesticated plants and animals had been introduced to Europe from Anatolia around 6000 BC. Correlating the two innovations, Renfrew identified the carriers of the new agricultural procedures with speakers of the Indo-European languages.

Renfrew's proposal received a great deal of publicity and elicited vigorous comment. It seemed very attractive to have economic advances associated with the spread of new speakers. And diffusion was much more likely around 6000 BC than even small-scale migrations. But the proposal lacked linguistic and cultural bases.

There is no evidence for Indo-European languages in Anatolia until the entry of the Hittites in the last part of the third millennium. And the iconography of central Anatolia gives evidence for a totally different type of religion and other cultural practices from that of the Indo-Europeans. The Indo-Europeans recognised a sungod, whose name is reflected in Zeus and Jupiter, accompanied by few other divines, notably two horsemen, reflected as Castor and Pollux. There were no goddesses, even in Vedic times, with the minor exception of dawn. By contrast, the Mediterranean world recognised many goddesses, as is clear from those added to the Greek and Latin pantheons. Accordingly, the proposed basis for solving the puzzle came to be seen as weak.

Many further counterarguments have been advanced to Renfrew's hypothesis, such as the introduction of new terms for domesticated plants in the northern European languages. If Indo-European speakers had introduced the plants, they would have had names for them. But that argumentation is outside our basic concern. What interests us here is the methodology by which the "puzzle" may be solved.

Renfrew's book has shown definitively that economic developments may have nothing to do with the spread of languages. Like linguistics, archaeology must determine its methods through examination of comparable phenomena. Archaeologists studying the spread of corn in North America have found that it was brought out of Mexico to the north without spread of languages (Smith, 1989). By making such prominent use of a failed comparison between economic and linguistic change, Renfrew has made clear that we will be able to determine the early location of the Indo-European peoples only through ever finer analysis of linguistic and textual as well as archaeological data.

Increase in Precision of Archaeological as well as Linguistic Data

While Renfrew's book was being reviwed, David W. Anthony was carrying on precise research that reaffirmed the homeland in southern Russia while illustrating the methods that must now be used to draw conclusions from archaeological as well as linguistic data. Through painstaking analysis of horses' teeth, Anthony determined how one might detect the wear caused by rope bridles. After such determination he analysed large quantities of horses' teeth from various sites. Using elaborated techniques currently available, he found the earliest evidence in teeth excavated at Dereivka and dated around 4000 BC. There is, of course, no direct correlation between that finding and the Indo-Europeans or their language. But we have long known that Indo-Europeans were among the earliest to ride horses. It is, then, a simple matter to relate the horse buried at Dereivka with the homeland of the Indo-Europeans.

The evidence fits with Specht's based on his analysis of the inflectional system. Moreover, it is in accord with the proposals of Gimbutas on the Sredniy Stog culture. Linguists and prehistorians will no doubt continue to examine the evidence. Whatever the outcome, it is clear that any further statements must be based on precise linguistic analysis, like that of Specht, and equally precise archaeological analysis, like that of Anthony.

A similarly minute topic has been elegantly treated by Watkins (1990). Taking a phrase from Varro, *tarentum Accas,* Watkins subjects it and its cognates to meticulous analysis. In addition, the examines associated cultural practices, the *ludi Saeculares,* secular games preformed at Rome once a century. On the basis of meanings of the root *$terh_2$-"overcome" in Hittite and *tīrat-* "crossing" in the *Rigveda,* he concludes that "the Roman ritual for the dead at the Tarentum, the 'crossing place,' is at the same time a ritual to assure the long life and orderly succession of the generations; it is a reaffirmation of the crossing of the *saecula* of a hundred years" (1990). In the way he reconstructs Indo-European ritual, largely from a passage that had to be resorted to provide its meaning.

These illustrations may indicate procedures that are now necessary to make further advances in correlating data provided from archaeological finds and linguistic analysis. The advances are built on information that has been assembled since the days of Bopp and Grimm. As in other scientific fields, the methodology is meticulous. The two illustrations may also suggest that careful work based on thorough knowledge of the previous contributions will result in additional understanding of the Indo-European family of speakers as well as those of other languages.

Linguistic Inferences in Prehistoric Periods

Although our earliest texts date from around 3000 BC, archaeological finds give us evidence about much earlier cultures. Relating those finds to residues in the languages provides important opportunities for fuller understanding of the speakers of the proto-languages in their background. Conclusions may be based on tenuous evidence. Yet new procedures in applying technologies in the sciences, such as molecular biology and genetics, make available data were totally unavailable to our predecessors. Further, as Watkins has demonstrated, residual data in the texts may be interpreted to illuminate those data. We may note briefly two examples, the first based chiefly on archaeological finds.

In an elegant book, Barber (1991) treats "the development of cloth in the neolithic and bronze ages," with special reference to the Aegean and deals with language. The remainder presents in great detail the evidence for producing cloth from 20,000 BC. By limiting its treatment to such a restricted set clarifies terms or the technology that had previously been obscure or misinterpreted. Distinct subsets within the set are recognised, one from the proto-language; others are borrowings, probably from two different languages. One of these is located in the Balkans, suggesting that the Greeks came to the Hellenic peninsula by that route, in contrast with Renfrew's notion of spread from Asia Minor.

Moreover, for many of the items there are two terms, one derived from the proto-language, the other borrowed. Such arrays of synonyms leave little doubt that the Greeks adopted the technology, as well as technical terms, from indigenous speakers.

The concentrated attention to the set of words enables Barber to correct previous lexicographers, who glossed *ēlakátē* as "distaff" rather than "spindle," as Barber has determined it to be. In this way she has improved our understanding if the Greek as well as the Indo-European lexicon.

A prime interest here is an inference made by Barber in an appendix to the first chapter, about the borrowing Lat. *cannabis,* Gk *kánnabis,* Eng. *hemp.* It has long been assumed that the word was borrowed into these languages, probably from Thracian. Further, since the word underwent the Germanic consonant shift [k > h, b > p], the borrowing is placed early in the first millennium BC. Pointing out that the Indo-Europeans "knew and were using hemp since 5000 BC," Barber suggests that the word was taken over because it referred to a narcotic-bearing hemp, adding that there is evidence for such use of narcotics from this time. The inference is of great interest, for it assumes that "enough people were travelling *back and forth* between Iran [where (the THC-bearing hemp) grew] and eastern Europe that they could spread a *habit" (ibid.*). We leave further support for the hypothesis to specialists. Our prime interest here has to do with an inference based on extensive study of a restricted sphere and on an assumption about a change in culture of the speakers. Before Barber's hypothesis, the terms for "hemp" were cited largely to date the time of the Germanic consonant shift.

In connection with a second such hypothesis we recall Schmandt-Besserat's determination of the origins of writing. Moreover, we note again that the tokens referred to quantities of specific substances, rather than to abstract numerals as in our system today. That is to say, the tokens were comparable to number systems with mandatory classifiers, like those in languages of southeast Asia, including Chinese, and of Central America. In those languages any listing of quantities must be accompanied by a classifier, as in our expression "a hundred head of cattle." While the pre-Sumerian languages using the system of tokens are unknown, we may assume that they had number systems like those with classifiers. As testimony for that inference we may note that the Sumerian word for "one," *as,* means 'man," and that for "two," *min,* means "woman"; at this point such references stop, for *eš* "three" means "many," and *geš* "the great unit" comes to stand beside *aš* for "one." Moreover, Joran Friberg has determined numerical references that correspond to measures (1984). Presumably, a number system resembling use of tokens was first developed, and then superseded by one with a word for each numeral.

When by contrast, we examine the Indo-European set of numbers we find that **oinos,* the primary word for "one" is based on the root

*ʔey- "this," that for "two" on the root **dew-* "distant," that for three on the root **ter* "beyond." That is to say, the words are based on pointing to objects, rather than on specific references like Jap. *ichi-nin* "one man," etc.

While tokens have been found throughout the Middle East, none have been discovered in southern Russia, the presumed homeland of the Indo-Europeans. Accordingly, it has been proposed that the Indo-Europeans used a totally different basis for their number system from one based on classifiers (1990). The inference may be supported by further numbers that can be identified. The term for "five", **penkwe*, has been determined to refer to a total set; that is, in pointing system, use of the whole hand provided the number. And Hittite has given us the presumable Indo-European word for "four," *mi-ia-u-e-es,* which Neu has related to the root **mey-* "lessen," that is, the "lesser hand, the hand without counting the thumb." The remaining numbers, including the etymon of our word "four," are obscure in origin, and may well have been borrowed.

These two illustrations may suggest further opportunities in use of linguistic and archaeological data for determining in greater detail the linguistic as well as the cultural situation of social groups in prehistoric times. Barber concludes her chapter on 'word excavation' as follows:

> We have shown that languages, like habitation sites, can contain "excavatable" strata that turn out to correlate with tangible cultures. And we have demonstrated that as linguistics and archaeology pass their information back and forth and build on each other's findings, both fields stand to gain enormously from this process of word excavation. (1991)

Many opportunities, then, are open for better understanding of the early periods of languages families. But they can be exploited only on the basis of minute control for the linguistic and the archaeological data.

7

Syntactic Devices

The meaningful structure of a sentence can best be stated in terms of a hierarchy of ICs. The immediately obvious structure of a sentence as spoken or heard is as a linear sequence of elements. Words or morphemes seem to come one after another, but they are not necessarily significantly related to the ones they precede or follow. They do, of course, have important relationships, but these may be to elements at some distance, and they may be of various kinds. To understand the sentences, the hearer must somehow identify what these relationships are. That is, he must deduce the IC structure, or something having many of the same properties. Otherwise the meaning will elude him.

Anyone who has studied a foreign language knows that this can happen. He has come upon a sentence in which he knows all the words. Yet it is not at all apparent what the sentence means. He does not know how the words fit together, and apart from these relationships they cannot form one meaningful whole. Such an experience merely shows that the student has not yet gotten control of the devices by which the IC structure of the sentence is signalled. It also demonstrates, as should be expected, that the structural signals may be very different from one language to another. The crucial task in learning a second language is precisely to master these structural signals.

What some of these signals are, and how they operate, can be seen by considering a sentence such as:

The iggle squiggs trazed wombly in the harlish goop.

Only three words of the nine are recognised. Nevertheless, to any native speaker of English the structure is clear, however obscure the meaning may be. It is almost unmistakably marked by these three words and by the four word fractions *-s,-ed*, *-ly*, and *-ish.*

Just how these seven items mark structure is not at all simple to describe. Their function in the process differ somewhat from one to another. For the most part they do not mark structure, either directly or decisively. But they do suggest certain facts about some constituents or hint at certain constructional patterns. Only part of the intricate web of evidence can be mentioned:

For example, *-ish* is commonly a derivational suffix forming adjectivals or words with similar functions. (Not always, or course, witness *starfish.)* This scrap of evidence is strengthened by the fact that *harlish* occurs in a position where such a word might be expected. This in turn, together with the position of *in the,* suggests that *goop* is most probably a noun. This would make *in the harlish goop* a construction of a quite common type. As the native speaker responds to such a sentence, it is probably not so formal process, but perhaps effectively equivalent. These several clues might suggest to him that this portion of the sentence is comparable with some others that are familiar enough:

. . . .	*in the harlish goop.*		
He lived	*in the red*	*house.*	
I read it	*in the big*	*book.*	etc.

Other comparisons are, of course, possible but of various reasons seem less likely:

He wandered *in the forest alone.*
He gave everybody *in the family money.*

The first word in the sentence, *the,* signals in a somewhat different way. This must always be the first word (unless preceded by *all, both,* or *half)* of a nominal phrase. After *the,* perhaps separated by one or more adjectives and their modifiers, must usually be a noun. Thus the noun phrase must be: *The iggle,* or *The iggle squiggs,* or *The iggle squiggs trased,* or some longer sequence. There is nothing that will surely identify the noun, though the ending *-s* is certainly suggestive. There is a common noun suffix of this form, and it is not at all common for adjectives to end this way. Thus *the iggle squiggs* seems more probable as a nominal phrase than does *the iggle squiggs trazed.* Following a nominal phrase, probably a sentence subject, the most likely element would be some sort of verbal phrase. This would normally consist of either a single verb, or of a verb form preceded by one or more auxiliaries. If the latter were present, they would be very helpful in signalling the beginning of the verbal phrase. Since no auxiliary is present, the verbal phrase is most likely a single word, perhaps with one of the verb inflectional suffixes. Either *squiggs* or *trazed* would qualify: both have endings that look likely. But *wombly* looks rather unlikely as a verb, though it would be risky to rule it out absolutely. Thus we have two reasons, each a bit tenuous, to reject the following:

The iggle squiggs trazed	*wombly*	*in the harlish goop.*
subject	verb	

But taken together, they strengthen each other. We are left with two possibilities:

The iggle	*squiggs*	*trazed*	*wombly*	*in the harlish goop.*
subject	verb	?	?	
The iggle	*squiggs*	*trazed*	*wombly*	*in the harlish goop.*
subject		verb	?	

Which of these would seem best depends largely on the possibility of identifying the elements marked with question marks. *Wombly* in the second analysis looks like words such as *happily, daily.* Like them it has the ending *-ly* and it occurs immediately after the verb, a very suitable position. That is to say the whole sentence might be comparable to:

The little pigs wallowed happily in the muddy puddle.

This is not the only possibility. The following will also fit:

The little boys threw gravel in the empty pool.

But somehow this seems less felicitous, and most people would prefer the first solution. To make *squiggs* the verb is also possible, but even less satisfying:

The boy throws gravel idly in the empty pool.

It does not seem a happy solution to make *trazed* a noun, and the whole sentence seems a bit stilted, though possible. A choice must be made of the one solution that seems most probable, but at best errors will be made. The interesting thing is the generality (not usually unanimity!) with which Americans will agree on the structure of such sentences. Though hard to calculate formally, the probabilities are sensed in much the same way by many hearers.

If, starting with a sentence such as the one discussed above, the constituent classes of the words are given one by one, it is found that the analysis becomes very rapidly more certain. For example, if the only bit of additional information is that *trazed* is indeed a verb, the structure becomes quite unambiguous. Identification of the class of another constituent will strengthen the cast a bit more, If the constituent class of every word is known, there is very little room for doubt, even in the most unusual sentence type. If, the first bit of additional information is that *iggle* is an adjective, that will strengthen the case, but not as much as when *trazed* was revealed as a verb. Information as to constituent class is not equally valuable in all cases, but it is always of some help.

Suppose that, instead of revealing the constituent class of a word, a familiar word is substituted. Thus the first substitution might be:

The little squiggs trazed wombly in the harlish goop.

and the second:

The little squiggs trazed happily in the harlish goop.

and so forth. This would have much the same effect. After each substitution the structure becomes clearer. At the same time some meaning begins to emerge. But as far as structure is concerned, the analysis is just as clear when there is merely the information that *iggle* is an adjective as it is when *little* is substituted. The substitution of *little* can reveal nothing of structural importance which identifying *iggle* as an adjective cannot do. The only thing which is structurally revealing about a word like *little* is the constituent class to which it belongs. Not only so. If there is positive information that *iggle* is an adjective, more is known about the structure than if *little* is substituted. The best that can be said in the latter case is that *little* is very probably an adjective. English words have a habit of turning up in the constituent class where they are least expected! *Little* is about as thoroughly dependable as any word in the language. But it can occur as a noun very rarely.

Suppose instead that the first substitution has been for *squiggs*. Among the possibilities are:

The iggle pigs trazed wombly in the harlish goop.
The iggle hogs trazed wombly in the harlish goop.

These two give very different results. In the first, *pigs* is very probably a noun. In the second, *hogs* is probably a noun, but with a very appreciable possibility of being a verb. English words vary widely in the certainty with which they can, by themselves, be assigned to classes. Real ambiguity seldom occurs since only a coincidence of complementary uncertainties in several words will permit it.

Constituent class membership of various elements in a sentence is thus an important clue to structure. But like other clues discussed above, seldom definitive or decisive. It is not possible to deduce The structure, only the most probable structure.

An example such as that just discussed seems like an excursion into unreality. One may well raise the question whether it does really have anything to do with the actual functioning of a language. The answer to this question must be that it does. Seldom do we see a sentence in which all the major words are unknown. But any student commonly sees sentences in which one or several words are unfamiliar. In a book used in some university courses is found the following:

The protonema is fixed to its substratum by rhizoids.

Up to three words in this sentence may be unfamiliar (depending on the reader's background, of course). But the sentence structure is absolutely clear to any native speaker of English. This structural clues which might be yielded by the unfamiliar words are not needed; there are enough others.

Faced with a sentence of this sort, one might go to a dictionary for the meanings of the words. This is seldom done. Instead, the meanings are discovered from the context. The context consists of the whole discourse in which it occurs, the other words in the sentence, and particularly the sentence structure. If the sentence structure cannot be understood, there will be considerable difficulty in deducing the meaning of the hitherto unknown words. The ability to find the sentence structure without knowing the meaning of some of the words is an essential language skill.

The following sentences are not significantly more complex than that just given:

Die Gametangien entwickelnden Zweige unterscheiden sich bei den thallösen Jungermanien wenig von den sterilen.

Assez généralement, il est constitué par des graines mitochondriaux associés à de petits chloroplasts fusiformes ou lenticulaires privés d' amidon.

Unless you are a botanist, these will be good tests of your knowledge of German or French. If you really know these languages they should give you no more trouble than the English sentence above. Whether you know the meaning of *Gametangien* or *mitochondriaux* should not affect the matter at all. After all, very few Germans or Frenchmen know them either. If you cannot see the structure—easily—you will find great difficulty in discovering their meaning, with or without a dictionary. Indeed, some of these words are not likely to be in ordinary bilingual dictionaries at all.

One of the most serious weaknesses in American language teaching has been just here. Students are told in school that they must be absolutely sure of the meaning of every word. They learn rather well how to use a dictionary, but very poorly how to guess. In effect, they are being prohibited from learning to read German as the Germans do. Dictionaries are useful, of course, but they must be used properly. That means first guess, and then look it up. But the guess must be based on the sentence structure.

Throughout the argument given above was a constant appeal to word order. This is certainly one of the most fundamental of structural markers. Yet it is one which is easily overlooked or minimised. The significance becomes plain if the words are scrambled.

Goop harlish iggle in squiggs in the trazed wombly.

The native speaker sees no structure. This is not simply because the ICs are no longer adjacent. Such is not a necessary condition. Consider the utterance:

What are you looking for?

What . . . for and *are . . . looking* are constituents. They are not, however, merely discontinuous; they are discontinuous in a set and regular way. To make them continuous will just as surely destroy the intelligibility as to jumble the words in any other way:

**What for are looking you?*

At first sight word order is simple enough. If there are two elements A and B, there are only two possible orders, AB and BA. Often enough one of these is required and the other excluded. Thus in English, articles precede nouns: *the man* not **man the*. But this sort of simplicity characterised only part of sentence structure, and word order is often most difficult to describe meaningfully. Some constituents are positionally quite free. Thus either *Today I'm going to town* or *I'm geving to town today* is acceptable. Sentence elements of the class of *today* show this sort of freedom in English.

Much more difficult are the cases where order is neither very rigidly fixed nor very free, but generally fixed with a very minor degree of freedom. In English the common order is subject—verb—object. It is also possible to have object—subject—verb. The latter is very much less frequent. Moreover, it seems not at all natural with many sentences. It is most common in a few rather stereotyped utterances: *This I must see.* The limitations are subtile and have not yet been satisfactorily defined. It is particularly difficult to determine what part of the restrictions are grammatical and what stylistic. Yet a satisfactory statement is contingent upon distinguishing these two clearly.

Word order may be affected by the presence or absence of some third element. Again the frequent and simple cases are easily stated. Thus in German the order is typically subject—verb, but this is reversed if certain elements precede. *Er geht . . . .* 'He goes' but *Dann geht er . . . . 'Then he goes'.* The rarer and more complex situations can be puzzling. Worst of all are the instances where the presence of some other element merely conditions a change in the degree of freedom or a change in preference, the order being somewhat free.

Word order and constituent class membership, the two basic structural markers, are of course completely interdependent. Constituent classes are defined by the ability of the members to occur in certain characteristic positions. These positions can be recognised or stated only in terms of relationships involving order. Word order can be defined only in terms of classes.

A recent newspaper carried the headline

Beethoven Works On Hess Program

Probably a number of other readers were startled as I was, taking *works* as a verb. Taking *works* to be a noun gives a less incongruous meaning, one which the article clearly confirms as the headline writer's intention. This kind of ambiguity is characteristic of a very special style of written English, largely restricted to headlines and telegrams. It arises, of course, from the omission of certain "small words," elements which contribute little or nothing to meaning, but function as pure structural signals.

These "small words" are commonly grouped as function words. The term is useful, but the concept is very difficult to define. There is a complete intergradations from items which are almost purely structural markers, to ones which have considerable lexical meaning and for which the function of marking structure is incidental. A function word is any word near one end of this continuum. How purely a structural signal it must be to qualify cannot be specified, and the limit of the group must be somewhat vague, and a matter of each linguist's opinion and convenience.

Perhaps the clearest examples in English are the **articles,** *the, a, some.* The greater number of nominal constructions contain one of these, almost always as the first member. They serve to signal the presence of nominal and to mark one limit of the construction. In these functions, all three are equivalent. The differences mark either the subclass of the nominal phrase or the position of the nominal in the discourse. In rather rare cases none of these grammatical factors exerts control, and the occurrence of one rather than another may signal a meaning difference. This is very much less common than it is popularly supposed, or than what the traditional grammars would lead one to believe. The pairs of contrasting sentences commonly advanced to illustrate the differences in meaning *(The man come.: A man came.)* are, for the most part, either artificial or cited out of context. Much of the grammatical control over the articles operates within stretches larger than single sentences, and so easily escapes the notice of grammarians.

Since articles are primarily structural devices, it is not surprising that languages show extreme variation in the matter. Many languages have none, others only one, others several. Apart from this the usages may be different not only in detail but also in broad outline. It is hardly ever safe to give, as many textbooks do, English articles as glosses for those of a second language.

The treatment of the articles of one language as equivalents of those in another has sometimes led to strange misunderstandings. For example, it has been said that Hebrew thought is less abstract than English, because, where an American would say *Gold is good.*, a Hebrew speaker would say /ṭóob hazzaháab./, allegedly to be translated as 'The gold is good.', the latter being a less general statement than the regular English form. The fallacy is patently in equating the prefixed articles /haC–/ with *the,* so that /hazzaaháab/ must be 'The gold' in contrast with /zaaháab/ 'gold,' and then reading the English distinctions into the resulting translation. The reason that there is no *the* in *Gold is good.* is that *gold* is a mass noun and is signalled as such by the absence of *the.* With an English mass noun, *the* particularises. In Hebrew there is no contrast of this sort. Therefore the argument about Hebrew being less able to generalise is irrelevant. Moreover, in a sentence of the pattern of /ṭóob hazzaaháab./, /haC–/ is used as a structural signal to mark the subject. It has nothing whatever to do with abstractness or concreteness in a context such as this. The whole alleged contrast fails, because /haC–/ is required by Hebrew structure in such a general statement, while the omission of *the* is required by English structure in an equivalent statement. Nothing which is required by the structure can signal any meaning.

Another instance in which the English article serves as a structural signal is seen in the contrast *a bowl or vessel: a bowl or a vessel.* The first implies that *bowl* and *vessel* are synonyms and no contrast between the two is intended. In the second, the intention is to contrast the two and imply that if the object is a *bowl,* it is not also a *vessel.* Such a contrast is not inherent in the *a* as such, but in the different structural relationships which the presence or absence of the *a* signals. Such a contrast may be marked by radically different means in various other languages.

Prepositions are another type of English function words. They most commonly occur as the initial word in prepositional phrases, and thus clearly mark this construction type. Prepositions differ markedly from articles in one very important respect. It is quite commonly the case that one preposition can be substituted for another with attendant change of meaning. That is to say, prepositions contrast very much more sharply with one another than do articles. For this reason they have a much greater part in signalling meaning.

It is, therefore, the mere fact that a word is a preposition which is structurally most significant. That is, the structure-signalling function is a property, not of any given preposition as much as it is of the constituent class of prepositions. In this respect a preposition is not greatly different from a noun. It may be no more significant structurally that a given word is a preposition than that another is a noun. This observation would seem to seriously weaken the distinction between function words and other word types.

There are, however, some other ways in which prepositions differ from nouns, and these may partially justify the distinction. For one thing there are comparatively few prepositions, in contrast to a very large number of nouns. Moreover, the stock of nouns in English is continually changing. Of the new words that flood the English language every year, most are nouns. New prepositions are rare. The probability of a new article in the next decade is entirely negligible. The distributions of nouns and prepositions are quite different. For example, *man* is a very common noun. Yet there are whole books in which the word does not appear at all. *In* is a common preposition. It would probably be possible to write a book without *in,* but it would be a very artificial exercise. Whether a given noun occurs in a book depends very largely on the subject matter. Not so with prepositions. They have less meaning, and more direct involvement in grammar, and hence occur more uniformly through English texts of all sorts.

These remarks indicate the characteristics of the ideal function word. It should be a member of a relatively small constituent class with a fixed membership. Its occurrence in a corpus should be highly independent of the subject matter, literary type, or style. Any item approximating these qualifications is likely to be highly involved in structure signalling and easily recognised as such. They may conveniently be called function words.

In many languages there occurs a special syntactic device known as **government**. This mean that certain inflectional forms are used primarily to signal the place of the word in a construcion. When nouns are involved (the most familiar instance), these special categories are known as **cases.** In such a language, each noun occurs in a small paradigm of forms. Each form is restricted to a certain list of syntactic positions, and hence contributes to marking the structure. Each form in this paradigm is said to represent some case. There is considerable variation in the number of cases and the ways in which the several cases contrast within the system.

The minimum number of cases is, of course, two. This is found in many languages, among them Masai of East Africa. Both subject and object follow the verb, but are clearly distinguished by the case of the noun. The cases differ only in tone, and the morphology is quite complex with numerous inflectional subclasses, two of which are illustrated:

/έdɔ́l ɛmbártá/	'He sees the horse.'
/έdɔ́l ɛmbartá/	'The horse sees him.'
/έdɔ́l entíto/	'He sees the girl.'
/έdɔ́l entitó/	'The girl sees him.'

In Sanskrit there are eight cases:

	'love	'goddess'	
nominative	/kaamas	deevii	subject of a sentence
accusative	kaamam	deeviim	direct object
instrumental	kaame ena	deevyaa	attributive to predicate or sentence
dative	kaamaaya	deevyaai	indirect object
ablative	kaamaat	deevyaas	attributive to predicate or sentence
genitive	kaamasya	deevyaam	attributive to a noun
locative	kaamee	deevyaam	attributive to predicate or sentence
vocative	kaama	deevi/	loosely connected to sentence

The uses listed are merely typical. Most of the cases have subsidiary uses of various sorts. Three, the instrumental, ablative, and locative, are used in very much the same syntactic positions (not identically!) but often contrast in the semantic relationship signalled. The instrumental is commonly translatable by English 'with,' ablative by 'from,' and locative by 'in,' but again, there is considerable variation in this.

Latin and Greek have case systems very similar to that of Sanskrit, but with fewer cases. In Latin the instrumental is lacking, and the locative is found in only a few nouns. In Greek the instrumental, ablative, and locative are missing.

In Finnish there are fifteen cases:

nominative	*talo*	'house'	subject
genitive	*talon*		'of'
accusative	*talon*		object
inessive	*talossa*		'in'
elative	*talosta*		'out of'
illative	*taloon*		'into'
adessive	*talolla*		'on,' 'at'
ablative	*talolta*		'from'
allative	*talolle*		'to'
essive	*talona*		'as'
partitive	*taloa*		'(part) of'
translative	*taloksi*		'(changes) into'
abessive	*talotta*		'without'
instructive	*taloin*		'with,' 'by'
comitative	*taloine*		'together with'

Such a system is different from that of Sanskrit in two very important ways. A great deal more of the contrasts between the cases seem to be semantic rather than merely structural. As a result it is easiest to describe the use of these cases in terms of positions of objects or the like rather than simply by the syntactic structure they signal. In this respect they are much like English prepositions: classes of cases signal structure, but the specific case signals something else. Moreover, it is comparatively simple to cut off the case endings in Finnish, and very much more difficult is Sanskrit. The Finnish case system seems in many respects intermediate between the Sanskrit system and the English system of prepositions. Indeed, we might think of the Finnish case-suffixes as essentially a system of postpositions ("prepositions" is usually reserved for elements which precede) lightly fused onto the noun. Case is thus very similar to certain kinds of systems of function words. If many languages are examined, various intergradations between systems of case and systems of function words may be found.

Hindi shows one kind of intergradations rather clearly. There are three patterns to consider: (1) Nouns occur in two forms, the selection of which is determined by the structure. /lərke/ 'boy' occurs before postpositions, /lərka/ in most other places. These are traditionally called oblique and nominative. (2) Certain postpositions occur directly after nouns: /mẽ/ 'in,' /se/ 'from,' /pər/ 'on', /ko/ 'to,' /ka/ 'of,' /ke/ (not translatable), /ne/ (marks agent of past transitive verbs). These all have a large element of structure marking in their use. (3) A much longer list of postpositions, including /nice/ 'under', /sath/ 'with'... occur after /ke/. /lərke ke sath/ 'with the boy', /lərke ka bap/ 'the father of the boy,' /lərke ne keha/ 'The boy said,' /lerke ka bap/ 'the father of the boy,' /lerke ne keha/ 'The boy said,' /lerka kehta hæ/ 'The boy is saying.' The contrasting forms typified by /lərka/ :/ lərke/ are clearly case, though they have very little signalling function, since a postposition is almost always present after the oblique, and never after the nominative. The set including /mẽ/, /se/, might be considered, with a bit less justification, also as case markers. O these /ko ka ke ne/ have very nearly pure structure-marking function. Moreover, pronouns have fused forms: /mere sath/ 'with me,' not /*mujh ke sath/, /mera bap/ 'my father' not /*mujh ka bap/. The remaining postpositions, however, are very clearly not case markers but function words. It is relatively unimportant what labels we apply, of course; the important thing is that we must recognise that there are here three types of structure: One clearly case, one clearly a system of function words, and one intermediate between the two. If we call the latter "case," then we must be clear that there are two layers of case structure; if we call them function words, we must be clear that there are two very different systems of function words.

In English, case is restricted to pronouns. The difference between *I* and *me* or *he* and *him* is one of case. Thus in *I saw him.,* the form *I* and *him* rather than *me* and *he* assist in marking the structure. However, in English, word order alone is used for this purpose with most nominals. The sentence, *Paul saw Mary.,* is fully as clear, though there is one less structure marker. The result of this is that most Americans rely very little on the case forms, even when they are available. If a group of Americans are instructed to correct such sentences as **Me saw Paul.* Or **Mary saw he.*, a majority will make them *I saw Paul.* and *Mary saw him.*, rather than *Paul saw me.* and *He saw Mary.* This may be taken to indicate that, when the facts of word order and case form are in conflict, native speakers of English will consider word order as the more significant. Case is a very marginal feather in English syntax.

The situation is quite otherwise in some other languages. In Latin, most nouns show case forms which mark the sentence structure much more clearly than do the cases of English pronouns. Moreover, they have much greater functional significance in Latin than in English. For example, 'Paul saw Mary.' might be expressed:

Paulus Mariam vidit.	*Mariam Paulus vidit.*
Paulus vidit Mariam.	*Mariam vidit Paulus.*
Vidit Paulus Mariam.	*Vidit Mariam Paulus.*

Any one of the six would be clear, since the inflectional suffix—*us* marks *Paulus* as subject, and *-am* marks *Mariam* as forming, with *vidit,* the predicate. Though all are intelligible, not all are equally "good." There are strong preferences for one as against the others, but at various periods in the history of the language these preferences have been different.

It is sometimes said that because of the highly developed inflectional system of Latin, word order was unimportant. This is a gross overstatement. In every language word order has important syntactic functions. The example just quoted is exceptional in Latin in allowing absolute freedom of word order. Every language has some definable instances of rigidly fixed word order and some definable freedom of word order. All that can fairly be said is that in Latin, word order is less important as a syntactic device than in English. It is still of great importance. Languages differ more in the relative importance assignable to various syntactic devices than they do in the inventory of such devices. Only the very specialised syntactic devices, such as government, are not essentially universal in languages.

Government is not restricted to nouns. In some languages other parts of speech occur in two or more forms which serve primarily to signal the place of that word in the sentence structure. Thus is Zulu, adjectives have different forms when attributive to a noun than when forming a predicate:

Umuntu omkhulu uzwa.	'The big man hears.'
Umuntu mkhulu.	'The man is big.'
Inkosi endala izwa.	'The old chief hears.'
Inkosi indala.	'The chief is old.'

Omkhulu and *endala* are adjectives in the attributive position following the nouns *umuntu* and *inkosi. Omkhulu* and *indala* are adjectives in the predicate position. There is a very similar contrast marking the position of a verb in a sentence:

Umuntu uyohamba	'The man will travel.'
Umuntu oyohamba uzwa.	'The man who will travel hears.'

Uyohamba is a form of the verb use as a predicate. *Oyohamba* is a form used attributively to a noun. Note the close parallelism of the verb forms with the adjective forms, and the very sharp contrast in the English equivalents. In English, predicate use of an adjective is marked by the function word *is;* attributive use of a verb phrase by the function word *who.*

It is not unusual to have special forms of verbs to indicate attribution of the verb or its clause to another verb. For example, in Kâte of New Guinea:

/nɔnɔ nɔpe valeve?/	'I ate, then he came.'
/nɔnɔ nɔme valepo/	'He ate, then I came.'

/vleve?/ 'he came' and /valepo/ 'I came' are main verbs; /nɔpe/ 'I ate' and /nâme/ 'he ate' are subordinate verbs. The endings /-ve?/ and /-po/ signal not only the subject, but also the place of the verb in the sentence, and similarly with /-pe/ and /-me/.

Another device to indicate structure is concord. This means that certain words are required to take forms which correspond in specified ways with certain other words. There is very little concord in present-day English. The clearest instance is with the words *this* and *that,* which are required to show concord in number with any noun with which they are associated. Thus we say *that boy* but *those boys,* and similarly *this boy* and *these boys.* These are clear instances of concord, but they have relatively little functional value in English because they are isolated vestiges.

Latin has a much better-developed system of adjective-noun concord. Every adjective must agree with its noun in three categories: number, gender, and case.

filius bonus	'the good son'	(sing. masc. nominative)
filii boni	'of the good son'	(sing. masc. genitive
puella bona	'the good girl'	(sing. fem. nominative)
puellarum bonarum	'of the good girls'	(plur. fem. genitive)

Moreover, Latin concord serves a syntactic function, since occasionally only the concord indicates the immediate constituents. Consider the following examples:

filius domini bonus	'the good son of the master'
filius domini boni	'the son of the good master'

Concord may involve various inflectional categories. In Hebrew, nouns in apposition must show concord in gender, number, and definiteness. The latter refers to the presence or absence of a prefix usually translated 'the,' or to certain equivalent conditions. For example:

/mélek gaadóol/	'a great king' (sing. mase. indef.)
/hammélek haggaadóol/	'the great king'(sing. masc. def.)
malkáa gədooláa/	'a great queen' (sing. fem. indef.)
/məlaakíim gedoolíim/	'great kings' (plur. masc. indef.)
/hamməlaakíim habberuukíim/	'the fortunate kings' (plur. masc. def.)

Concord of the head noun of the subject with the verb or other head word of the predicate is also common. By head is meant the constituent which seems to serve as the centre of any construction. Here also, there is some trace in English. The $\{-Z_3\}$ form of the verb is a concord form indicating that the subject is third person singular. It occurs only in the present.

Latin shows a comparable type of subject-verb concord much more fully developed. All verb forms have distinct singular and plural forms:

Filius vidit	'The son saw.' (sing.)
Filii viderunt	'The sons saw.' (plur.)

This type of concord differs from the adjective-noun concord of Latin in that gender and case are not involved.

Hebrew has a similar type of concord. In this instance both gender and number are involved:

/zaakár hammélek/ 'The king remembered.' (masc. sing.)
/ zaakearáa hammaláa/ 'The queen remembered.' (fem. sing.)
/ zaakərúu hamməlaakíim/ 'The kings remembered.' (masc. sing.)

In Hebrew a predicate can be a verb, a noun, or various longer constructions. When the predicate is a noun, the same type of concord occurs as when it is a verb. That is, there must be agreement in number and gender. Since the subject is always definite and the predicate indefinite, a subject-predicate sentence is clearly distinguishable from a construction of two nouns in apposition. By the different type of concord:

/gaadóol hammélek/ 'The king is great.' (a sentence)
/mélek haggaadóol/ 'The great one is king.' (a sentence)
/hammélek haggaadóol/ 'The great king' (not a sentence)

Concord is one instance of a relationship which may exist between constituents other than those which are ICs of some construction. For example, in the Latin sentence *Filius bonus est.* 'The son is good.', gender concord occurs between *filius* and *bonus*. The immediate constituents of the sentence, however, are *filius* and *bonus est*. The relationship may be diagramed:

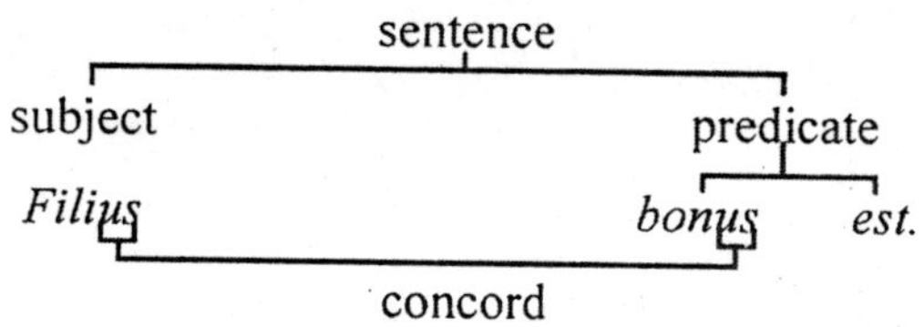

Government may also cut across IC structure in this way.

Both the English sentence, *The man carries.*, and the Latin sentence, *Vir portat.*, show concord between subject and predicate. But there is a very significant difference, which comes out if a longer series of sentences is examined:

Vir portat. 'The man carries.'
Viri portant. 'The men carry.'

Portat. 'He carries.'
Portant. 'They carry.'

The difference is that the Latin verb may stand alone, whereas the English verb must have an expressed subject. The reason for this is that the Latin verb contains within it an expression of the subject; the English does not. In a sentence such as *Vir portat.,* there are two indications of the subject: *vir* 'man' in the nominative, the usual case for the subject, and the suffix *-t* 'he.' The subject-predicate concord of Latin is a requirement that the two expressions of the subject must be consistent. The subject-predicate concord of English is merely a requirement that a third-person singular subject must have a certain verb form, but this form does not express the subject. Some consider this distinction sufficient that the two types should be differently labelled. In this case, the Latin type is called **cross-reference,** and the English type concord. But there is so much that the two have in common that it seems better to consider cross-reference as merely a special form of **concord**. The two are sometimes quite difficult to distinguish clearly.

The English examples discussed up to this point were deliberately presented in orthography rather than phonemic transcription. Enough structural signals are commonly present in spelled English to make sentences intelligible. But this is not always true. In an earlier draft of this text I wrote: *What thinking Americans do about language is.....* When I reread the script, this sentence seemed irrelevant until I realised that the written form is ambiguous. I had read it as meaning 'What is done about language by thinking Americans is....' whereas I had written it to mean 'What thinking about language is done by Americans is ....' If this sentence is read aloud, there is no ambiguity. It can be read to carry either meaning, but not both simultaneously.

The ambiguity rests in different ways of organising the words into constituents. The intention was that *Americans do about language* should be a constituent, not *thinking Americans.* There is nothing in the written form to signal this. But in speech these relationships are clearly marked by stress and intonation. Perhaps the most usual way of reading this sentence in either sense will be with two intonation contours, the first of which ends with /→/. The position of this /→/ will always mark a major division in the utterance. If the /→/ occurs at the end of *thinking,* only the intended meaning is possible. If there is no /→/ here but there is one after *Americans,* the other meaning is indicated.

We may see how this system works by considering again the sentence which was discussed so extensively in the last chapter. This can be read several ways. Probably the most usual would be

/^{2}ðìy^{+}ôwld^{+}mæ̂n^{+}huw^{+3}lívz^{+}ðêr$^{2\rightarrow 2}$hə́z^{+}gɔ́Hntuw^{+}ɨz^{+3}sə́nz+hâws^{1}↘/

There are two intonation contours in this pronunciation. The terminal of the first falls at the major constituent break in the sentence. If the sentence were spoken more slowly, a different pronunciation would probably occur. One possibility would be

/^{2}ðìy^{+3}ówld^{+}mæ̂n$^{2\rightarrow 2}$hùw^{+3}lívz+ðêr$^{2\nearrow 2}$hə́z^{+3}gɔ́Hn$^{2\rightarrow 2}$tùw^{+}ɨz^{+3}sə́nz^{+}hâws^{1}↘/

In this pronunciation, the four intonation contours coincide with the four constituents at the second level in the hierarchy. Moreover, the terminal falling at the first cut is /↗/, while those at the second cuts are /→/. The intonation thus serves to mark the two top levels of IC cuts with precision.

We may arrange the English open transition and terminals in order of rank /+ → ↗ ↘/. In general, higher ranking cuts in the discourse are marked by higher ranked phonemes in this set. However, not only the terminals but also the pitch contours as wholes serve to mark structure. If instead of /232 → 232 ↗ 232 → 231↘/, the sequence of intonation contours had been /232 → 233 ↗ 232 → 231↘/ the structure would probably have been quite different. /233 ↗ / ordinarily occurs at the end of a sentence, whereas /232 ↗/ seldom does.

A system of transitions and terminals of this sort can often mark structure quite unambiguously. However, it is likely that there is no language in which such a system always does so. There are certain difficulties which must inevitably upset it. First, there are not enough kinds of markers. In English there are four ranked elements which might mark cuts. If the highest were to mark only sentence ends, then four levels of cuts could be marked within the sentence, the lowest being marked by the absence of any of these. But many sentences even of moderate length, have more levels of IC cuts than this. Indeed, this is true of the sentence just discussed. In very complex sentences, of course, a very extensive system would be needed. Second, to mark the structure when some constituents are discontinuous requires something more than mere marking of cuts and their rank. Third, the contrasts between /↘/ and /↗/ in particular, and with /→/ to a lesser extent, are used for other purposes as well. In association with preceding pitches, not only do they mark constituents; they also mark the kind of such constituents and the type of construction in which they are found. Thus sentences ending in /233 ↗/ are usually questions. Inevitably there must be conflicts between the use of terminals to mark rank of IC cuts and to mark other things. Fourth, there are occasional situations in which terminals or transitions are not used where the IC structure has a cut, or where one occurs but there is no cut.

For example, short sentences generally have at least /+/ between subject and predicate. In moderately long sentences there is usually a /→/ at this place, and in long sentences there may be a /↗/. Quite often this is the highest ranking cut within the sentence, and it is marked by the highest ranking of /+ → ↗/ within the sentence. However, if the subject is a personal pronoun and the first element in the predicate is *is, are, has, have, had, will, or would,* there is not even a /+/ in normal fast speech.

/^{2}àyl^{+3}gów^{1}↘/	*I will go*	also spelled	*I'll go.*
/^{2}hìyz^{+3}gɔ́Hn^{1}↘/	*He has gone.*		*He's gone.*

In both these sentences the cut marked by /+/ is of lower rank than the one before it without such a marker. The structure is clear enough, because the list of exceptions is familiar to every speaker of English and easily stated by a linguist. The converse is illustrated by certain words which are said with /+/ even some which seem to be best treated as single morphemes, e.g., /pléy^{+}tów/ *Plato.*

English stress and intonation is far from being an automatic marker of sentence structure. It is not possible to deduce the IC structure simply from the stress and intonation in all cases, though in a very large number of sentences it is possible. In many sentences these features are the decisive evidence for the structure. In most they lend support to and are supported by the various other markers. That is, stress and intonation function as part of a whole system of structure markers, and it misleading to try to separate them from the others. In spoken English, however, these features are probably the dominant elements in the syntax-signalling system.

It is probable that all or very nearly all spoken languages have some sort of intonation or intonation-like system. In many, including some that are otherwise rather well known, we cannot even identify this system in speech. This does not mean that it does not exist, but probably only that it is so intertwined with other features of the structure that we have not as yet been able to sort the systems out correctly. In other languages intonation systems have been identified, but their functioning is not as yet understood. In spite of this, it would seem safe to assert that intonation or intonation-like systems are highly important structure markers in most languages, and more important than more obvious systems in many.

We have very little idea of the range of phenomena that will be found when more intonation systems have been studied. We would expect, a *priori,* that there would be some rather obvious differences from the type exemplified by English. Perhaps there may be some basic similarities, but we cannot at present identify what we may expect these to be. In short, we do not as yet know enough about intonation systems that any significant generalisations can be made. We may, however, feel confident that progress in the understanding of intonation systems, and the development of better methods of analysis of intonation, may have tremendous importance for the further development of descriptive linguistics, and particularly for syntax.

8

Transformations

A favourite exercise in public school English has been the changing of sentences from one form to another. Thus from a sentence like

John is writing a letter.

may be formed among others; the following:

John isn't writing a letter.
Is John writing a letter?
A letter is being written by John.

Very little is ordinarily given by way of clearly formulated rules for these processes yet students seem to learn the technique more or less readily. Given the same sentence to start with, and the same rather simple instructions (*e.g.*, "Make this negative."); there will be a very high degree of agreement in the answer. All this would suggest that such exercises must reflect some significant structural relationships in the English language. If so, they are worth careful investigation and formal statement.

When such changes are discussed at all, it is generally in terms of the meanings of the sentences. But this cannot be very exact, and is seldom very helpful. For example, it is easy enough to label *Is John writing a letter?* as a question. But what is the meaning of a question? Indeed, we cannot even give a good definition of the word 'question.'

There is, of course, nothing unusual in finding difficulties in describing meanings, or in making clear statements about language on the basis of meaning. But with questions, it seems particularly difficult and unsatisfactory.

On the other hand, a little examination will show that changes of the sorts illustrated above can be described structurally—that is, in terms of the addition of elements, the rearranging of elements, or the altering of the form of elements. What specific portions of the sentence are involved, and how, can be very exactly stated. This is done, not in terms of their meanings, but on the basis of their structural position within the sentence. Moreover, the descriptions so arrived at have very wide applicability. For example, almost any English sentence not already negative, may be made into a negative sentence in a way very similar to that shown. This can then be formulated into a rule of considerable power, precisely the kind of rule that we desire in grammars.

Not all changes are of this sort. Thus the same sentence might be altered to

John is penning an epistle.

Native speakers of English will recognise a very significant relationship between this sentence and its prototype. But they also sense that the relationship here is of an entirely different sort. The sentence structure is not changed; substitutions are made within the same structural framework. From a structural point of view

Mary is baking a cake.

is just as closely related to the original. There is a difference, of course. It lies in the fact that *penning* is a "synonym" of *writing*, whereas *baking* is not. Synonymy is not a precisely definable concept, nor indeed a structural concept. Changes of this sort are, therefore, not structurally describable. Moreover, they are of much more restricted scope. Clearly, not all operations of altering sentences to related sentences have the same linguistic interest. The ones involving structural changes stand apart from all the others. They will be called transformations.

A **transformation** is a statement of the structural relation of a pair of constructions which treats that relation as though it were a process. Hence, it is normally stated in the form of rules which may be applied to one of the pair—an **input**—altering it to produce the other—an **output**. Note that transformations are directional. Some can be described in either direction, though practically we must choose one. Others can be described effectively only in one way.

As an example we might consider the following set of sentence pairs. These are obviously a sample from a very much larger number.

1.	*Johan is writing a letter.*	*Johan isn't writing a letter.*
2.	*Jim has been trying to do it.*	*Jim hasn't been trying to do it.*
3.	*James will come tomorrow.*	*James won't come tomorrow.*
4	*Ruth was a beautiful girl.*	*Ruth wasn't a beautiful girl.*
5.	*Mary could have been there.*	*Mary couldn't have been there.*
6.	*His father walked home.*	*His father didn't walk home.*
7.	*My friend like chess.*	*My friends don't like chess.*
8.	*The car runs well.*	*The car doesn't run well.*
9.	*Sam started running immediately.*	*Sam didn't start running immediately.*

If we can find a single clearly statable rule to cover all of these, we may describe these nine sentence pairs as examples of a single transformation. The sentences seem to fall into two groups. For sentences 1 to 5 a simple rule is immediately evident :—*n't* is added as a suffix to the first word in the verb phrase. This is true weather the verb phrase consists of a single word as in 4, or several as in 2 and 5. There is a minor complication in 3: *will* + *-n't* yields *won't.* We can easily show that this is quite regular, a fact about the language which would have to be described in any case. Pairs 6 to 9 seem to follow a different rule. Before the *-n't* is added, *walked* is changed to *did walk* and comparable changes are made in the other cases. If we try applying the pattern of the first five pairs without this intermediate step we get such very strange outputs as

**His father walkedn't home.*

These two rules may be combined into one, if certain conditions can be met. The first of these is that we find a clear conditioning which determines which applies. This we can do: *-n't* is never added to words like *walked.* Which of the two rules applies is determined by whether or not the first word is one of the small list (*is, are, was, has, can, might*—an English-speaking student can easily complete the list) to which *-n't* can be added. If not, it is changed to a verb phrase which starts with *did, do, does*. A second condition which must be met is to find a clear statement as to how this change, *walked* to *did walk*, etc., is to be described.

The following sentence pairs may help with this problem:

10. *The boy ran away.* *The boy didn't run away.*
11. *The boy did run away.* *The boy didn't run away.*

These present no difficulty for the rules just mentioned for the negative transformation. In 11 the verb phrase begins with *did*, and *-n't* is added directly. In 10 *ran* is a word to which *-n't* cannot be added; it is therefore changed to *did run*. The interesting feature is that the outputs in the two pairs seem to be identical. Actually this is something of an illusion. There are a number of different pronunciations for a writing like *The boy didn't run away*. Only one factor, the position of the sentence stress, needs to be noted here. There are at least the following pairs:

10. a. *The boy ran away.* *The boy didn't run away.*
    b. *The boy rán away.* *The boy didn't rún away.*
    c. *The bóy ran away.* *The bóy didn't run away.*
11. *The boy díd run away.* *The boy didn't run away.*

This seems clearly the natural way to match them up. The sentences in each pair have the sentence stress in the same place. *Did run* occurs in the input only when the sentence stress falls on *did*. (A sentence like *The boy did run awáy.* sounds at best extremely archaic, and certainly cannot be considered normal modern English.) It follows, then, that *did* occurs in such sentences only either when *-n't* is suffixed or when it receives the sentence stress. There are other uses of *did*, but most of them fit into the same pattern. The auxiliary *did* occurs in English only where sentence structure demands it. It is never required by the meaning, and it never means anything at all. The difference between *The boy ran awáy.* and *The boy díd run away.* is not a matter of the presence or absence of *did*, only of the stress position. *Did* is there only to provide a meaningless carrier for that stress in the required position. If anything else were available, *did* would not occur. Compare

The boy will run awáy. *The boy wíll run awạy.*

Did, do, does, done (the verb *do* in all its forms) as auxiliaries are always completely meaningless—mere position makers. *Do* may also occur as a main verb, in which case it does have meaning: *I did do my homework.*

The morphemes {-Z_3} and {-D_1} can occur only in the first word of a verb phrase. If that word ceases to be first by addition of {do}, these morphemes must shift to the new first word. Thus

walked	(={walk} + {-D_1})	becomes *did walk*	(= {do} + {-D_1} +{walk})
like	(= {like })	becomes *do like*	(= {do} + {like })
runs	(= {run }+{-Z_3})	becomes *does run*	(= { do} + {-Z_3} + {run})

Both these rules (addition of *do* and position of {-Z_3 } and {-D_1} are ones that will be needed anyway. They are not proposed merely to facilitate the definition of the negative transformation. Thus is, of course, the best possible recommendation of the result so far: All the rules are quite general. All the sentence pairs we have discussed can then be subsumed under one rule—the negative transformation—plus in some cases the operation of certain other rules, but these are also quite general.

We cannot speak of "the question transformation" in English, since there are a number of different ones, no one of which has any clear pre-eminence. But we can readily describe each of this rather heterogeneous family of transformations. Some are of considerable interest. Among them are

12.	*John is writing a letter.*	*Who is writing a letter?*
13.		*Is john writing a letter?*
14.		*What is john writing?*
15.		*John is writing a letter, isn't he?*

Of these, number 12 seems the simplest. A question word (*who* or *what*) is merely substituted for the subject of the sentence. The intonation remains the same. This is a simple example of a transformation which can be described in only one direction. *Mary is writing a letter., That old man over there is writing a letter.,* and many other input sentences all yield this same output. If the process is reversed, taking the question to be the input, how is the proper output to be selected from the multitude of sentences which are paired with it?

Number 13 is more complex. The first word in the verb phrase is transposed to the first position in the sentence. It must be one of the same list of forms as was found taking the suffix *-n't*. if it isn't, the verb phrase is first altered by the addition of a *do*, thus:

> *John wrote a létter.*→ **John did write a létter.*→
> *Did John write a létter?*

The intermediate stage is marked with *because it does not occur in that form in normal use. In pronunciation there is, of course, also a change in intonation. Commonly it is from /231↘\ to /233↗/.

Number 14 is also best described as involving a series of changes. First, the first word in the verb phrase is moved, as in number 13. Then a question word is substituted for some sentence element, and this is transposed to the initial position:

> *John is writing a letter.*→ *Is john writing a letter?*→
> **Is john writing what?* → *What is john writing?*

This illustrates another very common characteristic of transformations. When two or more apply in one sentence, it is usually easier to describe them in one fixed order; sometimes it is extremely difficult or impossible to use another order. Almost always the form in which the rules are stated must be changed if they are not applied in the same order.

Number 15 involves both change of the intonation (commonly to /232→/) and the addition of a second clause. This consists of only two words. The first is identical with the first word in the input's verb phrase, except that only one of the two must have the suffix -*n't*. The other word is the proper pronoun to substitute for the subject. This is pronounced with the intonation /233↗/.

Describing various types of questions in this way does not merely elucidate their structure. It also provides a good basis for understanding some of the dialectal or stylistic variations which occur. The following two outputs from a single input will illustrate:

16.	*John is writing to his mother.*	*To whom is John writing?*
17.		*Who is John writing to?*

Examined as they stand, these two results have quite different sentence structure. But looked at in terms of transformations, they are seen to be very much more similar. The intermediate steps are something like the following:

John is writing to his mother.→ *Is John writing to his mother?*

$$\rightarrow {}^{*}\textit{Is John writing to} \left\{ \begin{array}{l} \textit{whom} \\ \textit{who} \end{array} \right. \rightarrow \left\{ \begin{array}{l} \textit{To whom is John writing?} \\ \textit{Who is John writing to?} \end{array} \right.$$

In the last stage they differ as to how much of the sentence is transposed. The transposition of a whole phrase, *to whom*, is found almost exclusively in literary and quite formal English. Colloquial usage very seldom transposes more than a single word. (Colloquial usage, including informal writing, is also much more likely to use *who* than *whom,* particularly when separated from its conditioning context.) The result is sentences with final prepositions and various other "errors." As is often the case, these "errors" are not the result of "loose grammar," but of very rigid and explicit patterns. Most colloquial English usage calls for transposition of the single question word, result what may.

In this discussion there is no desire to evaluate either pattern. The intention is rather to point out that much of our prescriptive grammar, and equally much of the rebellion against it, is vitiated by bad diagnosis. Linguistic description is neutral in such questions. Its task is to give a clear and significant description of usages which actually occur, and when usages differ, to make clear and significant statement as to how they differ. That is, descriptive linguistics can provide the diagnosis on the basis of which an evaluation can be made. Every thoughtful speaker must evaluate conflicting usages; he will do so more effectively with a clearer understanding of the facts. One of the strengths of a transformational description of this type of question is the clarity with which it sets forth this particular difference in usage.

In the process of operating these transformations we find that not only are words shifted around in sentences, but even affixes are moved from one word to another. Not infrequently this causes rather complex changes in forms. For example, applying two of the transformations we have just discussed in succession:

John will go.→ *John won't go.*→ *John won't go, will he?*

With the addition of *-n't,* the form of *will* was changed. Then in the second operation the *-n't* had to be removed, restoring the original form of *will*. This constant shifting of forms is awkward and wasteful. As long as every stage in our description is plagued with these operations, many of them only to be later undone, transformational description is unnecessarily complex.

One way around this difficulty is to operate not with sentences but with "strings" of morphemes, leaving the adjustment to the proper form to the last:

{John} {will} {go}→ /²ǰâHn⁺wìl⁺³gów¹↘/ *John will go.*
↓
{John} {will} {-n't} {go}→/²ǰâHn⁺wòwnt⁺³gów¹↘/*John won't go.*
↓
{John} {will} {-n't} {go} {will} {he}
→/²ǰâHn⁺wòwnt⁺³gów²→²wíliy³↗/*John won't go, will he?*

So described, there are two quite distinct sets of operations. The vertical arrows indicate transformations. They carry one string of morphemes into another. The horizontal arrows represent **morphophonemic** operations. They give any string of morphemes a phonemic shape. (Or, if a written language is being described, a comparable set of operations gives it a graphic shape.) Morphophonemic operations are described as applying only after all transformations have been completed. This, of course, will require some restatement of the transformational rules discussed above. It will also require a slight redefinition of transformation, since transformations do not alter one sentence into another, but one string of morphemes into another. These strrings may be said to underlie the sentences which we used in the presentation above.

The word "string" might easily be misleading. We must certainly mean more than merely some assortment of morphemes arranged in some linear order. Several reasons for this should be apparent from the discussion above. Many of the transformations must be stated in terms of an operation performed on a certain element in a certain position in the string. For example, many of these we have discussed involve the first word in the verb phrase. But if a string were merely a sequence of elements in linear order, the only position we might define would be something like "second element" or "third from the end." Some of the question transformations involve substitution of a question word for a constituent. This might consist of a single morpheme, or of a considerable number. If transformations are to apply to strings, strings must be assemblages of elements having constituent structure. When used in description in terms of transformations, "string" must mean a special sort of sequence of elements, which, because it is characterised by a constituent structure may be called a **structured string**.

Since transformations operate on structured strings, a grammar which is to describe transformations must first describe the construction of a set of structured strings. This can best be done in terms of very much the same concepts as have been described.

When carried out consistently, the ideas just sketched result in a grammar quite characteristic in its organisation and form of statement. Such a description is called a **transformational grammar**. It is claimed by some linguists that this type of statement can attain to a degree of precision, completeness, and conciseness not possible in any other way—in fact, that this technique can overcome certain limitations which are inherent in any other known form of description. Needless to say, these claims are not universally accepted. Both the technique and the claims imply a certain distinctive general theory of linguistics. This differs from other descriptive linguistic theories in certain ways that produce characteristic features in grammatical statements. Certain of these should be pointed out:

1. A transformational grammar is organised in three sections. The first of these describes certain strings of comparatively simple structure. The basic theory here is similar to that underlying all descriptions in terms of immediate constituents. For this reason, it is called the **constituent structure**, or by others, the **phrase structure**, segment of the grammar. The second, or **transformational** section, describes all the transformations by which the output strings of the first section of the grammar are carried into **terminal strings**, sufficient in number to underlie all of the sentences of the language. The third is the **morphophonemic** section. Here are described all of the processes by which terminal strings are given shapes which can be identified as utterances or portions of utterances. Any transformational grammar must have all three, but some individual sentences may involve no

transformations. That is to say, the transformational section may be by-passed in some sentences; the other two cannot.

2. Since in such a scheme, no matter of phonemic (or orthographic) form comes in until the third, morphophonemic, portion of the grammar, the greater part of the statement, is properly in terms of quite abstract symbols. If the symbols used should have a form reminiscent of a familiar spelling or of a phonemic transcription, this is of no particular significance. In most instances the symbols are more or less arbitrary letters representing classes of structures, often with subscripts representing subclasses. Some of these symbols bear no obvious meaning, being selected merely for convenience. The use of such abstract symbols gives a thoroughgoing transformational grammar an algebraic appearance. This is often enhanced by the fact that the terminology and phraseology used in such grammars has been strongly influenced by that of mathematics. However, a transformational grammar is not properly any more mathematical than any other type of grammar in its basic features.
3. The statement is largely in the form of a set of rules. These are of two kinds. The first is of the form "X → Y + Z." This should be read as "X is to be rewritten as Y + Z." Such rules are referred to as rewrite rules. They have the effect of changing a symbolisation, generally in the direction of making it more specific and explicit. For example, in one formulation of English grammar the starting point is the symbol S, roughly to be read as "sentence." The first rule is S → NP + VP. This substitutes for the very general representation, S, the more specific and explicit representation, NP + VP, roughly to be interpreted as "noun phrase plus verb phrase." This is not a statement that a sentence consists of a noun phrase and a verb phrase. Many do, of course, but not all: *e.g.*, *Come here!* lacks the noun phrase. Rather it is a statement that all sentences (or only one set if there is another rewrite rule that starts from S) must be DESCRIBED IN TERMS OF a noun phrase and a verb phrase. Subsequent rules may have the effect of cutting out some of these structures.

The rewrite rule applies to any string wherein the proper symbols are found. The second type of rule, the **transformational rule,** is similar in many respects, but operates only on certain symbols in certain places within a constituent structure. Thus a rewrite rule applying to NP, will apply to any NP. But a transformational rule may apply to certain NPs only. For example, a transformation involving the moving of an NP in object position relates the following pair of sentences:

18. *I saw John yesterday. John I saw yesterday*

But cannot apply to an NP in some other position:

19. *I gave the money to the man with John.*
**John I gave the money to the man with.*

4. Transformational grammars are generally very explicit about the conditions under which any given rule can be applied. Careful attention is given to the order of application of rules. An effort is made to distinguish clearly between **optional** and **obligatory** rules, and between **recursive** rules (ones that can be applied repeatedly) and **non-recursive** rules. Properly, this is not a peculiarity of transformational grammars as such, but of all grammars which attempt to be thoroughly rigorous in their description.
5. A key word in all transformational grammar is **generate**. This is used in a sense taken from mathematics.

$$(x - a)^2 + (y - b)^2 = c^2$$

may be said to generate a set of circles in a plane defined by x and y. That means that for any given a, b, and c this equation defines one specific circle. For all possible values of a, b, and c it defines all possible circles in the plane concerned. In the same way, a transformational grammar consists of a set of statements which generate all possible sentences in a given language. Depending on the choices made wherever a choice is possible (whether to apply a certain optional rule, or which alternative to select when several are offered), it defines each specific sentence. In this sense, a particular running through of the grammar is not to be considered as CREATING a sentence, but more nearly as SELECTING a sentence from a

> pre-existing stock (the language) of all possible sentences. Thus the grammar might start with the symbol S and in a particular application of it end with /[2]ǰâʜn[+]wìl[+3]gǿw[1]↘/. But the last expression does not represent anything not represented by the first. Rather S stands for ALL sentences in the language, and thus represents, among others, /[2]ǰaHn[+]wìl[+3]gǿw[1]↘/. The process of running through the grammar and making the required choices is a matter of singling out a specific sentence to replace the general symbol S. Nothing is created, increased, or added to; the meaning is instead very much narrowed. In much the same way $(x-2)^2 + (y-5)^2 = 32$ represents nothing not already completely covered by $(x-a)^2 + (y-b)^2 = c^2$, but only one specific instance out of the total set of circles. The selection is made by choosing values 2, 5, and 3 for *a, b,* and *c.*

At the beginning of this chapter a few transformations were described in terms of familiarly spelled sentences. Later it was shown that it would be preferable to work, not with sentences, but with structured strings. In the last section it was suggested that a transformational grammar, when formally stated would be quite different from the non-rigorous description above. Here will be given a more formal description of the pair of sentences with which the discussion began. Not all alternatives are stated at every step, but some are mentioned so that it will be clear where choices must be made and how it is that more than one sentence might come out. At each step the rule being applied is listed at the left and the form resulting from its application at the right. Braces around morpheme symbols have been omitted.

The description starts, of course, with the general expression for a sentence.

Step 1. S

The first rewrite rule is generally described as obligatory, that is, there is no other choice at this step:

Step 2. S → NP + VP NP + VP

There are a variety of ways in which the VP might be developed leading to a variety of sentence patterns: . . . *ran.,* . . . *is good.,*

. . . *saw him.*, etc. At this point a choice of rewrite rules will determine which type, in the broadest sense, will result.

Step 3. VP → Verb + NP   NP + Verb + NP

At the next step there are two alternatives, between which a choice must be made. In such a case a rewrite rule giving the alternatives can be stated in the following form:

Step 4. $NP \rightarrow \begin{Bmatrix} NP_{sing} \\ NP_{pl} \end{Bmatrix}$ NP_{sing} + Verb + NP

The import of this rule is to demand a choice between singular and plural for each NP. It must be applied twice, since there are two occurrences of NP in the form resulting from Step 3. These must be considered as two separate steps, since they are quite independent of each other. Moreover, one basic principle of this sort of grammar is that each rewrite in the constituent structure must replace just one symbol.

Step 5. NP_{sing} + Verb + NP_{sing}

Step 6. Verb → Aux + V NP_{sing} + Aux + V + NP_{sing}

Step 7. Aux → C(M) + (have + en) + (be + ing)

NP_{sing} + C + be + ing + V + NP_{sing}

The parentheses in this rule mean that a choice may be made. C must be used, M (which stands for *can, may, shall,* etc.) may be omitted, have + en and be + ing can be omitted. Of the optional elements only be + ing was selected. The next rule also presents some choices, but these are partly controlled by the context.

Step 8. $C \rightarrow \begin{Bmatrix} Z_3 \text{ in the context } NP_{sing} \\ \text{Ø in the context } NP_{pl} \\ \text{past in any context} \end{Bmatrix}$

NP_{sing} + Z_3 + be + ing + V + NP_{sing}

Next there are several alternatives for the rewriting of NP_{sing}, of which only two are listed here.

Step 9. $NP_{sing} \rightarrow \begin{Bmatrix} D + N + \text{Ø} \\ NP_{prop} \\ \text{etc.} \end{Bmatrix}$

NP_{prop} + Z_3 + be + ing + V + NP_{sing}

Step 10. $NP_{prop} + Z_3 + be + ing + V + D + N + Ø$

The Ø in the last rule points out the lack of an inflectional suffix in contrast to $NP_{pl} \rightarrow D + N + Z_1$.

The result of step 10 is an expression consisting of some symbols for specific morphemes, either affixes like Z_3 or stems of function words like *be,* and some symbols standing for classes of stems or words. The next four steps consist of substituting an actual member of the class for each class symbol:

Step 11. N_{prop} → Mary, John, Henry, . . .
John + Z_3 + be + ing + V + D + N + Ø

Step 12. V → write, read, take, . . .
John + Z_3 + be + ing + write + D + N + Ø

Step 13 D → the, this, a, . . .
John + Z_3 + be + ing + write + a + N + Ø

Step 14. N → ball, man, letter, . . .
John + Z_3 + be + ing + write + a + letter + Ø

The result of step 14 is a possible terminal string. Two courses of further development are open. We may apply certain transformations, or we may pass to the morphophonemic section of the grammar immediately. In the latter case there will be a variety of rules which must be applied, and no attempt will be made to give them in detail here. However, one type needs to be noticed. Certain affixes will regularly be combined with the following verbal element. In spelling the effect is as follows:

John + Z_3 + be + ing + write + a + letter + Ø

John is writing a letter.

Or we may apply to the result of step 14 a transformation:

Step 15. $NP + C + \begin{bmatrix} M \\ have \\ be \end{bmatrix} \ldots \rightarrow C + \begin{bmatrix} M \\ have \\ be \end{bmatrix} + NP \ldots$

$\underbrace{Z_3 + be}_{Is} + John + \underbrace{ing + write}_{writing} + a + \underbrace{letter + Ø}_{letter?}$

Is John writing a letter?

Again, the morphophonemic steps are not given in detail, but only suggested by showing the final result in spelling. Much the same set of rules applies, however, as did above.

At first reading, the last section seems to be a very elaborate and complex way of describing a pair of quite simple sentences. But such an evaluation is not entirely appropriate. To be sure a very much more simple description is possible: In *John is writing a letter.*, the first word is *John,* the second word is *is,* the third word is *writing,* . . . But such a description tells us very little if anything about the sentence. It might be possible to make a somewhat more sophisticated description of the same anecdotal sort, but however detailed this might be, it would tell nothing whatever about the grammar of the sentence. A sentence has a grammar only as it stands in relation to other sentences as part of a language. Any speaker of English immediately sees something of the grammar in a sentence like *John is writing a letter*. This is only possible because he knows the language, and can fit this sentence into its place within the language. The sentence *apko kya cahiye.* 'What do you want?' is just as grammatical, but the grammar is inaccessible to most readers of this book, simply because they cannot relate it to other sentences in Hindi. A grammatical description must place any given sentence in a framework which can be used to describe any sentence in the language, even though this requires making some statements which do not seem, superficially, to be of any great pertinence to the sentence at hand. Many features of the statement in the last section are not demanded by anything in the sentences being discussed, but by things in other (perhaps very many other) English sentences. At every point where a choice was presented, these two sentences were related to, and set off from, a host of other sentences. The statement did not merely describe the sentences in themselves, but rather put the two sentences into their place within the whole structure of the English language. The English language is an immensely complex thing, ramifying in many directions, and a description which does actually relate a single sentence to this complex structure cannot be very simple. One of the marvellous things about language is that any statement as short as that just given could in fact approach adequacy in relating these two sentences to the billions of other sentences in the language.

In a statement of this sort, given with just two sentences in focus, the reasons for some of the features of the statement could not be made clear. To understand them, it would be necessary to trace out some of the consequences of other alternatives. An excerpt from a grammar cannot be as meaningful as a full grammar. To have given a full grammar of English, even if very much lacking in detail, would have been impossible here. What was given is a little like a full recounting of all the moves of the king's bishop in a championship chess game, mentioning the other pieces only when they fall directly in the path of the bishop.

There is another very important reason why the statement may seem unduly cumbersome. It attempted to state explicitly a number of things which are quite easily taken for granted. Every grammar leaves a great deal unsaid which the user must supply somehow from his "common sense" or "Sprachgefühl" or some other undefinable source. Much of this seems so obvious that to state it seems gratuitous. But research consists very largely of attempting to state the phenomena as explicitly as possible. Thus, Newton's law is traditionally said to have been found through dissatisfaction with treating the fall of an apple as simple and obvious, and was nothing more than an attempt to explain explicitly how it falls. Progress in linguistics must come largely by raising questions about the unstated phenomena, probing into them and attempting to make explicit statements in places where it had not previously been done. An explicit statement is not necessarily an acceptable statement. But it is often a testable statement. It always calls the attention of investigators to the question, and often provides a starting point toward a better formulation. Work on a transformational grammar of English has forced explicit statement at some points in the structure of the language and in general linguistic theory which had previously been passed by.

The introductory sections of this chapter centred around a small selection of sentence pairs related through a few transformations. The rules were not explicitly stated. Indeed, it would have been rather pointless to have given an explicit statement of the transformations without building this on and explicit statement of the underlying constituent structure. It should be pointed out, however, that a formal statement is possible. None of the sentences discussed would require the use of any very complex rules, and most of the rules would be quite general in application. Indeed, a proper writing of the rules might lead to a further step in generalisation. For example, pairs 12 and 14 were described differently. But this is not necessary. Instead, the same sequence of transformational rules can be applied to produce both. The first fifteen steps in the generation are identical with that described earlier. Step 14 gives the string which, if taken directly through the morphophonemic rules, would give *John is writing a letter.* In the same way, the product of Step 15 would yield *Is John writing a letter?*. As a string it is of the form:

Step 15. Z_3 + be + John + ing + write + a + letter + Ø

The next step replaces an NP by a question word. There are two NPs in this string, *John,* and *a letter.* They belong to different classes, one which requires *who* as a substitute, and one that requires *what.*

Step 16. Z_3 + be + who + ing + write + a + letter + Ø
OR Z_3 + be + John + ing + write + what

This is followed by an obligatory transformation which shifts any such question word to the initial position:

Step 17. who + Z_3 + be + ing + write + a + letter + Ø
what + Z_3 + be + John + ing + write

To these the same morphophonemic rules would apply. They would have the effect of taking them into a phonemic form familiarly associated with the spellings of examples 12 and 14:

Who is writing a letter?
What is John writing?

The other transformations discussed can be formally stated in much the same way.

A complete transformational grammar of English would, of course, list many more transformations than this small sample. Some of them would be rather different in general form and effect. In the following sections a few more will be mentioned in order to show the range of possibilities. All are, of course, capable of formal statement. But for the present purpose, it will be better to revert to the less rigorous style of discussion in which sentences are compared rather than strings, and in which only certain outstanding features are mentioned.

One type of transformation uses two or more inputs, combining them into one output. A very simple case is the following:

	Inputs	Output
20.	*The car stopped suddenly.* *I was thrown against the windshield*	*The car stopped suddenly and I was thrown against the windshield.*

This particular transformation can be described in terms of nothing more than concatenation, the addition of a marker *and*, and appropriate adjustment of the intonation (or in writing of the punctuation). But the situation can be more complex:

	Inputs	Output
21.	*You have some bananas.* *I would like about a dozen.*	*If you have any bananas, I would like about a dozen.*

At first sight, sentence 21 would seem to come from **You have any bananas.* and *I would like about a dozen.* But the first of these two sentences seems quite unnatural. A little investigation will show that there is a very special relation between *any* and *some.* The one occurs in certain types of sentences, the other in other types. An adequate set of transformational rules will have to include a rule which has the effect of substituting *any* for *some* to produce sentences like that in 21. This is not as special a rule as it might seem. Very much the same relationship is seen in other pairs of sentences, so that the same rule can be applied in the series of transformations which connect them.

22. *I have some bananas.* — *I haven't any bananas.*
23. *You have some bananas.* — *Have you any bananas?*

Another somewhat similar phenomenon is illustrated in the following:

24. *I will come.* — *He said he would come.*

Only one of the two input sentences is shown here; the other will be discussed later. There is a change of *will* to *would,* and of *I* to *he*. These changes are conditioned by the occurrence of *said* and *he* in the first part of the sentence, as may be seen by comparing the set of sentences in 25, all having the same input:

25. *I will come.* — *He says he will come.*
I said I would come.
I say I will come.

Transformations which have the effect of putting two or more inputs together into one output involve a number of rules. There is the addition of various construction markers, *and, either . . . or, because, therefore, if . . . then,* etc. There may be changes of certain specific items, *some* → *any, sometime* → *ever,* etc. Verb forms may be changed to bring them into the proper relationship. (Traditional grammar gives a partial treatment of these phenomena under the rules of "sequence of tenses.") Pronouns may undergo various changes. As all of these can be structurally defined, they belong in a grammar and can be formulated in transformational rules.

Example 24 illustrates another feature of some transformations. The other underlying sentence cannot easily be *He said.* Such a sentence does occur, but rather infrequently, and in a quite specialised situation. Rather it must come from something like *He said it.* In the transformation, *it is* replaced by *he would come.* This sort of transformation does not merely connect strings; it inserts one into another so that it becomes an element in the structure of the other. In doing so it removes and replaces some element. Sometimes it is fairly obvious what this replaced element must be. In other cases it is not clear from the final result what such an element should be considered to have been in the input. In this respect, such a transformation is exactly like some of the question transformations. In example 12, the transformation involved the substituting of *who* for *John*. Looking at the output alone, it would not be clear what nominal was involved. It might have been *Mary, the man, my neighbour who grows daffodils,* or innumerable other possibilities. But it could not be *the pen* or *that typewriter,* or many others, which would require the substitution of *what* rather than *who.* Perhaps it is just this uncertainty which lies behind calling a sentence like *Who is writing a letter?* a question. It is not possible to go from the output sentence backward and reconstruct in detail every step of the generation. But it is possible to know that *who* substitutes for an NP, and equally to know that *he would come* must substitute for an NP.

Another type of transformation which inserts one input into another is exemplified by the following two sentences:

26. *The man who drives the yellow Cadillac hit a lamppost yesterday.*

27. *The man who hit a lamppost yesterday drives the yellow Cadillac.*

Both these sentences can be generated from the same pair of inputs.

The man hit a lamppost yesterday.
The man drives the yellow Cadillac.

To be usable in this transformation, the two inputs must have some part in common, in this case, *the man*. For this constituent in one input may be substituted *who* or *which*, whereby the whole S becomes attributive to the matching noun in the other, and is inserted in the position after the noun. When the NP replaced by *who* or *which* is not initial, then additional changes have to be specified.

By means of various transformations of these types, it is possible to take care of all those sentence types which are traditionally labelled as "compound" or "complex." So conceived, the phrase structure sector of the grammar generates certain clauses, and the transformational sector unites these into sentences. In the light of this, it is not, strictly speaking, correct to read the symbol S as meaning "sentence" as used in traditional grammar. Nor indeed is it necessarily much better to read it as meaning "clause" in the sense of traditional grammar, since some transformations will carry an S into some structure other than what is traditionally called either a "clause" or a "sentence." But this does not mean that S does not designate some real and significant unit, only that it is not a unit identical with any one of those defined in traditional grammar. It is better to consider S as a designation for a unit which is basic to English grammatical patterns as described by a transformational grammar. If read as "sentence" it means only "sentence" as understood in this kind of grammar. It should not be expected to match precisely any unit in any other statement of English grammar. A transformational grammar is not merely a restatement of, or a minor amendment to, a traditional grammar or an immediate constituent grammar, but a basically different approach to language structure. It must find different units.

Once it is recognised that transformations can be applied to a pair of input strings to reduce one to the status of an element within the other, a vast panorama of possibilities opens up. Certain types of what are traditionally labelled "phrases" seem quite similar in important ways to "subordinate clauses" and suggest that a similar treatment is possible. As examples the following sentences will serve:

28. *His coming and going like that gives me the willies.*
    from *He comes and goes like that.*

29. *His continual drumming on the table makes me nervous.*
    from *He continually drums on the table.*

These both have a great deal of the underlying sentence pattern still remaining, and therefore have a great deal that commends such treatment.

If it is permissible with sentences like 28 and 29, why not also with similar phrases with less of the sentence elements preserved? The following all seem to be related in some way to example 29, and should perhaps be treated as having the same origin:

30. *His continual drumming makes me nervous.*
    His drumming on the table makes me nervous.
    Continual drumming on the table makes me nervous.
    His drumming makes me nervous.
    Continual drumming makes me nervous.
    Drumming on the table makes me nervous.
    Drumming makes me nervous.

but not
    **His continual on the table makes me nervous.*,
    etc.

All of these differ from 29 only in the omission of certain parts. Any element or combination of elements can be omitted except *drumming.* They might accordingly be described in terms of a special type of transformation which merely deletes certain statable constituents.

This sort of transformation has a very wide usefulness, but it requires caution. It would be quite possible to generate 29 by a series of deletions from something like:

31. *His continual drumming on the table with his knife and fork while the toastmaster is introducing the speaker of the evening makes me nervous.*

But this is quite unnecessary. There seems to be no reason to start from the longer sentence. *He continually drums on the table.* is sufficient as an input. But if so, why not merely *He continually drums.* for the first sentence in 30? In this case a deletion transformation would be unnecessary. But this is not true of all these sentences. The input may be *He continually drums.*, or *He drums on the table.*, or simply *He drums.*, but it must have *he* or some other

NP in the subject position. Those sentences in 30 without *his* must be derived by the use of a deletion transformation if the *drumming* is to be gotten from the VP of an S. Unnecessary deletions are not justifiable, but some deletions are necessary in a transformational grammar of English.

One of the commonest criticisms of traditional school grammar has been directed at the use of "understood" sentence parts. For example, an imperative sentence like *Come here!* is commonly described as having as subject "*you* understood." *You* in such sentences is quite rare and exceptional. Some linguists reject the use of such "understood" elements in a grammatical statement. Here, as in many other instances, a transformational grammar parallels traditional grammar in some respects. This sentence can be derived by the same first rewrite rule as used earlier, S → NP + VP. If so, at a later point in the grammar, a deletion transformation must remove the NP. The question is, then, is it necessary to have the NP in the derivation? There is some evidence that it is. *Myself* occurs, generally speaking, only in sentences in which *I* occurs in subject position. *Yourself* occurs commonly in two kinds of sentences, those with *you* for the subject, and imperatives. All these facts can be brought under one rule if *you* could be the subject of imperative sentences at the point in their generation at which the rules introducing *yourself* apply. That is, if something like **You go chase yourself!* were one stage in the generation of the imperative sentence *Go chase yourself!*

Within the framework of a transformational grammar deletion transformations seem to have a place when they are required to explain existing patterns. Unnecessary deletion transformations have no such place—no unnecessary rule of any kind can be tolerated. In other types of grammars the use of "understood" elements may be less easily justified, and whether they will be used or not is a decision which the linguist must make, just as he must decide which of several possible forms of statement he will follow. There is, however, one special danger in "understood" elements which explains, and at least partly justifies, the condemnation of many linguists. This is the use of "understood" elements in field linguistics. It requires a very profound knowledge of a language to be able to assess when such a device is justified by the structure of the language itself. The temptation in preliminary stages is to supply "understood" elements in order to bring the structure into line with that of some other language. For example, in Hebrew /ṭóob haaʔíiš/ 'The man is good.,' /ṭóob/ means 'good' and /haaʔíiš/ means 'the man.' There is no direct equivalent to 'is,' though of course the sentence structure as a whole is in some way equivalent to the structure of the English sentence as a whole. Some grammarians have stated that 'is' is understood, or even that /haayáa/ is understood. (This is glossed in some dictionaries as meaning, among other things, 'to be.') But it is difficult to see how /haayáa/ can be "restored" to this sentence without utterly changing it. In no instance can there be any justification for "understood" elements or deletion transformations except in the STRUCTURE of the language. That "the meaning requires"—or the exigencies of translation, or any other non-structural indication, real or imaginary—is totally irrelevant.

If individual words can be introduced into a sentence by means of a transformation combining two structured strings, it would seem possible to give a similar treatment to a great deal more of what has in the past been taken care of in the IC structure, or handled by traditional grammatical devices of various kinds. For example, it has been proposed that attributive adjectives can be introduced into noun phrases by this means.

32. *I see the house.*
The house is red. } *I see the red house.*

In favour of this suggestion is the fact that *I see the red house.* does seem to be related in some way to *I see the house which is red.* The latter clearly can be gotten from the inputs of 32. It is claimed that this procedure does result in a considerable simplification of description, but some linguists are less convinced of the value of such transformations than of those described earlier in this chapter.

Such a proposal seems to be pointing in the direction of making all of sentence structure a matter of transformations. But this is not the case. While it is easy enough to derive *red house* from an input *The house is red.*, it does not seem possible to generate *the house* in this way. Certainly it cannot be done in a strictly parallel way, since there is no sentence of the form **House is the.* In any case, it would seem that there must be at least a small collection of sentences in the derivation of which no transformations are applied. Nevertheless, one of the important issues in regard to transformational grammars is determining the proper apportionment of the task of description between the phrase structure sector and the transformational sector of the description. Some would push the use of transformational description much farther than others.

The use of transformations in grammar, in any rigorous sense, has been a new development in the decade of the 1950's. Involving as it does a reorientation of linguistic theory and a significantly different technique of description, it has necessarily been the centre of a vigorous controversy. At the time of writing, several of the issues are not as yet clearly defined. Not enough has been published in the way of transformational grammars of a variety of languages. It is, therefore, not yet possible to evaluate its potentialities adequately. It may be expected, however, that the theory will continue to play a significant role in the development of linguistics by virtue of having raised some important, previously overlooked issues, and perhaps by contributing to their solution.

9

Linguistic Phonetics and the Science of Speech and Hearing

Phonetics is the scientific study of the medium of the spoken language and as recent studies in this field attest, it has a subject all to itself. As study in the medium of spoken language it covers every aspect of the basic speech science i.e., speech physiology, speech acoustics and speech perception. In aim and objectives, it *draws* parameters on which all potentially possible human vocal sounds can be systematically arranged and classified in a natural order. As a theory, phonetics is capable of handling the three distinct stages—(i) stage of the allocation of speech-sounds to contrasting categories, (ii) stage of the designation of relative values of each category, and (iii) stage of the interpretation of these values in terms of measurable units. (Ladefoged 1967) The three stages correspond to three levels of phonetic sciences—(1) level of systematic phonemics, (2) the level of systematic phonetics, and (3) the level of physical phonetics. These three levels can be said to represent the hierarchy of generalisation and abstraction which a speech-sound undergoes in the speech-communication process.

It should be observed that when a phonetician indulges in the study of speech-sound it is this process of generalisation and the nature of interrelationship between these three levels of phonetic sciences which motivate him to ask specific questions and direct him to design specific models for experimental research work.

Specific and Applied Phonetics

The fact that phonetics deals not with *any* sound but speech-sounds conditioned by biological, psychological and communicational factors, forces us to recognise its specific and applied fields of investigation. The scope of two fields are given in Tables 1 and 2 respectively.

Table 1

	Basic speech science	
Speech physiology	speech acoustics	speech perception
	Descriptive phonetics	
articulator	acoustic	auditory

Table 2

Discipline of speech science	*Related disciplines*	*Applied field*
phonetics (specific)	Linguistics Psychology Medical sciences Information sciences Others	Functional phonetics (phonology) Psycho-acoustics Speech-pathology Speech communication

Obviously, phonetics as a basic speech-science forms its specific field of descriptive phonetics but as an applied field, it interacts with different dinstinct disciplines. The various directions of investigation on the frontiers of autonomous field of phonetics show how complex is the speech process and how many different aspects of the basic speech science are to be explored in order to formulate any composite theory of phonetics.

The Speech Process

A model of speech process common to both speaker (speaking) and hearer (listening) is proposed in the schematic representation given in Table 3 (which is self-explanatory). It is a matter of interest to note that according to the proposed model, the stage of recognition process

Table 3

Schematic Representation of Speech-process

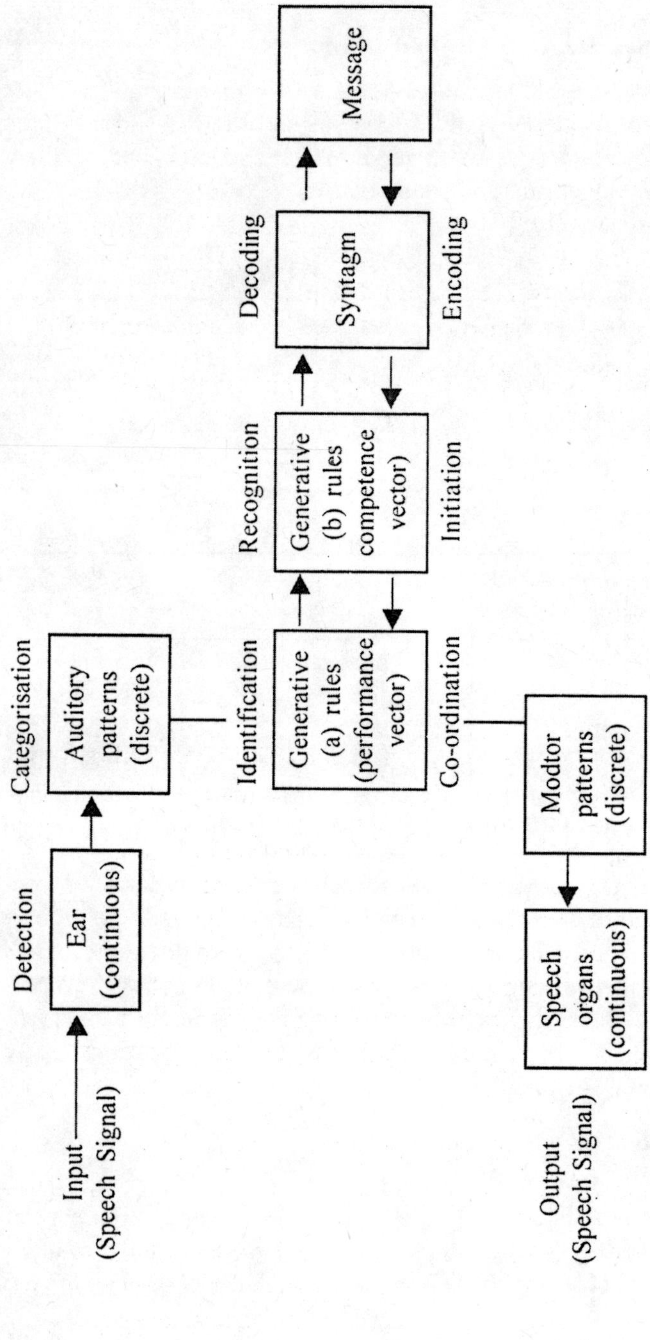

has a vector more towards the competence (ability with regard to the grammar of a language) while the vector of identification process is more toward the performance scale (ability with regard to the production and perception of particular utterances). Though the competence and performance aspects shade into each other, based on their results of experiments on the auditory perception of temporal intervals in speech and on the findings of their investigation on some of the aspects of the control of the vocal organs which are independent of the language being spoken. Ladefoged and Fromkin (1968) have convincingly shown that wherever the differences between them (competence and performance) have been lost, wrong assumption have led to inadequate models.

Many relevant problems related to speech science have been raised—what is the mechanism and stages in the production and perception of speech? What are the minimal units for the different stages? Is the mechanism for production and perception same? etc.

The complexity of speech process poses another serious limitation in the formulation of any genuine phonetic theory. It is often seen that a hypothesis proposed from one aspect is often challenged and contradicted in the light of empirical evidence of the other aspect of the speech process. For example, on the question whether or not there is an isomorphism between speaking and hearing processes, available literature often offers conflicting hypothesis.

In our flow-chart of speech process (Table 3) we have suggested a common central mechanism for both speaking and hearing (see especially the dual role of our boxes 3, 4 and 5) primarily because separate mechanisms for production and perception seem to be too uneconomical. The conflation of the speaking and listening process is supported by the *motor theory* of perception which states that "articulatory movements and their sensory effect mediate between the acoustic stimulus and the even we call perception' (Liberman, 1957). The hypothesis is that kinesthetic memory serves as stimulus where . . . exterocepter is invariably translated into . . . propriocepter sensations before reaching to any stage of recognition. Thus, writers Kozhevnikov and Chistovich (1966). 'In the process of imitation are provided conditions that are favourable to the forming of the conditioned-reflex correlations between groups of sound signals and complexes of articulatory motion . . . . It is assumed that these conditioned reflex correlations play an important part also in the process of speech recognition by an adult." Results of electromyography (EMG) studies led Ladefoged, Draper and Whitteridge (1958) to conclude that the phenomena of prosodic feature like stress can best be stated in terms of 'speakers' muscular behaviour (or statements about the actions of the listeners's muscles which would have to be made in order to produce similar sounds). Similarly, Leontev's (1959) findings in pitch also adduce "conclusive demonstrations of the significance of the motor representation of signals for their evaluation."

On the other hand, research work in some of the related fields offers an opposite view *i.e.*, the auditory patterns are not necessarily integrated with or structured similarly to the patterns of motor commands. Based on their case-analysis of anarthria, aphasia and cerebral palsy, MacNeilage, Rootes and Chase (1967), Lebrun (1968), Lenneberg (1962) etc., hold the view against the conflation of speaking and hearing processes. Lebrun's case study of a patient with cortical anarthria without any concomitant dysphasic impairment supports the view that for normal speech perception there is no reference back to articulatory movement and, in a sense, is in consonance with Penfield and Robert's (1959) earlier suggestion that there are two distinct language centres for motor and sensory functions.

If one wants to resolve such conflicting views and contradictory hypothesis, much more research work is needed and as Halle and Stevens (1964) correctly suggest that this research work must "take physiological factors into consideration more directly, through the use of cineradiography, electromyography and other techniques." But research alone is not enough; there must be a contant demand to integrate the findings of the research work conducted in the different aspect of the unitary speech process. Evidence from one aspect and the counter-evidence adduced from another aspect alone can lead us to formulate hypothesis of higher order. It is only in the context of the explanatory power of such higher hypothesis under unified theory of speech-process that conflicting evidence from different sub-parts of the unitary process can be given the right perspective.

Experimental Phonetics

The principal new instruments and techniques that have appeared in the field of phonetics have been discussed in details by Ladefoged (1957), Catford (mimeo), Cooper (1965) etc. A classified listing of the various instruments available in any sound phonetics laboratory is given in Table 4.

The very set up of phonetics laboratory is indicative of the fact that research work in phonetics cannot be effectively carried out without the active co-operation of acousticians, engineers, linguists, psychologists, logicians and neuropathologists. For example, the interest in the innervation process and aerodynamic phase have encouraged phoneticians to ask for the help from medicine department; interest in speech acoustics have prompted the phonetics department to seek the co-operation of the experts in electronics and engineering while the emphasis on speech-perception have led them to co-operate with psychologists, telecommunication engineers and scholars working in the theory of information.

Phonetics Laboratories and Researches in Phonetics in India

Phonetic laboratories in India are in bad shape; they are not only poorly equipped but are not manned by trained personnel. The irony of the situation is that where there is a trained phonetician, either there are no proper instruments to carry on the experiments or there are no funds to keep the laboratories in a working condition. Over and above, different departments in the universities try to maintain their autonomy in such a manner that there arises no question of conducting research by cutting a common cake. Research work in phonetics in India therefore, is mainly confined in the area of functional phonetics. For any significant work done in other applied fields of phonetic research like psycho-acoustics, speech pathology, speech-engineering etc., one has to look for laboratories locate outside India.

* * *

It is high time that some of the phonetic laboratories in India were equipped with appropriate instruments and manned by trained phoneticians where it should be possible to demonstrate all the methods of instrumental phonetics and where it would be possible to investigate the various problems of speech and hearing processes. Furthermore, every endeavour should be made to keep in touch with

Table 4

A Speech physiology		*B* Speech-acoustics	
Innervation	*Articulation*	*Aerodynamic*	*Acoustics*
	(1) Lungs		
(myo- and neuro-motor Phase EMG	(a) Direct Cine-photography (b) X-ray photo-graphy (c) Pneumato-graphy (d) Plethysmo-graphy	(1) Volume of air: spirometry (2) Pressure: Pres-sure trans. ducerattached with osciollo-scope	(1) Spectrograph (2) Speech syn-thesis (3) Trans Pitch meter
	(2) Larynx		
	(a) Cinephoto-graphy (b) Laryngo-scopy (Strobosscopy) (c) Photo-electric gllotography	(3) General: Electro-aerometer (4) Velacity: anemometer	(4) Intensity meter (5) Cathode ray oscilloscope (6) Kymograph (deal more directly with articulation)
	(3) Lower-jaw		
	Photo-electric jaw-movement transducer	*C* Speech perception	
	(4) Tongue		
	(a) Direct} Palato (b) Still} graphy (c) Dynamic} (d) X-ray photography	(1) Tape-splicing (2) Speech Synthesiser (3) Delayed Auditory Feedback (4) Automatic speech-recogniser	

the recent developments and achievements in other allied fields of investigation. The basic fact about this discipline must not be overlooked that "speech and hearing science is peripheral to many other disciplines as other disciplines are peripheral to it." (Peterson and Fairbanks, 1963) And perhaps this is the reason why "phonetics/ phonology has contributed to and shared in whatever success has been enjoyed by all of speech-research, and in the process has experienced the same shifting of its goals." (Chala, 1970).

The fact which I want to emphasise is that only by a comprehensive approach to the study of speech process, an approach embacing the current achievements both in linguistics and psychology and assimilating knowledge about the normal physiological functioning of the higher nervous system and language disorders due to the local brain lesions, is it possible to adduce hypotheses which go beyond the limits of narrow questions of phonetics. Is it not self-revealing that the famous Research Institute of Logopeadics and Phoniatrics, University of Tokyo, Japan, though under the faculty of medicine, has a full programme for electro-communication, phonetics, linguistics etc.? And is it not self-instructing that one of the most stimulating books on the science of speech and hearing—*"Speech: Articulation and Perception,* presents the results," of an original experimental investigation of the speech process conducted by a group of physiologists, linguists, mathematicians and engineers.

In summing up the present status of phonetics in India, it might be said that it is a long borne underdeveloped bastard-child struggling for its existence under the inadequate care of mentally handicapped foster-mother-phoneticians and disowning foster-father-linguists.

10

Linguistic Perspective to the Communicative Functioning of the Deaf

Communication is the life-principle for all living organisms—be they plants, insects, animals or human-beings (Sovak, 1979). The fact that plants communicate, with animals has been proved by so-called herbo-galvanic reflex. Insects are said to utilise chemical releasers (pheromones) which are probably the first signal, put to service in the evolution of animal communication (Wilson, 1968). Various kinds of visual and acoustic communication signals are used in varying degrees by various animals. But it is with the man that we get a qualitatively distance model of language which is both specific and species-consistent. The evolution of this Model is hidden in the series of transformations, structural and functional, that took place in the course of the formation of modern man. It is tied to the history of physiological adaptations, of cognitive specialisations, of sensory specifications (Lenneberg, 1968). Chomsky has shown that the basic form of this model (Universal Grammar) is innate in character, in fact, it is the reflex of the human mind accountable in terms of human biology (Chomsky, 1975). Thus, according to him, "Some intellectual achievements, such as language learning, fall strictly within biologically determined cognitive capacity." (Chomsky, 1975).

Certain facts regarding the nature of cognitive capacity, as conceived by Chomsky, should be mentioned before we discuss the communicative potentials of deaf shown through his behaviour. It is emphasised that one of the basic faculties of human mind which is common to the species is the faculty of language. Secondly, the intrinsic nature of the language faculty is free of stimulus control. Thirdly, given appropriate stimulation, it is this faculty which constructs a grammar. Fourthly, Universal Grammar—the system of principles represented in the genetically determined initial state, and Grammar—the system of knowledge represented in the mind and the brain in the eventual steady state—are real objects, part of the physical world (Chomsky, 1983). It is true that a typical human language has the vocal-auditory channel of communication. But the exploitation of vocal-auditory channel belongs to the area of performance. A channel of communication has nothing to do directly with the cognitive faculty or linguistic competence. If a child has a normal mind (a normal control of nervous system) it is hypothesised that he can be trained to exploit linguistic signs for communication purposes. There exist a number of interesting circumstances wherein spoken speech is either totally or partly in abeyance. Thus arise various sign-languages, as they are called: (Critchely, 1939)

Even Indian language philosophers like Bhartrhari make distinction between covert speech (implicit speech element) and overt speech (external manifestation in the form of spoken language). According to him there cannot be any cognitive state of human mind without the imprint of implicit speech element (inner speech). His familiar metaphor for revealing the intrinsic relationship between consciousness and language is fire and illumination: just as fire and illumination cannot exist without each other so can't consciousness and language. Like a child, a deaf may not use language overtly, but he is obviously endowed with implicit speech. The external world in fact awakens the 'word seed' in the light of which child cognises the person—normal speaking being or a deaf—does have the ability to construct the fictional world. It is a different matter whether he is physiologically competent to externalise the fictional world through overt speech or not. One may argue here that in adverse circumstances such as impaired hearing one may adopt another sensory channel such as visual and tactile.

The most important fact to be remembered is that sign languages are produced by human agents through visual-gestural channel of communication. These sign languages are also the result of the cognitive faculty of human mind. There are many kinds of evidence to prove that the speech and gesture have developed side by side demanding a common type of communicative competence. It is our common-day observation that our discourse is often accompanied by non-verbal but parallel system of communication: intonation, mimicry, gesture etc. Our talk is often accompanied on the one hand by non-verbal sounds like interjections, onomatopoeia, voice modulation and the like, and on the other hand by shrugging the shoulders, raising the eyebrow, nodding or shaking head etc. These non-verbal codes of communication are often integrated with the verbal code of sign system in such an inextricably interwoven way that without a composite conceptual framework it is not possible to reveal the significance of either the vocal symbol or visual sign system. As referred to by Critchley, Abraham has mentioned that the spoken language of the Brazilian Puris is so meagre that it has only one word—'day' for the concepts 'yesterday,' today,' and 'tomorrow.' For the sake of comprehensibility, the Brazilian Puris supplement the vocal symbol with that of gestures; he indicates 'yesterday' by saying 'day' along with a concurrent visual symbol *i.e.* pointing behind him, for 'today' he points to the sky and for 'tomorrow' indicates forwards (Critchley, 1939).

When two normal human beings communicate with each other by way of talking they generally employ an admixture of verbal and non-verbal codes controlled by a common cognitive plane of action. This is possible because for a normal man both the channels of communication, vocal auditory and visual-gestural, are available for sign production. It is interesting to note what happens when one of the channels for communication is completely blocked because of interlocutors' physical impairment. For example, in the case of blind we find that the channel related to sight is completely blocked while in case of deafs it is the vocal-auditory channel which becomes dysfunctional. But while blinds can acquire a language in a normal way and converse with themselves, as well as with other normal human beings by using the vocal-auditory channel of communication deaf people are left only with the visual-gestural channel of communication. Because man is basically a sign producing animal, a social being that cannot exist without communicative function, he is forced to exploit the system of visual sign to the maximum. He inverts a sign language with a system of signs parallel to the vocal code. The underlying principle behind the system of signs is the same as we find in the verbal code because both kinds of sign manifestations—non-verbal as well as verbal—flow from the same cognitive faculty (i.e., central nervous system).

I will call this perspective of looking at the system of signs employed by deaf people during their act of communicative functioning Semio-Linguistic. It has been called semio-linguistic because firstly, it involves a study in semiotic theory which relates the two aspects of signs—*signans* which are immediately perceptible and *signatum* which are inferable and apprehensible, and secondly, it proposes that all man-created sign-systems have the same deep seated principles or schemata which language as a verbal system displays. This semio-linguistic perspective directs us to study the sign language employed by deaf persons not as an *ad-hoc* use of gesture but as a system of gestural signs based broadly on linguistic principles. What is being emphasised here is that the semio-linguistic orientation has a breadth of perspective which is on one hand wider than what linguistic theories at present are able to offer because it includes in its orbit those non-verbal components of communicative behaviour which get manifested and on the other hand narrower than what a general theory of semiotics would like to include in its scope because it excludes from its orbit all those sign delineations which are no species-specific and species-consistent.

This semio-linguistic perspective to the study of sign languages can dispel some of the major misunderstandings about the semiotic nature of the true Sign language, say American Sign Language (ASL). Some of such misunderstandings are as below:

Sign Languages are Infra-Human

Such a type of misunderstanding is based on the belief that the sign languages of deaf (mutes) is based on instinctive gestures which are shared commonly by lower animals. The reason for this misunderstanding lies in our failure to differentiate between non-verbal signs .which are exclusively human (anthroposemiotic) .and those gestures which are shared commonly by human beings and other animals of lower order (Zoosemiotic). According to Sebeok the two are often confused but it is important to distinguish the purely anthroposemiotic systems, found solely in man, from the zoosemiotic systems which man shares with at least some ancestral species (Sebeok, 1968). As pointed out by Diebold there are some recurrent gestural responses which are part of the shared bodily and behavioural characteristic of phylogenetically closely related species, but there also exist gestural responses which are highly socio-culturally conditionable categories which can easily be labelled as 'ethnic gesture' (Diebold, 1968). Existence of such vehicles proves that sign languages are not sub-human.

Sign Languages are not Language-like

It has been reiterated by many scholars that as sign languages are basically mimetic (iconic and indexical) in nature, they are in their manifestation also universal and pancultural. According to them, gestural signs employed by deaf (mutes) during their act of communication involve instinctive gestures which belong to the category of 'natural signs.' Contrary to this, it has been stressed by many structuralists that symbolism involved in verbal communication is not iconic but arbitrary. According to Hockett, it is this principle of arbitrariness which puts human language at an advantageous position because then there is no limit to what can be communicated about (Hockett, 1960).

Recent researches in the field of linguistics and semiotics disprove the above-mentioned points of view. On the question whether there exists a simple and constant relation between the gestural signifiers and their denotative signatum or on the issue whether sign languages employed by deaf (mutes) are universally and panculturally understood or not, there is no ambiguity left over. It has been shown by Stokoe (1972) that the relations between gestural vehicles and what they denote are anything but simple and iconic—at least his semiotic study of ASL dispels such a naive assumption. Similarly, researches conducted by Battison and Jordon (1976), on seventeen different national sign languages categorically answer that a sign language is neither universally understood nor is pancultural in orientation. They have also convincingly shown that like different verbal languages, different sign languages are also not mutually intelligible, In addition to this while studying historical changes which

ASL has undergone, Frishberg (1975) has pointed towards a universal tendency which sign languages exhibit, a change in the direction from iconic to arbitrary.

Linguists, on the other hand, are now becoming convinced that the principle of arbitrariness is a legacy of earlier intellectual trends (Lehmann, 1968). According to Friedrich (1978), the multiple fallaciousness of the principle of arbitrariness suggests that it is time to make a 180° turn and state the antithetical position: the lexical symbol is non-arbitrary. According to him non-arbitrariness is the unmarked condition. In fact, it is a matter of degree describable in terms of trends and frequencies. In the light of the above facts, it becomes obvious that to say sign languages are not language—because their signs are iconic while verbal signs are arbitrary, holds no validity.

Sign Languages cannot be Studied Linguistically

Though there are some attempts made in the direction of studying sign languages used by deaf (mutes) on the basis of linguistic theories, it is held by a section of scholars working in the field of non-verbal behaviour that linguistics alone cannot provide a conceptual framework of multidimensional aspects of a sign system in general and inherently specific nature of manual alphabets in particular. Among those who have worked on deaf-sign system linguistically, names of McCawl (1965), Stokoe (1966, 1972), Schlesinger (1969), Cicourel and Boese (1971), Battison (1974), Frishberg (1975), and Fischer and Gough (1978) can be mentioned. It is true that gesture symbols or manual alphabets used by deaf persons are tertiary symbol sets (a normal man uses vocal symbols) and are manifested in three dimensional space and time simultaneously. But what is more important to remember is that these are the signs of a sign language. They are not isolated instances of gesticulation. It is the syntactic orientation which differentiates signs from gestures. Signs occur in phrases and sentences. Similar or identical gestural phenomena which are not signs signify messages which need no parsing because the vehicles have no syntactic structure; each one means what it means by virtue of being what it is. Signs, however, in a sign language mean what they mean by virtue of relation to other signs used with them as much as by being signs

(Stokoe, 1972). This relationship between signs of ASL have been dealt with in detail within the transformational-generative model in some of the papers included in a recent book edited by Klima and Bellugi (1979); however, it is commonly upheld by scholars that "linguistics as the science of the internal structure of spoken languages may not be the best discipline for analysis of human sign languages" (Stokoe 1980). Unless all the three aspects of sign act—what acts, what it does and where (configuration, action and location of sign) are taken into account and unless a general theoretical conspectus is evolved that includes in its scope essentials and strategies of non-verbal behaviour, no linguistic theory could provide a model for explicating the true nature of sign languages. A semio-linguistic perspective, as defined in the earlier part of the paper, is thus inevitable for studying sign languages used by deaf (mutes).

It is true that visual-manual sign languages employed by deaf persons, which have been developed as a system of communication, do perform almost all the functions of a language which operates on vocal-auditory channel. It is equally true that these sign languages satisfy the inner urge of deaf persons to communicate with their fellow-beings. However, to whatever extent such a sign language may not possess the basic properties of the usual verbal system it is also equally true that its communicative potential is basically restricted to the intra-group of deafs. Such an intra-group communication has resulted in the social segregation of the deaf (Blanton, 1968). Deaf persons are generally well adjusted in their own community (Baroff, 1963). The result is that they are left with no motivation to communicate with the normal hearing section of society. An attempt has therefore been made to develop communicative potential in them which could enable them to become a member of the broader speech community in which they live. This is achieved by compensating for their sensory deficit of auditory perception by providing them hearing aids. I would like to call this dimension of study on deafness Audio-Lingual.

The audio-lingual perspective raises many theoretical and empirical questions related to verbal behaviour. However, it dispels first the belief that a deaf child cannot learn a verbal language because his audition is defective. It also refutes the view that the cognitive development of the deaf cannot follow the same learning process as that of hearing children. It also asserts that there is never a case of total deafness and further points out that whatever small the potential of hearing a deaf child has it can be utilised in the development of speech. The Nuffield Hearing and Speech Centre of London has convincingly shown that with proper audio-metric criteria for testing and with linguistically correct method of observation and classification of acoustic cues, child and adult with impaired hearing can be trained to develop responses to sounds. As a result, the clinic has produced many instances of children with very severe hearing losses (70-80 and 90dB over the whole audible range in the better ear) who have developed excellent speech, sometimes, indistinguishable from normal, and who have consequently been educated successfully among normally hearing children in an ordinary school (Fry, 1966).

The audio-lingual perspective of the language development in the normal and the deaf child emphasises the following aspects of linguistic theory:

1. A linguistic theory is a theory of biological endowment capturable in terms of Universal Grammar (UG). UG, thus, is the theory of the human faculty of language and hence, underlies the acquisition and use of language. There is no *a priori* reason believing that the deaf child's cognitive faculty for learning a language is in quality different from that of the hearing child's . In fact, scholars have convincingly shown that the cognitive development of deaf children follows the same path as that of hearing children (Fry, 1966).
2. While UG appears to be unique in significant measure to the faculty of mind, within the framework to UG language specific grammars differ from language to language. Any particular grammar conforms to the principles of UG, but is further articulated; it presents as well accidental facts distinguish the particular language in question (Chomsky, 1977). This directs one to accept that the accidental facts of a language (which differentiate the grammar of one language from that of the other) is also a component of child's language faculty. They are learnt by the child through the linguistic data to which he gets exposed. It is to be emphasised that the peripheral hearing mechanism relays information to the brain in the form of nerve impulses, but the organisation of this information is solely the work of the central

mechanism (Fry, 1966). In the deaf children it is the hearing mechanism for receiving the acoustic cues which is defective (and not the central mechanism which organises the information in the form of linguistic competence).

Because of this defect in the hearing mechanism, a deaf child is unable to combine phonation with articulation during the babbling stage. A deaf child also tries out his vocalisation mechanism by way of coos and chuckles but as he is unable to establish a feedback loop, he is also unable to establish a link between auditory cues and kinesthetic impressions. As the deaf child is unable to set up connection between the auditory and motor aspects of babbling like a normal child, babbling soon ceases from his verbal behaviour. The above discussion goes to suggest that the onset of language is not dependent upon either acoustic impression or motor control, and hence as shown by Lenneberg (1962), it is quite independent of motor skills.

3. As the crucial component of the learning process lies in the brain in the form of speech-sound processor and organiser of acoustic sensation, the audiolingual perspective asserts that it is possible to bring the functional units of sound (like phoneme, phonological syllable etc.) to the psychological reality in the linguistic competence of even a deaf child. Three facts in this respect have to be noted—(a) the functional categories (like phonemes) are functionally discriminated from one another and are units of linguistic competence, (b) categorised perception of functional units is the consequence of the operation of speech-sound processor (which is located in the brain), and (c) the physical characteristics of speech sounds are not in one-to-one relationship with the phonologically relevant units of sound systems.

Those scholars who are working with deaf children within the audiolingual mode of speech training try to provide the child with a set of acoustic cues (which a deaf child is capable of perceiving after suitable amplification) so that with the suitable exposure to speech, he is able to develop the phonological system. Because of the fact that the amount of speech, a child develops, depends not so much on the amount of hearing *per se* as upon the use he is able to make of his hearing for language learning (Fry, 1966), an attempt was first made to measure the speech-perception potential a hearing impaired child or adult had. It was this hearing potential which was utilised for training these children. Attempts have also been made to evolve a technique for measuring the speech perception of hearing-impaired children. A conventional audiometric clinical testing generally includes pure tone detection threshold, a speech reception threshold and a sound discrimination power for each ear. According to Asp, the optimal field of hearing usually produces better speech discrimination scores than wide-band amplification or a frequency response that amplifies those frequencies that have the greatest hearing loss (Asp, 1975).

Taking into consideration the time of onset of the hearing impairment and speech development potential Kostic' (1980) has proposed the following classification of hearing impaired children:

Type	*Speech Potential*
Zero Group: Total deafness. No contact with sounds. Loss at birth.	Children can acquire elements of speech through kinsthetic feed-back or through visual symbols.
First Group: Severe hard-of-hearing. Contact with sound only through a narrow band (500 to 600 Hz). Loss between 2 f (1,2) and 9 months (period of early babbling).	Children can perceive only suprasignals-i.d, tonal patterns within frequencies of their remnants.
Second Group: Hard-of-hearing. Contact with sound at frequencies not less than 1000 Hz and not more than 1500 Hz. Loss between 9 and 24 months (period of Babbling).	Children can perceive with supra-signals a voice quality, like voicing, features associated with first formant of vowels and certain cues for consonants.

Contd..

Contd..

Type	*Speech Potential*
Third Group: Uneven pattern of hearing loss. Cannot develop speech without selective amplification. (Loss between 2 and 4 years of age).	Children can acquire normal speech with appropriate selective amplification.
Fourth Group: Slight to lineral Loss. (Loss between 5 to 7th year).	Children can acquire normal speech after speech training.

Under the general supervision of Kostic, Rudi Cajaree. Electronic Factory, Yugoslavia is now producing instruments (SAFA=Selective Auditory Filter Amplifier). The instrument has 27 independent units which process the frequency spectrum for 105 Hz to 9600 Hz. The main purpose of the instrument is to bring the hard-of-hearing child into contact with speech sound. after the diagnosis that leads to a quantitative and qualitative evaluation of the child's sensation and perception of speech and environmental sound stimuli (Gerdes, 1982).

The audio-lingual perspective on the deaf-education also takes into account the etiology of the hearing loss, the time of onset of deafness and the extent and degree of hearing impairment. The common etiologies are hereditary. rubella, meningitis, fever and premature birth (Asp, 1975). The time of onset divides deaf patients basically into two groups—prelingual and postlingual (*i.e.*, deafness before the acquisition of language or after). If it is a postlingual hearing loss, the task becomes relatively easy for any well-experienced speech pathologist. Here the problem is restricted to the area of perception and articulation (*i.e.* performance). In case of prelingual hearing loss, the problem is also to develop in the child the linguistic competence. It should be remembered "that onset off speech consists of a gradual unfolding of capacities" (Lenneberg, 1966), and thus, while enabling a child to develop language competence attention has to be paid to potentialities of behaviour—the underlying matrix for behaving—instead of to a speech etc.

This new audio-lingual perspective to the deaf education is quite different from the old method practised in traditional schools for teaching the deaf child to speak. It emphasises the need of early detection of deafness and its diagnosis preferably before the age of one year, extensive exposure to language in early age, fitting of two hearing aids one in each ear, developing in the child the language competence rather than restricting the teaching to the area of performance (skill-oriented) etc. This method minimise the role of formal instruction and gives low priority to the manual language which deprives the children of the experience of intrinsic properties and function of language.

The two perspectives—Semio-linguistic and audiolingual—for the deaf education, are built on linguistic principles. While the former perspective makes the deaf persons use visual signs in a system to communicate with members of their own intra-group, the latter perspective builds in the child an ability to talk with persons outside of its groups also. It is generally presumed that the second line of educational action has greater potential for the rehabilitation of deaf children because it provides them an opportunity to achieve the normal educational and vocational levels. But the situation is not that simple as is generally thought to be. Gorman (1960) points out that in Britain deaf children educated in oral school often leave the schools at the age of fifteen because they do not find their group identity, social stability and economic viability. They generally make contact with the non-oral deaf social group and prefer to enter that group after learning the sign language (Gorman, 1960). This simply proves that deafness is not merely a problem of semantics and cognition or of speech perception and production; it is one of the most severe social handicaps.

11

Communicative Grammar and Discourse Analysis

There is little argument that there exists a difference between **linguistic competence** (*i.e.* knowing a rule of a language) and **communicative competence** (*i.e.* how to use a rule appropriately). While Chomsky is of the opinion that "acceptance of rules must be distinguished from the existence of the related practices" (Chomsky, 1976). Dell Hymes holds the view that "competency for use is part of the same developmental matrix as competence for grammar" (Hymes, 1971). What is important to note is that scholars focusing on the two kinds of competence tend to advocate two different kinds of models for language. Those who keep linguistic competence at the centre of their theory advocate a model of language with an orientation toward biologically determined cognitive capacity of human being with a view to construct **Theoretical (Universal) Grammar**. Contrary to this, those who are inclined to include in their theory also the competency for use, aim at developing a model of language "with a face toward communicative conduct and social life" (Hymes, 1971). It is this second group of scholars who are concerned with developing the notion of **Communicative Grammar**.

Since the difference between theoretical and communicative grammar is based on two distinct kinds of orientation, it is better that we grasp those salient features which diametrically oppose each other in the two types of grammar. We summarise below their differences in tabular form:

S.No.	*Theoretical*	*Communicative*
(1)	*Object of Inquiry*	
	—language faculty as an element of cognitive capacity.	—functional potential of language in act of communication.
(2)	*Perspective of Inquiry*	
	—language as verbal —structure-dependent formal semantics.	—language as social semiotic. —use-dependent communicative intention.
(3)	*Context of Investigation*	
	—replication of uniformity.	—organisation of diversity.
(4)	*Modality of Investigation*	
	—replication of uniformity.	—organisation of diversity.
(5)	*Unit of Analysis*	
	—sentence.	—speech event.
(6)	*Nature of Analysis*	
	—rule-oriented.	—role-oriented.
(7)	*Form-function Dichotomy*	
	—emphasis on form.	—emphasis on function.

Language is the communicative system *par excellence.* According to Searle, "the purpose of language is communication in much the same sense that the purpose of the heart is to pump blood. In both cases it is possible to study the structure independently of function but pointless and perverse to do so, since structure and function so obviously interact" (Searle, 1969). It is this functional and international perspective which we find behind the model proposed by Hymes (1972), Halliday (1973) etc., and in the work on discourse analysis by Allen and Widdowson (1975), Munby (1978), Widdowson (1978), and Wikins (1976).

The sentence-bound theoretical orientation to the language study is of marginal interest to the scholars working on communicative intention. They draw insights for developing their model from socio-linguistics, discourse analysis and stylistics. Those interested in applying communicative orientation to the discourse analysis employ principles of speech acts, ethnomethodology and pragmatics. For example, Widdowson is in favour of exploiting these three dimensions of verbal behaviour of explicating the structure of discourse (Widdowson, 1978).

Most of the language theories accept sentence as the largest natural unit of language. However, as Harris (1952) has noted, "language does not occur in stray words or sentences, but in connected discourse. . . ." A discourse or text is formed by sentences in a logical sequence. It is in respect of such features that scholars have now pleaded for an 'upward extension' of linguistic analysis, *i.e.* the extension of linguistic analysis 'beyond the sentence.' Gleason (1964) speaks of the need "for an upward extension of the scope of grammar." Armstrong (1959) pleads for the structural analysis of sub-units which are higher than a sentence.

The concept of a discourse /text as indicated by Harris overcomes two basic limitations of sentence-based linguistic models:

(1) It transcends the limitation of a sentence which is a minimal monologue, and
(2) It carries information about certain correlation of language with other behaviours.

It has been argued by scholars that the inter-sentential gap is filled in by the implicit link provided by the dialogue structure (Volsoinov, 1930) and that the dialogue provides the conceptual bond between the autonomous sentences (Baxtin, 1929).

It is being argued here that for the purpose of the evaluation of a text we have to take into account the analysis of the implicit link that fills in the inter-sentential gap and the conceptual bond which exists between two sentences. A given text invariably includes the information about its structural properties, the linguistic markers of inter-sentential cohesion and the situational features which connect the information content to its outward context.

Some attempts have been made to evolve techniques of analysis of given texts. Hasan (1968) discusses cohesion features as anaphora and exophora; Halliday (1967) analyses the information structure under three functions:

(1) the ideational: expressive content,
(2) the interpersonal: maintaining social relations, and
(3) the textual: enabling links to be made with the situation and the cohesive texts to be constructed.

Widdowson (1978) considers that there are only two basic functions of language—(a) conceptual, and (b) communicative. In his framework of analysis, 'interpersonal' and 'textual' functions of Halliday fall under communicative function. According to him these two functions conceptual and communicative—"potentially in conflict, have to be reconciled by negotiation on every occasion of social use. This negotiation is realised in discourse." (Widdowson, 1980)

Hasan and Halliday's models of textual analysis deal primarily with the contextual relevance of a clause/sentence. These do not take note of the information structure of the theme and its presentation. Sinclair and Coulthard (1975) have tried to systematic the analysis by integrating the situational and grammatical categories with their discourse category equivalents in the following manner:

Discourse categories	*Situational categories*	*Grammatical categories*
Informative Elicitation Directive	Statement Question Command	Declarative Interrogative Imperative

One of the basic assumptions behind a written text is that writing is a thinking process, and a written text is an organised thought. Writing is an organisation of experiences and structures of thought. However, thoughts and experiences are controlled by the purpose of the writing. "This purpose determines the selections and organisation of the thought content, *i.e.* one may find three types of expository prose: prose which reports (reporting), prose which explains (explaining), and prose which evaluates (evaluating). It is obvious that the form and structure of discourse with respect to the above stated three functions will differ from each other. A wrong selection of form and structure in respect of the function of the text will create confusion and result in incomprehensibility. It is also important to note that certain elements of rhetoric are employed for making a text effective in so far as it gets the message across to the reader. (Kaplan, 1966)

Scholars have tried to redefine the rhetoric function. They want to stress that the object, speakers set out to know, may not be the same as the object known conventionally. It is therefore many of them are motivated to study the gap between the words of the speaker and of the audience. (Richards, 1936) It is in this light that Kenneeth Burke (1950) had tried to free rhetoric from the narrow limits of genres of discourse and defines it as "the consciousness required for communication." Similarly, McNally proposes that rhetoric be viewed as sign-behaviour exhibiting a pragmatic concentration of meaning. (McNally, 1970)

Pragmatics is that part of verbal behaviour which conditions the appropriate use of language in communication. If syntax is the study of signs in relation with other signs and semantics is the study of signs in relation with designata, then pragmatics is the field of linguistic inquiry which studies signs in relation to their users. It is the most general level of study and includes non-linguistic (an encyclopaedia) knowledge. With the interaction between linguistic knowledge (a grammar) and non-linguistic knowledge (encyclopaedia), it sets out inference rules (a logic) for getting at communicative intent. Consider the following exchange as given by Smith and Wilson (1979):

(1) A: Where's my box of chocolates?
B: Where are the snows of yesteryear?

(2) A: Where's my box of chocolates?
B: I was feeling hungry.

(3) A: Where's my box of chocolates?
B: I've got a train to catch.

(4) A: Where's my box of chocolates?
B: Where's your diet sheet?

(5) A: Where's my box of chocolates?
B: The children were in your room this morning.

In none of the cases, B's reply is a direct response to A's question. All of them bring together the communicative intent by inference rules based on the interplay between linguistic and non-linguistic knowledge of the participants in the communication.

Apart from the pragmatic orientation, discourse structure exhibits its own rhetoric strategies. A common discourse structure with Question (Q)—Answer (A) format reveals a structure, (Q_1 A_1) Q_2A_2) (Q_3 A_3) . . ., for example:

Q_1: कल आप कहाँ जा रहे हैं ?
A_1: बनारस।

Q_2: क्यों ?
A_2: इण्टरव्यू है।

Q_3: किस चीज का ?
A_3: संपूर्णानन्द संस्कृत विश्वविद्यालय में प्रोफेसर की पोस्ट है।

However, conversational discourse may employ the following embedding strategy [Q_1,{Q_2(Q_3 A_3)A_2 }A_1]

Q_1: आज शाम सिनेमा चल रहे हो ?
Q_2: और कौन–कौन जा रहा है ?
Q_3: इससे कुछ फ़रक पड़ेगा क्या ?

A_3: हाँ पड़ेगा।
A_2 मोहन और शीला चल रहे हैं।
A_1: तब मैं भी चलूँगा।

In order to evaluate a given text for comprehension we have to look at both the linguistics as well as the rhetorical factors.

Textual processing thus demands two types of abilities:

(1) the ability to recognise and manipulate the formal devices which are used to combine sentences to create a continuous passage of prose, and
(2) the ability to recognise how sentences are used in the performance of acts of communication. Allen and Widdowson (1974) call these two abilities, grammatical cohesion of text and rhetorical coherence of discourse. Both these abilities, according to them, interpenetrate each other.

Rhetorical coherence of discourse deals with the communicative orientation; language here no longer exists as an independent subject. Content itself becomes both the form and function of language *i.e.* learning science is not to be seen as merely process of learning facts, but of learning how language is employed to take the role of reasoning. It should be made clear that by rhetorical elements of discourse we mean judgements concerning the order of presentation of information within the text and judgement about the clarity and precision of presenting the facts for communication and exposition.

Discourse can be defined, for the purpose of the present analysis, as any sequence of two or more sentences interacting with another. A discourse topic can be defined as a topic which seeks new information; a proposition or a set of propositions can be accepted as an answer to the question related to the topic, *i.e.* a statement adding new information.

Discourse may develop in several ways. Broadly, these can be divided into two major types: (i) continuous discourse, and (ii) discontinuous discourse. (Keenan and Schiflelin, 1976) Continuous discourse contains a series of linked discourse topics. The discourse topics are linked in the sense that the prepositional content of each is drawn from one or more of the sentence articulations already existing in the text. On the contrary, a discontinuous discourse may consist of topics which are not linked in any obvious way, *i.e.* a discourse topic may not draw on resources of already mentioned propositions.

A continuous discourse can be of two types—(i) a collaborating discourse topic, and (ii) an incorporating discourse topic. In the former case the discourse topic matches exactly that of the immediately preceding proposition; in the latter it does not. The important factor in this distinction lies in the fact that in the former case the same topic is sustained over two or more propositions, while in the latter a related topic gets integrated on the basis of a presupposition of an immediately preceding proposition.

Similarly, discontinuous discourse may have two types of topics: (i) reintroducing discourse topics, and (ii) introducing discourse topics. The first type reintroduces a topic that has appeared in the discourse proposition. (Constructions such as 'जैसा पहले बताया जा चुका है' or 'जहाँ तक इसका सम्बन्ध है' mark this type of discourse. The second type of discontinuous discouse introduces a topic which is in no way related to the preceding proposition and does not draw from the already created texts. It generally needs a new paragraph or a new subsection.

These can be diagrammatically represented as:

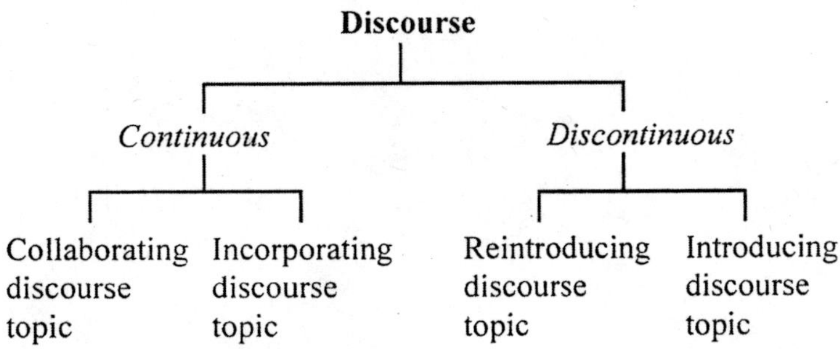

Index